SPOTLIGHT

SAVANNAH & THE GEORGIA COAST

JIM MOREKIS

Contents

SAVANNAH &
THE GEORGIA COAST

SAVANNAH

Rarely has a city owed so much to the vision of one person than Savannah owes to General James Edward Oglethorpe. Given the mission by King George II of England to buffer Charleston's plantations from the Spanish, this reformer had a far more sweeping vision in mind.

After befriending a local Creek tribe, Oglethorpe laid out his settlement in a deceptively simple plan that's studied today the world over as a model of nearly perfect urban design. Many of his other progressive ideas—such as prohibiting slavery and hard liquor, to name two—soon went by the wayside. But the legacy of his original plan lives on to this day.

Savannah would comprise a series of rectangular "wards," each built around a central square. As Savannah grew, each square took on its own characteristics depending on who lived on the square and how they made their livelihood. It's this individuality that instilled Savannah's innate individualism, so well-documented in John Berendt's *Midnight in the Garden of Good and Evil.*

The squares of Savannah's downtown—since 1965 part of the National Landmark Historic District—are also responsible for the city's walkability, another defining characteristic. Just as cars entering a square must yield to traffic already within, pedestrians are obliged to slow down and interact with the surrounding environment, both built and natural. You become participant and audience simultaneously, a feat made easier by the local penchant for easy conversation.

In an increasingly homogenized society,

HIGHLIGHTS

◖ River Street: Despite River Street's tourist tackiness, there's still nothing like strolling the cobblestones amid the old cotton warehouses, enjoying the cool breeze off the river, and watching the huge ships on their way to and from the bustling port (page 14).

◖ First African Baptist Church: The oldest black congregation in America still meets in this historic sanctuary, a key stop on the Underground Railroad (page 20).

◖ Owens-Thomas House: Possibly America's best example of Regency architecture and definitely an example of state-of-the-art historic preservation in action. Savannah's single greatest historical home (page 29).

◖ Telfair Museums: Old-school meets new-school in this museum complex comprising the traditional collection of the Telfair Academy of Arts and Sciences and the ultramodern Jepson Center for the Arts, both within a stone's throw of each other (page 30).

◖ Cathedral of St. John the Baptist: This soaring Gothic Revival edifice is complemented by its ornate interior and its matchless location on verdant Lafayette Square, stomping ground of the young Flannery O'Connor (page 35).

◖ Monterey Square: Perhaps Savannah's quintessential square, with some of the best examples of local architecture and world-class ironwork all around its periphery (page 38).

◖ Forsyth Park: A verdant expanse ringed with old live oaks, with memorials chockablock. The true center of downtown life, it's Savannah's backyard (page 43).

◖ Bonaventure Cemetery: This historic burial ground is the final resting place for some of Savannah's favorite citizens, including the great Johnny Mercer, and makes great use of its setting on the banks of the Wilmington River (page 47).

◖ Fort Pulaski National Monument: This well-run site, built with the help of a young Robert E. Lee, is not only historically significant, its beautiful setting makes it a great place for the entire family (page 53).

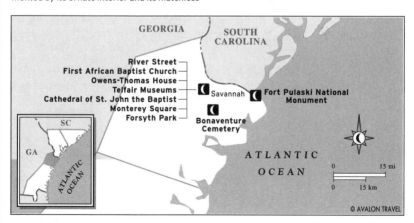

LOOK FOR ◖ TO FIND RECOMMENDED SIGHTS, ACTIVITIES, DINING, AND LODGING.

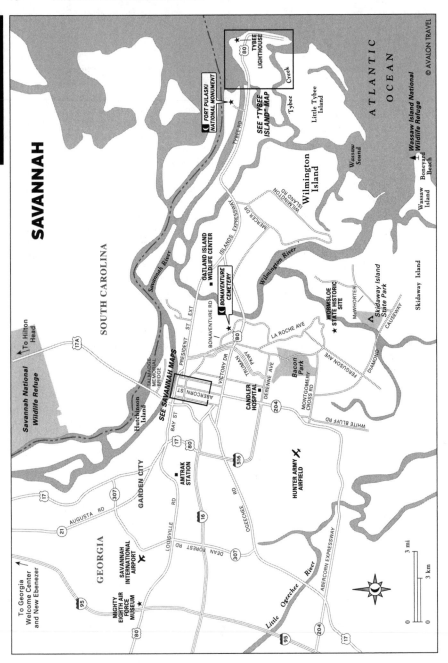

Savannah is one of the last places left where eccentricity is celebrated and even encouraged. This outspoken, often stubborn determination to make one's own way in the world is personified by the old Georgia joke about Savannah being the capital of "the state of Chatham," a reference to the county in which it resides. In typical contrarian fashion, Savannahians take this nickname, ostensibly a pejorative, as a compliment.

Savannah is also known for being able to show you a rowdy good time. It's not only about the massive, world-famous St. Patrick's Day celebration each year—though certainly that's something everyone should experience at least once in their lives. Savannahians, like New Orleanians, will use any excuse for a party, and any excuse to drink in the full flavor of natural beauty here—whether in the heady glory of a spring day with all the flowers blooming, or the sweet release of the long-awaited autumn, brisk and bracing but not so crisp that you can't wear shorts.

While Charleston's outlying areas tend to complement the history and outlook of the Holy City itself, Savannah's outskirts are more self-contained. Despite the fact that Tybee Island is largely dependent on Savannah's economy, it has willfully kept its own fun and funky persona. More rural areas outside town, such as New Ebenezer and Midway, are reflective of a wholly different side of the state—a Georgia of country churches and tight-knit descendants of original plantation owners.

HISTORY

To understand the inferiority complex that Savannah feels to this day with regards to Charleston, you have to remember that literally from day one, Savannah was intended to play second fiddle to its older, richer neighbor to the north. By the early 1700s, the land south of Charleston was a staging area for attacks by the Spanish and Native Americans. So in 1732, King George II granted a charter to the Trustees of Georgia, a proprietary venture that was the brainchild of a 36-year-old general and member of Parliament, General James Edward Oglethorpe.

On February 12, 1733, the *Anne* landed with 114 passengers along the high bluff on the south bank of the Savannah River. Oglethorpe bonded with Tomochichi, the local Creek Indian chief, and the colony prospered. (Contrary to what locals might tell you, Savannah did not get its name because it resembles a grassy savanna. The city is christened for the Savannah River, which itself is named for a wandering, warlike offshoot of a local Shawnee tribe.)

Ever the idealist, Oglethorpe had a plan for the new "classless society" in Savannah that prohibited slavery, rum, and—wait for it—lawyers! But as the settlers enviously eyed the economic dominance of Charleston's slave-based rice economy, the Trustees bowed to public pressure and relaxed restrictions on slavery and rum. By 1753, the crown reclaimed the charter, making Georgia America's 13th colony.

Though part of the new United States in 1776, Savannah was captured by British forces in 1778, who successfully held the city against a combined assault a year later. After the Revolution, Savannah became the first capital of Georgia, a role that lasted until 1786.

Despite hurricanes and yellow fever epidemics, Savannah's heyday was the antebellum period from 1800 to 1860, when for a time it outstripped Charleston as a center of commerce. By 1860, Savannah's population doubled after an influx of European immigrants, chief among them Irish workers coming to lay track on the new Central of Georgia line.

Blockaded for most of the Civil War, Savannah didn't see much action other than the fall of Fort Pulaski in April 1862 when a Union force successfully laid siege using rifled artillery, a revolutionary new technology that instantly rendered the world's masonry forts obsolete.

War came to Savannah's doorstep when General William T. Sherman's March to the Sea concluded with his capture of the town in December 1864. Sherman sent a now-legendary telegram to President Lincoln granting him the city as a Christmas present with these words: "I beg to present you as a

Christmas gift, the City of Savannah with 150 heavy guns and plenty of ammunition and also about 25,000 bales of cotton."

After a lengthy Reconstruction period, Savannah began reaching out to the outside world. From 1908 to 1911, it was a national center of road racing. In the Roaring Twenties, native son Johnny Mercer rose to prominence and the great Flannery O'Connor was born in downtown Savannah.

World War II provided an economic lift, with Savannah being a major center for the building of Liberty Ships to transport soldiers and equipment overseas. But the city was still known as the "pretty woman with a dirty face," as Britain's Lady Astor famously described it in 1946. Almost in answer to Astor's quip, city leaders in the '50s began a misguided program to retrofit the city's infrastructure for the automobile era. This frenzy of demolition cost such civic treasures as Union Station, the City Auditorium, and the old DeSoto Hotel. Savannah's preservation movement had its seed in the fight by seven Savannah women to save the Davenport House and other buildings from similar fates.

Savannah played a pioneering, though largely unsung, role in the civil rights movement. Ralph Mark Gilbert, pastor of the historic First African Baptist Church, launched one of the first black voter registration drives in the South, which led the way for the historic integration of the police department in 1947. Gilbert's efforts were kept alive in the '50s and '60s by the beloved W. W. Law, a letter carrier who was head of the local chapter of the NAACP for many years.

Savannah's longstanding diversity was further proved in 1970, when Greek American John P. Rousakis began his 21-year stint as mayor. During Rousakis' tenure, the first African American city alderman was elected, the movie industry discovered the area, and Atlanta was awarded the 1996 Summer Olympics, which brought several venues to Savannah. Once-decrepit River Street and Broughton Street were revived. The opening of the Savannah College of Art and Design

(SCAD) in 1979 ushered another important chapter in Savannah's renaissance.

After the publication of John Berendt's *Midnight in the Garden of Good and Evil* in 1994, nothing would ever be the same in Savannah. Old-money families cringed as idiosyncrasies and hypocrisies were laid bare in "The Book." Local merchants and politicians, however, delighted in the influx of tourists.

Savannah's first African American mayor, Floyd Adams Jr., was elected in 1995. Immediately succeeding him in the office was Otis Johnson, the first black Savannahian to graduate from the University of Georgia.

PLANNING YOUR TIME

Much more than just a parade, St. Patrick's Day in Savannah—an event generally expanded to include several days before and after it—is also a time of immense crowds, with the city's usual population of about 150,000 doubling with the influx of partying visitors. Be aware that lodging on and around March 17 fills up well in advance. Unless you know someone that lives here, it's best not to just spontaneously show up in Savannah on St. Patrick's weekend.

Like Charleston, you don't need access to a car to have a great time and see most sights worth enjoying. A strong walker can easily traverse the length and breadth of downtown in a day, though less energetic travelers should consider a central location and/or use of the free downtown shuttle.

To fully enjoy Savannah, however, you'll need access to a vehicle so you can go east to Tybee Island and south to various historical sights with spottier public transportation. You'll appreciate downtown all the more when you can get away and smell the salt air.

And also like Charleston, it's hard to imagine fully enjoying Savannah in a single day. Plan on two nights at an absolute minimum—not only to enjoy all the sights, but to fully soak in the local color and attitude.

ORIENTATION

It's tempting for newcomers to assume that Savannah jumps across the river into South

OGLETHORPE: VISIONARY ARISTOCRAT

One of the greatest products of the Enlightenment, James Edward Oglethorpe was a study in contrasts, embodying all the vitality, contradiction, and ambiguity of that turbulent age.

A stern moralist yet an avowed liberal, an aristocrat with a populist streak, an abolitionist and an anti-Catholic, a man of war who sought peace – the founder of Georgia would put his own inimitable stamp on the new nation to follow, a legacy personified to this day in the city he designed.

After making a name for himself fighting the Turks, the young London native and Oxford graduate would return home only to serve a two-year prison sentence for killing a man in a brawl. The experience was a formative one for Oglethorpe, scion of a large and upwardly mobile family now forced to see how England's underbelly really lived.

Upon his release, the 25-year-old Oglethorpe ran for the "family" House of Commons seat once occupied by his father and two brothers, and won. He made a name for himself as a campaigner for human rights and an opponent of slavery.

Another jail-related epiphany came when Oglethorpe saw a friend die of smallpox in debtors' prison. More than ever, Oglethorpe was determined to right what he saw as a colossal wrong in the draconian English justice system. His crusade took the form of establishing a sanctuary for debtors in North America.

To that end, he and his friend Lord Perceval established the Trustees, a 21-member group who lobbied King George for permission to establish such a colony. The grant from the king – who was more interested in containing the Spanish than in any humanitarian concerns – would include all land between the Altamaha and Savannah Rivers and from the headwaters of these rivers to the "south seas."

Ironically, there were no debtors among Savannah's original colonists. Nonetheless, the new settlement was indeed a reflection of its founder's core values, banning rum as a bad influence (though beer and wine were allowed), prohibiting slavery, and eschewing lawyers on the theory that a gentleman should always be able to defend himself.

Nearing 40 and distracted by war with the Spanish, Oglethorpe's agenda gradually eroded in the face of opposition from settlers, who craved not only the more hedonistic lifestyle of their neighbors to the north in Charleston but the economic advantage that city enjoyed in the use of slave labor.

In nearly the same hour as his greatest military victory, crushing the Spanish at the Battle of Bloody Marsh on St. Simons Island, Oglethorpe also suffered an ignominious defeat: being replaced as head of the 13th colony which he had founded.

He went back to England, never to see the New World again. But his heart was always with the colonists. After successfully fending off a political attack and a court-martial, Oglethorpe married and commenced a healthy retirement. He supported independence for the American colonies, making a point to enthusiastically receive the new ambassador from the United States, one John Adams.

At age 88, the old general died on June 30, 1785. Fittingly for this life-long philanthropist and humanitarian, his childhood home in Godalming, Surrey, is now a nursing home.

statue of Gen. James Oglethorpe in Chippewa Square

Carolina. But this is not the case, as Savannah emanates strictly southward from the river and never crosses the state line. (Don't be confused by the spit of land you see across the main channel of the Savannah River, the one bearing the squat Trade and Convention Center and the towering Westin Savannah Harbour hotel. That's not South Carolina, it's Hutchinson Island, Georgia, annexed by the city of Savannah for development. South Carolina begins farther north, after you cross the river's Back Channel.)

The downtown area is bounded on the east by East Broad Street and on the west by Martin Luther King Jr. Boulevard (formerly West Broad St.). For quick access to the south, take the one-way streets Price (on the east side of downtown) or Whitaker (on the west side of downtown). Conversely, if you want to make a quick trip north into downtown, three one-way streets taking you there are East Broad, Lincoln, and Drayton. Technically, Gwinnett Street is the southern boundary of the National Historic Landmark District, though in practice locals typically extend the boundary several blocks southward.

When you're driving downtown and come to a square, the law says traffic within the square *always* has the right of way. In other words, if you haven't yet entered the square, you must yield to any vehicles already in the square.

Many of the following neighborhood designations, like City Market and the Waterfront, are well within the National Landmark Historic District, but locals tend to think of them as separate entities, and we'll follow their lead.

While largely in private hands, the Victorian District—with historical certification and protection of its own—contains some wonderful architecture that unfortunately is often overshadowed by the more ornate buildings in the Historic District proper.

The Eastside includes many areas that are technically islands, but their boundaries are so blurred by infill of the marsh and by well-constructed roads that you'll sense little difference from the mainland.

To most locals, "Southside" refers to the generic strip mall sprawl below Derenne Avenue, but for our purposes here the term also includes some outlying islands. I include them in the southern part of town because of the general direction and length of travel.

Sights

It's best to introduce yourself to the sights of Savannah by traveling from the river southward. It's no small task to navigate the nation's largest contiguous Historic District, but when in doubt it's best to follow James Oglethorpe's original plan of using the five "monumental" squares on Bull Street (Johnson, Wright, Chippewa, Madison, and Monterey) as focal points.

WATERFRONT

It's only natural to start one's adventures in Savannah where Oglethorpe's adventures themselves began: on the waterfront, now dominated by scenic and historic River Street. Once the bustling center of Savannah's thriving cotton and naval stores export industry, the waterfront is also generally thought of as including Factor's Walk and Bay Street.

◖ River Street

It's much tamer than it was 30 years ago—when muscle cars cruised its cobblestones and a volatile mix of local teenagers, sailors on shore leave, and soldiers on liberty made things less-than-family-friendly after dark—but River Street still has more than enough edginess to keep things interesting. Families are safe and welcome here, but energetic pub crawling remains a favorite pastime for locals and visitors alike.

If you have a car, park it somewhere else and walk. The cobblestones—actually old ballast

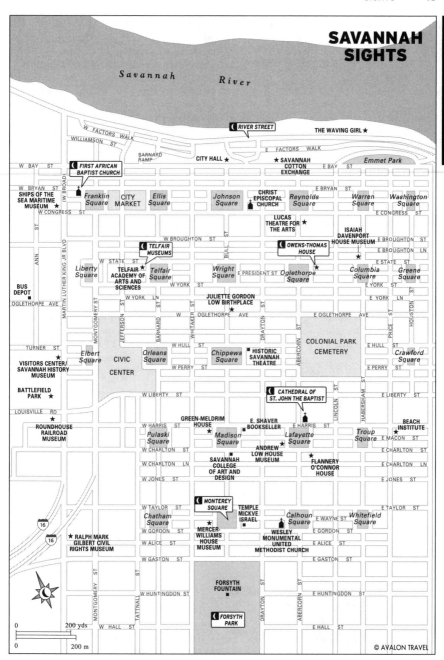

SAVANNAH SIGHTS

Savannah River

RIVER STREET
THE WAVING GIRL ★
W FACTORS WALK
WILLIAMSON ST
E FACTORS WALK
BARNARD RAMP
CITY HALL ★
★ SAVANNAH COTTON EXCHANGE
Emmet Park
W BAY ST
FIRST AFRICAN BAPTIST CHURCH
E BAY ST
W BRYAN ST
E BRYAN ST
SHIPS OF THE SEA MARITIME MUSEUM
Franklin Square
CITY MARKET
Ellis Square
Johnson Square
CHRIST EPISCOPAL CHURCH
Reynolds Square
Warren Square
Washington Square
W CONGRESS ST
E CONGRESS ST
LUCAS THEATRE FOR THE ARTS ★
W BROUGHTON ST
ISAIAH DAVENPORT HOUSE MUSEUM
E BROUGHTON ST
TELFAIR MUSEUMS
OWENS-THOMAS HOUSE
E BROUGHTON LN
Liberty Square
W STATE ST
TELFAIR ACADEMY OF ARTS AND SCIENCES
Telfair Square
Wright Square
E PRESIDENT ST
Oglethorpe Square
E STATE ST
Columbia Square
Greene Square
BUS DEPOT
W YORK ST
E YORK ST
OGLETHORPE AVE
W YORK LN
JULIETTE GORDON LOW BIRTHPLACE ★
E YORK LN
W OGLETHORPE AVE
E OGLETHORPE AVE
TURNER ST
Elbert Square
W HULL ST
Orleans Square
Chippewa Square
HISTORIC SAVANNAH THEATRE
COLONIAL PARK CEMETERY
E HULL ST
Crawford Square
VISITORS CENTER/ SAVANNAH HISTORY MUSEUM
CIVIC CENTER
W PERRY ST
E PERRY ST
BATTLEFIELD PARK ★
W LIBERTY ST
E LIBERTY ST
LOUISVILLE RD
CATHEDRAL OF ST. JOHN THE BAPTIST
ROUNDHOUSE RAILROAD MUSEUM
GREEN-MELDRIM HOUSE
W HARRIS ST
E. SHAVER BOOKSELLER
E HARRIS ST
BEACH INSTITUTE
Pulaski Square
Madison Square
Lafayette Square
Troup Square
E MACON ST
W CHARLTON ST
ANDREW LOW HOUSE MUSEUM
E CHARLTON ST
W CHARLTON LN
SAVANNAH COLLEGE OF ART AND DESIGN
FLANNERY O'CONNOR HOUSE
E CHARLTON LN
W JONES ST
E JONES ST
W TAYLOR ST
E TAYLOR ST
MONTEREY SQUARE
TEMPLE MICKVE ISRAEL
Calhoun Square
Whitefield Square
Chatham Square
W GORDON ST
E WAYNE ST
E GORDON ST
MERCER-WILLIAMS HOUSE MUSEUM
W ALICE ST
WESLEY MONUMENTAL UNITED METHODIST CHURCH
E ALICE ST
RALPH MARK GILBERT CIVIL RIGHTS MUSEUM
W GASTON ST
E GASTON ST
FORSYTH FOUNTAIN
W HUNTINGDON ST
E HUNTINGDON ST
FORSYTH PARK
200 yds
W HALL ST
E HALL ST
200 m
© AVALON TRAVEL

stones from some of the innumerable ships that docked here over the years—are tough on the suspension, and much of River Street is dedicated to pedestrian traffic anyway. If you do find yourself driving here, keep in mind that the north–south "ramps" leading up and off River Street are all extensions of major downtown streets, so you can easily drive or walk up them and find yourself in the middle of bustling Bay Street and on to points beyond.

THE WAVING GIRL

Begin your walking tour of River Street on the east end, at the statue of Florence Martus, a.k.a. *The Waving Girl,* set in the emerald green expanse of little Morrell Park. Beginning at the age of 19, Martus—who actually lived several miles downriver on Elba Island—took to greeting every passing ship with a wave of a handkerchief by day and a lantern at night, without fail for the next 40 years. Ship captains returned the greeting with a salute of their own on the ship's whistle, and word spread all over the world of the beguiling woman who waited on the balcony of that lonely house.

statue of Florence Martus, the "Waving Girl"

© JIM MOREKIS

Was she looking for a sign of a long lost love who went to sea and never returned? Was she trying to get a handsome sea captain to sweep her off her feet and take her off that little island? No one knows for sure, but the truth is probably more prosaic. Martus was a life-long spinster who lived with her brother the lighthouse keeper, and was by most accounts an eccentric, if delightful, person—which of course makes her an ideal Savannah character. After her brother died, Martus moved into a house on the Wilmington River, whiling away the hours by—you guessed it—waving at passing cars.

Martus became such an enduring symbol of the personality and spirit of Savannah that a U.S. Liberty ship was named for her in 1943. She died a few months after the ship's christening at the age of 75.

ROUSAKIS PLAZA

Continue walking west to Rousakis Plaza (River Street behind City Hall), a focal point for local festivals. It's a great place to sit, feed the pigeons, and watch the huge container ships go back and forth from the Georgia Ports Authority's sprawling complex farther upriver (you can see the huge Panamax cranes in the distance).

The **African American Monument** at the edge of Rousakis Plaza was erected in 2002 to controversy for its stark tableau of a dazed-looking African American family with broken shackles around their feet. Adding to the controversy was the graphic content of the inscription at the base of the 12-foot statue, written especially for the monument by famed poet Maya Angelou. It reads: "We were stolen, sold and bought together from the African continent. We got on the slave ships together. We lay back to belly in the holds of the slave ships in each other's excrement and urine together, sometimes died together, and our lifeless bodies thrown overboard together. Today, we are standing up together, with faith and even some joy."

Nearby you can't miss the huge, vaguely cubist Hyatt Regency Savannah, another controversial local landmark. The modern architecture of the Hyatt caused quite a stir when it

THE TWO PAULAS

It's odd that this conservative Southern city's two biggest empire-builders are women who overcame contentious divorces to get where they are today. Odder still is the fact that they both share the same first name.

In any case, the empires that Paula Deen and Paula Wallace have built are two of the major reasons people enjoy Savannah today. Deen's empire centers on The Lady & Sons restaurant in City Market and her high profile on the Food Network. Wallace's empire centers on the Savannah College of Art and Design, one of the largest art schools in the nation (and growing).

Their names are similar, but that's about their only similarity. These two powerhouse women and the stories of how they rose to the top could not be more different in every other way.

Deen, an Albany, Georgia, native, came to Savannah after divorcing her first husband in 1989, arriving with only $200 and her two teenage sons, Jamie and Bobby (now Food Network stars in their own right). Always ready with a self-deprecating quip, Deen still refers to herself as a former "bag lady" – the name of her first catering company – who still has a yen for shopping at Wal-Mart.

Severely agoraphobic (fearing crowds), Deen gradually increased her public presence first with a job cooking at a local hotel and then with her own restaurant, Lady & Sons, initially on West Congress Street. Her gregarious "aw-shucks" style caught the attention of producer Gordon Elliott, formerly with the seminal tabloid show *A Current Affair*.

His first cooking show pilot with Deen fizzled in 1999. But soon after the 9/11 attacks, Elliott spotted an opportunity to market a good old-fashioned comfort food show, *Paula's Home Cooking* to the Food Network. The result was, as they say, ratings gold. Initially taped at Elliott's New York home, taping has now moved to Savannah.

Petite, soft-spoken, and often surrounded by a coterie of devoted assistants, Paula Wallace is Deen's polar opposite in temperament. She arrived in Savannah in 1979 with her then-husband Richard Rowan to establish an art school. The two twentysomethings, young children in tow, came armed with the guts to take a chance on depressed downtown real estate, the willingness to roll up their sleeves, and her parents' deep pockets.

The power couple soon became the toast of the town. Then came a bitter divorce. After the smoke cleared, Paula became the clear and undisputed *presidente* of SCAD.

It's hard to overstate the college's impact on Savannah. It has renovated nearly 100 historic properties and is estimated to own at least $200 million in assets, returning nearly $100 million a year into the local economy and employing approximately 1,500 people.

Now happily remarried, Wallace continues to expand SCAD's presence, with satellite campuses in Atlanta, Hong Kong, and Lacoste, France. In addition to her presidential duties, she authors children's and interior design books and manages the college's permanent art collection.

was first built in 1981, not only because it's so contrary to the area's historic architecture but because its superstructure effectively cuts off one end of River Street from the other.

"Underneath" the Hyatt—actually still River Street—you'll find elevators to the hotel lobby, the best way to get up off the waterfront if you're not up for a walk up the cobblestones. Immediately outside the west side of the Hyatt up towards Bay Street is another exit/entry point, a steep and solid set of antebellum

stairs, which, despite its decidedly pre–Americans with Disabilities Act aspect, is nonetheless one of the quicker ways to leave River Street for those with strong legs and good knees.

FACTOR'S WALK

One level up from River Street, Factor's Walk has nothing to do with math, though a lot of money has been counted here. In arcane usage, a "factor" was a broker, i.e., a middleman for the sale of cotton, Savannah's chief export during most of the 1800s. Factors mostly worked in Factor's Row, the traditional phrase for the actual buildings on River Street, most all of which were used in various import/export activities before their current transformation into a mélange of shops, hotels, restaurants, and taverns.

Factor's Walk is divided into Lower Factor's Walk, comprising the alleys and back entrances behind Factor's Row, and Upper Factor's Walk, the system of crosswalks at the upper levels of Factor's Row that lead you directly to Bay Street.

BAY STREET

Because so few downtown streets can accommodate 18-wheelers, Bay Street unfortunately has become the default route for industrial traffic in the area on its way to and from the industrial west side of town.

In front of the Hyatt Regency is a concrete bench, marking the spot on which Oglethorpe pitched his first tent. But dominating Bay Street is **City Hall** (2 E. Bay St.) next door, with its gold-leaf dome. The 1907 building was designed by acclaimed architect Hyman Witcover and erected on the site of Savannah's first town hall.

The large gray Greek Revival building directly across from City Hall is the **U.S. Custom House** (1 E. Bay St.), not "Customs" regardless of what the tour guides may say. Built on the spot of Georgia's first public building in 1852, the Custom House was also Georgia's first federal building and was the first local commission for renowned New York architect John Norris, who went on to design 22 other buildings in Savannah. Within its walls was held the trial of the captain and crew of the notorious slave ship *Wanderer,* which illegally plied its trade after a national ban on the importation of slaves. Local newspaper publisher and educator John H. DeVeaux worked here after his appointment as the first African American U.S. Collector of Customs.

Directly adjacent to City Hall on the east is a small canopy sheltering two cannons, which together comprise the oldest monument in Savannah. These are the **Chatham Artillery Guns,** presented to the local militia

group of the same name by President George Washington during his one and only visit to town in 1791. Today, locals use the phrase "Chatham Artillery" differently, to refer to a particularly potent local punch recipe that mixes several hard liquors.

Look directly behind the cannons and you'll see the ornate **Savannah Cotton Exchange** (100 E. Bay St.), built in 1886 to facilitate the city's huge cotton export business. Once nicknamed "King Cotton's Palace" but now a Masonic lodge, this delightful building by William Gibbons Preston is one of Savannah's many great examples of the Romanesque style. You'll become well acquainted with Preston's handiwork during your stay in Savannah—the Boston architect built many of Savannah's finest buildings. The fanciful lion figure in front—sometimes mistakenly referred to as a gryphon—represents Mark the Evangelist. However, it isn't original—the first lion was destroyed in 2009 in a bizarre traffic accident.

CITY MARKET

In local parlance, the phrase "City Market" generally refers not only to the refurbished warehouses comprising this tourist-friendly area of shops and restaurants in the Historic District's western portion, but its bookend squares as well—both of which had close scrapes with the bulldozer and wrecking ball before their current renaissance.

Ellis Square

Just across Bay Street on the western edge of the Historic District, Ellis Square has a history as Savannah's main open-air marketplace that goes back to 1755, when there was actually a single City Market building in the square itself. Three market buildings would come and go until the building of the fourth City Market in 1872, an ornate Romanesque affair with a 50-foot roofline.

In 1954, the city, under the thrall of auto-worship then sweeping the country, decided a parking garage in the square was more important than fresh food or a sense of community. So the magnificent City Market building—and Ellis Square—simply ceased to exist.

However, several large warehouses surrounding City Market survived. They carried with them the seed of real renewal, which grew with the nascent preservation movement in the '50s and '60s. Now a year-round hub of tourism, City Market's eclectic scene encompasses working art studios, hip bars, cute cafés, live music in the east end of the courtyard, cutting edge art galleries, gift shops, and restaurants. This is also where you pick up one of the horse-drawn carriage tours, which embark from Jefferson Street running down the middle of City Market.

The eyesore that was the Ellis Square parking garage is now gone, and the square has been literally rebuilt, complete with colorful fountain, all atop a huge underground parking garage. It cost taxpayers millions of dollars, but as any Savannahian will tell you, the return of one of their precious squares is priceless. Be sure to check out the bronze of native Savannahian and Oscar-winning songwriter Johnny Mercer.

THE REBIRTH OF ELLIS SQUARE

One of the great tragedies of Savannah's 1950s love affair with "urban renewal" was the paving over of Ellis Square, site of the original City Market, replaced by a squat, drab parking garage.

Savannah has finally made amends for its bad karma by bringing Ellis Square back from the grave. In the massive $22 million "Ellis Square Project" – also called "The Big Dig" in a nod to a similarly ambitious project in Boston – city taxpayers funded a complete facelift that boasts a new, modern landscape design including a colorful fountain.

While not everyone in town is enamored of the new look – many local landscape architects see its self-conscious modernity as a slap in the face to Oglethorpe's original design –

there's no doubt that Savannah welcomes the return of one of its most beloved squares.

There's also no doubt that the city welcomes the 1,000 or so new parking spaces available in the massive Whitaker Street Garage *under* the new Ellis Square.

Ellis Square is not the only one to have been partially or completely destroyed, however. A small plot of worn grass on the west side of the Savannah Civic Center is all that remains of Elbert Square, eviscerated by the construction of the block-long building.

And, ironically, Liberty Square was annihilated to make room for a place where some people lose their liberty – the new Chatham County Courthouse and Jail.

© JIM MOREKIS

the renovated Ellis Square

Franklin Square

Just west of City Market is Franklin Square, once known simply as "Water Tank Square" because that's where the city reservoir was. Don't be alarmed by the numbers of men hanging out in the square. Scruffy heirs to an old Savannah tradition, most of them are day laborers for hire.

Until recently, Franklin Square was, like Ellis Square, a victim of "progress," this time in the form of a highway going right through the middle of it. But as part of the city's effort to reclaim its history, Franklin Square was returned to its integral state in the mid-1980s.

◖ FIRST AFRICAN BAPTIST CHURCH

Without a doubt the premier historic attraction on Franklin Square—and indeed one of the most significant historic sites in Savannah—is the First African Baptist Church (23 Montgomery St., 912/233-2244, www .oldestblackchurch.org, tours Tues.–Sun. at 11 A.M. and 2 P.M., $5). It's the oldest black congregation in North America, dating from 1777. The church would also host the first African American Sunday school in North America, begun in 1826.

The church's founding pastor, George Liele, was the first black Baptist in Georgia and perhaps the first black missionary in America. He baptized his successor, Andrew Bryan, a slave who opted to stay in Savannah and preach the Gospel instead of leaving with many other blacks after the British vacated the city.

Third pastor Andrew Marshall was an ardent supporter of American independence and purchased his freedom shortly after the end of the Revolution. He served as George Washington's personal servant during his visit here. This founding trio is immortalized in stained-glass windows in the sanctuary.

The present building dates from 1859, and was built almost entirely by members of the congregation themselves, some of whom redirected savings intended to purchase their freedom toward the building of the church. It houses the oldest church organ in Georgia.

A key staging area for the fabled Underground Railroad, First African Baptist still bears the scars of that turbulent time. In the floor of the fellowship hall—where many civil rights meetings were held, because it was safer for white citizens to go there instead of black activists going outside the church—you'll see breathing

stained glass at the First African Baptist Church

© JIM MOREKIS

the Haitian Monument in Franklin Square

holes, drilled for use by escaped slaves hiding in a cramped crawlspace.

HAITIAN MONUMENT
This monument in the center of the square commemorates the sacrifice and service of "Les Chasseurs Volontaires De Saint Domingue," the 750 Haitian volunteers who fought for American independence and lost many of their number during the unsuccessful attempt to wrest Savannah back from the British in 1779.

HISTORIC DISTRICT
Johnson Square
Due east of City Market, Oglethorpe's very first square is named for Robert Johnson, governor of South Carolina at the time of Georgia's founding. It was here that Savannah's Liberty Pole was erected in 1774 to celebrate a new nation. And it was here that a gathering in 1861 celebrated Georgia's secession, ironically with a huge banner draped over the Greene Monument bearing the words "Don't Tread on Me"—a slogan used in the founding of the very union they sought to dissolve.

The roomy, shady square, ringed with major bank branches and insurance firms, is dominated by the **Nathanael Greene Monument** in honor of George Washington's second-in-command, who was granted nearby Mulberry Grove plantation for his efforts. Marquis de Lafayette dedicated the towering obelisk during his one and only visit to Savannah in 1825. At the time it did not honor any one person. Its dedication to Greene came in 1886, followed by the re-interment of Greene's remains directly underneath the monument in 1901. (In typically maddening Savannah fashion, there is a separate square named for Greene, which has no monument to him at all.)

A much smaller but more charming and personable little monument in Johnson Square, though, is the **William Bull Sundial** at the southside. Bull Street was named for this South Carolinian who accompanied Oglethorpe on his first journey to the new colony, helping him choose and survey the site—hence a sundial is an appropriate remembrance.

CHRIST EPISCOPAL CHURCH
The southeast corner of Johnson Square is dominated by Christ Episcopal Church (18 Abercorn St., 912/232-4131, www

.christchurchsavannah.org), a.k.a. Christ Church, a historic house of worship also known as the "Mother Church of Georgia" because its congregation traces its roots to that first Anglican service in Savannah, held the same day Oglethorpe landed. While this spot on Johnson Square was reserved for the congregation from the very beginning, this is actually the third building on the site, dating from 1838. Much of the interior is more recent than that, however, since a fire gutted the interior in 1895. In the northeast bell tower is a bell forged in 1919 by Revere and Sons of Boston.

For a special treat, walk right in to Christ Church's Compline service, held every Sunday evening at 9 P.M., and enjoy a selection of calming liturgical music sung by Christ Church's excellent Compline Choir. Colloquially known as "saying good night to God," the Compline service is free and open to those of all faiths.

Reynolds Square

Walk directly east of Johnson Square to find yourself at Reynolds Square, named for John Reynolds, the first (and exceedingly unpopular) royal governor of Georgia. First called "Lower New Square," Reynolds originally served as site of the filature, or cocoon storage warehouse, during the fledgling colony's ill-fated flirtation with the silk industry (a federal building now occupies the site).

As with Johnson Square, the monument in Reynolds Square has nothing to do with its namesake, but is instead a likeness of John Wesley dedicated in 1969 near the spot believed to have been his home. On the northeast corner of the square is the parish house of Christ Church, Wesley's congregation during his stay in Savannah.

A Reynolds Square landmark, the **Olde Pink House** (23 Abercorn St.), is not only one of Savannah's most romantic restaurants but quite a historic site as well. It's the oldest Savannah mansion from the 18th century still extant, as well as the first place in Savannah where the Declaration of Independence was read aloud. Pink inside as well as out, the Georgian mansion was built in 1771 for rice planter James Habersham Jr., one of America's richest men at the time, and a member of the notorious "Liberty Boys" who plotted revolution. The building's pink exterior was a matter of serendipity, resulting from its core redbrick seeping through the formerly white stucco outer covering.

At the southwest corner of Reynolds Square is the understated **Oliver Sturgis House** (27 Abercorn St.), former home of the partner with William Scarbrough in the launching of the SS *Savannah*. This is one of the few Savannah buildings to feature the stabilizing earthquake rods which are much more common in Charleston. Don't miss the dolphin downpour spouts at ground level.

LUCAS THEATRE FOR THE ARTS

The other major Savannah landmark on Reynolds Square is the Lucas Theatre for the Arts (32 Abercorn St., 912/525-5040, www .lucastheatre.com). Built in 1921 as part of Arthur Lucas' regional chain of movie houses, the Lucas also featured a stage for road shows. Ornate and stately but with cozy warmth to spare, the venue was a hit with Savannahians for four decades, until the advent of TV and residential flight from downtown led to financial disaster. In 1976, the Lucas closed after a screening of *The Exorcist*. Several attempts to revive the venue followed, including a comedy club in the '80s, but to no avail.

When the building faced demolition in 1986, a group of citizens created a nonprofit to save it. Despite numerous starts and stops, the 14-year campaign finally paid off in a grand reopening in December 2000, an event helped immeasurably by timely donations from *Midnight* star Kevin Spacey and the cast and crew of the locally shot *Forrest Gump*.

Administered by a public/private partnership between local taxpayers and the Savannah College of Art and Design, the Lucas now hosts world-class entertainment and civic events year-round. The theater's schedule stays pretty busy, so it should be easy to check out a show while you're in town. Once inside, be sure to check out the extensive gold-leaf work throughout the interior, all painstakingly done by hand.

© JIM MOREKIS

Lucas Theatre for the Arts on Reynolds Square

Columbia Square

Named for the mythical patroness of America, this square features at its center not an expected portrait of that female warrior figure, but the original fountain from Noble Jones's Wormsloe Plantation, placed there in 1970.

ISAIAH DAVENPORT HOUSE MUSEUM

Columbia Square is primarily known as the home of the Isaiah Davenport House Museum (324 E. State St., 912/236-8097, www.davenporthousemuseum.org, Mon.–Sat. 10 A.M.–4 P.M., Sun. 1–4 P.M., $8 adults, $5 children). The house museum is a delightful stop in and of itself because of its elegant simplicity, sweeping double staircase, and near-perfect representation of the Federalist style. But the Davenport House occupies an exalted place in Savannah history as well, because it was the fight to save it that began the preservation movement in Savannah.

In 1955 the Davenport House, then a tenement, was to be demolished for a parking lot. But Emma Adler and six other feisty Savannah women, angered by the recent destruction of Ellis Square, refused to go down quietly. Together they formed the Historic Savannah

Foundation in order to raise the $22,500 needed to purchase the Davenport House. By 1963, the Davenport House—built in 1820 for his own family by master builder Isaiah Davenport—was open to the public as a museum. Another major restoration from 2000 to 2003 brought the home back to its original early 1800s state as you enjoy it today.

Across the corner from the Davenport House is the Classical Revival masterpiece **Kehoe House** (123 Habersham St.), designed for local ironworks owner William Kehoe in 1892 by DeWitt Bruyn. Sadly, the proof of Kehoe's self-described "weakness for cupolas" is no longer extant, the cupola having rotted away. Once a funeral home and then an inn owned briefly for a time by football legend Joe Namath, the Kehoe House is now one of Savannah's premier bed-and-breakfasts. It's unique not only in its exuberantly Victorian architecture, but in its twin fireplaces and ubiquitous *rococo* ironwork, courtesy of the irrepressible Kehoe himself.

WARREN AND WASHINGTON SQUARES

Warren Square and its neighbor Washington Square formed the first extension of

Oglethorpe's original four, and still boast some of the oldest houses in the historic district. Both squares are lovely little garden spots, ideal for a picnic in the shade. Two houses near Washington Square were restored by the late Jim Williams of *Midnight* fame: The **Hampton Lillibridge House** (507 E. Saint Julian St.), which once hosted an Episcopal exorcism, and the **Charles Oddingsells House** (510 E. Saint Julian St.). Now a hotel, the **Mulberry Inn** on Washington Square was once a cotton warehouse and subsequently one of the nation's first Coca-Cola bottling plants.

GREENE SQUARE

Named for Revolutionary War hero Nathanael Greene, but bearing no monument to him whatsoever, this square is of particular importance to local African American history. At the corner of Houston (pronounced "House-ton") and East State Streets is the 1810 **Cunningham House,** built for Henry Cunningham, former slave and founding pastor of the **Second African Baptist Church** (124 Houston St., 912/233-6163) on the west side of the square, in which General Sherman made his famous promise of "40 acres and a mule." In 1818, the residence at 542 East State St. was constructed for free blacks Charlotte and William Wall. The property at 513 East York St. was built for the estate of Catherine DeVeaux, part of a prominent African American family.

Old Fort

One of the lesser-known aspects of Savannah history is this well-trod neighborhood at the east end of Bay Street, once the site of groundbreaking experiments and piratical intrigue, then a diverse melting pot of Savannah citizenry.

TRUSTEES GARDEN

At the east end of Bay Street where it meets East Broad rises a bluff behind a masonry wall—at 40 feet off the river, still the highest point in Chatham County. This is Trustees Garden, the nation's first experimental garden.

Modeled on the Chelsea Botanical Garden in London, it was intended to be the epicenter of Savannah's silk industry. Alas, the colonists had little knowledge of native soils or climate—they thought the winters would be milder—and the experiment was not as successful as hoped.

Soon Trustees Garden became the site of Fort Wayne, a defensive installation overlooking the river named after General "Mad Anthony" Wayne of Revolutionary War fame, who retired to a plantation near Savannah. The Fort Wayne area—still called the "Old Fort" neighborhood by old-timers—fell from grace and became associated with the "lowest elements" of Savannah society, which in the 19th and early 20th centuries were considered Irish and African Americans.

It also became known for its illegal activity and as the haunt of sea salts such as the ones who frequented what is now the delightfully schlocky Pirates' House restaurant. That building began life in 1753 as a seamen's inn, and was later chronicled by Robert Louis Stevenson in *Treasure Island* as a rogue's gallery of pirates and nautical ne'er-do-wells.

Find the **Herb House** on East Broad Street, the older-looking clapboard structure next to the Pirates' House entrance. You're looking at what's considered the single oldest building in Georgia and one of the oldest in the United States. Constructed in 1734, it was originally the home of Trustees Garden's chief gardener.

To the rear of Trustees Garden is the 1881 Hillyer building, now the **Charles H. Morris Center,** a mixed-use performing arts and meeting space that is heavily used during the springtime Savannah Music Festival.

EMMET PARK

Just north of Reynolds Square on the north side of Bay Street you'll come to Emmet Park, first a Native American burial ground and then known as "the Strand" or "Irish Green" because of its proximity to the Irish slums of the Old Fort. In 1902 the park was named for Robert Emmet, an Irish patriot of the early 1800s, who was executed by the British for treason. Within it is the eight-foot **Celtic Cross,** erected in 1983 and

THE IRISH IN SAVANNAH

It seems Savannah's close connection to St. Patrick's Day was ordained from the beginning. The very first baby born here, Georgia Close, came into the world on March 17, 1733.

Two hundred and fifty years later Savannah holds what's the second-largest St. Patrick's Day celebration in the world, second only to New York City's. Three presidents have visited during the shindig – William Howard Taft, Harry Truman, and Jimmy Carter.

With its fine spring weather and walkability – not to mention its liberal "to-go cup" rules allowing you to carry an adult beverage on the street – Savannah is tailor-made for a boisterous outdoor celebration. But most of all, what makes it a perfect fit is the city's large Irish-American population.

The earliest Irish in Georgia were descendants of the Calvinist Scots who "planted" Ireland's northern province of Ulster in the 1600s. Often called "crackers" – perhaps from the Gaelic *craic*, "enjoyable conversation" – these early Irish entered Georgia from upstate South Carolina and made their living trading, trapping, or soldiering. One such "cracker" was Sergeant William Jasper, mortally wounded leading the charge to retake Savannah from the British in 1779.

The main chapter in local Irish history began in the 1830s with the arrival of the first wave of Irish to build the Central of Georgia Railroad. The story goes that Irish were employed on the railroad because, unlike slaves, their bodies had no commercial value and could be worked to exhaustion with impunity. A second wave of Irish immigration followed two decades later when the Potato Famine in the old country forced many to seek new shores.

Though the Irish were initially subject to prejudice, their willingness to work long hours for low pay soon made them irreplaceable in Savannah's economy. And also as in New York, in short order Irish became major players in politics and business.

In the early days, Irish neighborhoods were clustered around East Broad Street in the Old Fort area, and on the west side near West Broad Street (now MLK Jr. Boulevard). It's no coincidence that those areas also had large African American populations. Because of their shared links of poverty and prejudice, in the early days Savannah Irish tended to live near black neighborhoods, often socializing with them after-hours – much to the chagrin of Savannah's elite.

Ironically, given St. Patrick's Day's current close association with the Catholic faith, the first parade in Savannah was organized by Irish *Protestants*. In 1813, 13 members of the local Hibernian Society – America's oldest Irish society – took part in a private procession to Independent Presbyterian Church. The first public procession was in 1824, when the Hibernians invited all local Irishmen to parade through the streets. The first recognizably modern parade, with bands and a "grand marshal," happened in 1870.

Today's parade is a far cry from those early beginnings. Organized by a "committee" of about 700 local Irishmen – with but a tiny sprinkling of lasses – the three-hour procession includes marchers from all the local Irish organizations, in addition to marching bands and floats representing many local groups. Rain or shine, the assembled clans march – amble is perhaps a more accurate word – wearing their kelly green blazers, brandishing their walking canes and to-go cups, some pushing future committee members in strollers, fair skin gradually getting redder in the Georgia sun.

the Celtic Cross in Emmet Park

© JIM MOREKIS

carved of Irish limestone. The Celtic Cross is the center of a key ceremony for local Irish Catholics during the week prior to St. Patrick's Day.

Close by is one of Savannah's more recent monuments, the **Vietnam War Memorial** at East Bay Street and Rossiter Lane. The reflecting pool is in the shape of Vietnam itself, and the names of all 106 Savannahians killed in the conflict are carved into an adjacent marble tablet.

Walk a little farther east and you'll find my favorite little chapter of Bay Street history, the **Beacon Range Light.** Tucked into a shady corner, few tourists bother to check out this masterfully crafted 1858 navigation aid, intended to warn approaching ships of the old wrecks sunk in the river as a defense during the Revolutionary War.

Broughton Street

Downtown's main shopping district for most of the 20th century, Broughton Street once dazzled shoppers with decorated gaslights, ornate window displays, and fine examples of terrazzo, a form of mosaic that still adorns many shop entrances. Postwar suburbs and white flight brought neglect to the area by the 1960s, and many thought Broughton was gone for good. But with the downtown renaissance brought about largely by the Savannah College of Art and Design (SCAD), Broughton was able not only to get back on its feet but to thrive as a commercial center once again.

Around the corner from the Lucas Theatre on Reynolds Square is the art moderne **Trustees Theatre** (216 E. Broughton St., 912/525-5051, www.scad.edu), a SCAD-run operation that seats 1,200 and hosts concerts, film screenings, and the school's much-anticipated spring fashion show. It began life in the postwar boom of 1946 as the Weis Theatre, another one of those ornate Southern movie houses that took full commercial advantage of being the only buildings at the time to have air conditioning. But by the end of the '70s it followed the fate of Broughton Street, laying dormant and neglected until its purchase and renovation by SCAD in 1989.

This block of Broughton in front of Trustees

Theatre is usually blocked off to mark the gala opening of the Savannah Film Festival each fall. Searchlights crisscross the sky, limos idle in wait, and Hollywood guests strike poses for the photographers.

Across the street is SCAD's **Jen Library** (201 E. Broughton St.), a state-of-the-art facility set in the circa-1890 Levy and Maas Brothers department stores.

An important piece of Broughton Street history happened further west at its intersection with Whitaker Street. Tondee's Tavern was where the infamous "Liberty Boys" met over ale and planned Savannah's role in the American Revolution. Only a plaque marks the site's contribution to Savannah's colonial history.

Wright Square

By now you know the drill. The big monument in Wright Square, Oglethorpe's second square, has nothing to do with James Wright, royal governor of Georgia before the Revolution, for whom it's named. Instead the monument honors **William Gordon,** former mayor and

William Gordon's monument in Wright Square

founder of the Central of Georgia Railroad, which upon completion of the Savannah–Macon run was the longest railroad in the world. Gordon is in fact the only native Savannahian honored in a city square.

But more importantly, Wright Square is the final resting place for the great Yamacraw chief **Tomochichi,** buried in 1737 in an elaborate state funeral at James Oglethorpe's insistence. A huge boulder of north Georgia granite honoring the chief was placed in a corner of the square in 1899 under the auspices of William Gordon's daughter-in-law.

However, Tomochichi is not buried under the boulder, but rather somewhere underneath the Gordon monument. So why not rename it Tomochichi Square? Old ways die hard down here, my friend.

On the west side of the square is the **Federal Courthouse and Post Office,** built in 1898 out of Georgia marble. The building's stately facade makes an appearance in several films, including the original *Cape Fear* and *Midnight in the Garden of Good and Evil.*

Across the square stands another Preston design, the **Old Chatham County Courthouse,** no longer an active judicial facility but still known as "the old courthouse." Note the yellow brick construction, quite rare for this area.

Next to the old courthouse is the historic **Evangelical Lutheran Church of the Ascension** (120 Bull St., 912/232-4151, www.elcota.org), built in the 1870s for a congregation that traced its roots to some of the first Austrian Salzburgers to come to Savannah in 1734. While most moved to adjacent Effingham County, many stayed and thrived in town, where they were universally well-regarded for their work ethic and honest dealings.

JULIETTE GORDON LOW BIRTHPLACE
Around the corner from Wright Square at Oglethorpe and Bull is the Juliette Gordon Low Birthplace (10 E. Oglethorpe Ave., 912/233-4501, www.juliettegordonlowbirthplace.org, year-round Mon.–Tues. and Thurs.–Sat. 10 A.M.–4 P.M., Sun. 11 A.M.–4 P.M., Mar.–Oct. Wed. 10 A.M.–4 P.M., $8 adults, $7 children),

USED BY PERMISSION OF THE JULIETTE GORDON LOW BIRTHPLACE, GIRL SCOUT NATIONAL CENTER

formal parlor at the Juliette Gordon Low Birthplace

SCOUT'S HONOR: JULIETTE GORDON LOW

Known as "Daisy" to family and friends, Juliette Magill Kinzie Gordon was born to be a pioneer. Her father's family took part in the original settlement of Georgia, and her mother's kin were among the founders of Chicago.

Though mostly known as the founder of the Girl Scouts of the USA, Daisy was also an artist, adventurer, and healer. Born and raised in the house on Oglethorpe Avenue in Savannah known to Girl Scouts across the nation as simply "The Birthplace," she was an animal lover with an early penchant for theater, drawing, and poetry.

After school she traveled, returning home to marry wealthy cotton heir William Mackay Low, son of the builder of Savannah's exquisite Andrew Low House. A harbinger of her troubled marriage happened on her wedding day, on the steps of Christ Church. A grain of rice, thrown for good luck, struck her eardrum and led to a painful infection and loss of hearing. Daisy and her husband moved to England, using the Andrew Low House as a rental property and winter residence. She maintained a home in England until her death, spending much of the year traveling in the United States and abroad.

Daisy returned to Savannah with the outbreak of the Spanish-American War in 1898. Because of the city's proximity to Cuba, one of the main theaters of the war, it became a staging area for U.S. Army troops from all over the country.

For Savannah, taking such an active role was an opportunity to make amends for the alienation of the Civil War and effectively rejoin the union again. For the first time since Sherman's March to the Sea, Savannahians proudly displayed the Stars and Stripes in an honest show of patriotism of which Daisy was a part, tending to wounded soldiers returning from Cuba.

After the war, Daisy returned to England to spend the last days of her marriage, which existed in name only until her husband's death in 1905. After settling his estate, she used the proceeds to fund some traveling.

In 1911 while in England she met another man who would change her life: Robert Baden-Powell, founder of the Boy Scouts and Girl Guides in Britain. Struck by the simplicity and usefulness of his project, she carried the seeds of a similar idea back with her to the United States.

"I've got something for the girls of Savannah, and all of America, and all the world, and we're going to start it tonight!" were her famous words in a phone call to a cousin after meeting Baden-Powell. So on March 12, 1912, Daisy gathered 18 girls to register the first troop of American Girl Guides, later the Girl Scouts of the USA.

Juliette "Daisy" Gordon Low died of breast cancer in her bed in the Andrew Low House on January 17, 1927. She was buried in Laurel Grove Cemetery on the city's west side. Girl Scout troops from all over America visit her birthplace, the Andrew Low House, and her gravesite to this day, often leaving flowers and small personal objects near her tombstone as tokens of respect and gratitude.

© JIM MOREKIS

gravesite of Juliette Gordon Low in Laurel Grove Cemetery

declared the city's very first National Historic Landmark in 1965. The founder of the Girl Scouts of the USA lived here from her birth in 1860 until her marriage, returning home to stay until her mother's death. The house was completed in 1821 for Mayor James Moore Wayne, future Supreme Court Justice, but the current furnishings, many original, are intended to reflect the home during the 1880s.

Also called the Girl Scout National Center, the Low birthplace is probably Savannah's most festive historic site because of the heavy traffic of Girl Scout troops from across the United States. They flock here year-round to take part in programs and learn more about their organization's founder, whose family sold the house to the Girl Scouts in 1953.

You don't have to be affiliated with the Girl Scouts to tour the home. Tours are given every 15 minutes, and tickets are available at the Oglethorpe Avenue entrance. Be aware the site is closed most holidays, sometimes for extended periods; be sure to check the website for details.

Oglethorpe Square

Don't look for a monument to Georgia's founder in the square named for him. That would be way too easy, so of course his monument is in Chippewa Square. Originally called "Upper New Square," Oglethorpe Square was created in 1742.

◖ OWENS-THOMAS HOUSE

The square's main claim to fame, the Owens-Thomas House (124 Abercorn St., 912/233-9743, www.telfair.org, Mon. noon–5 P.M., Tues.–Sat. 10 A.M.–5 P.M., Sun. 1–5 P.M., $15 adults, $5 children), lies on the northeast corner. Widely known as the finest example of Regency architecture in the United States, the Owens-Thomas House was designed by brilliant young English architect William Jay. One of the first professionally trained architects in America, Jay was only 24 when he designed the home for cotton merchant or "factor" Richard Richardson, who lost the house in the depression of 1820 (all that remains of Richardson's tenure are three marble-top tables).

The house's current name is derived from Savannah Mayor George Owens, who bought the house in 1830. It remained in his family until 1951, when his granddaughter Margaret Thomas bequeathed it to the Telfair Academy of Arts and Sciences, which currently operates the site.

Several things about the Owens-Thomas House stand out. First, it's constructed mostly of tabby, a mixture of lime, oyster shells, and sand. Its exterior is English stucco while the front garden balustrade is a type of artificial stone called coade stone.

Perhaps most interestingly, a complex plumbing system features rain-fed cisterns, flushing toilets, sinks, bathtubs, and a shower. When built, the Owens-Thomas House in fact had the first indoor plumbing in Savannah.

While inside the house, notice the unusual curved walls, with doors bowed to match. While many Owens family furnishings are part of the collection, much of it is representative of American and European work from 1750 to 1830. On the south facade is a beautiful cast iron veranda from which Revolutionary War hero Marquis de Lafayette addressed a crowd of star-struck Savannahians during his visit in 1825.

The 1990s marked the most intensive phase of restoration for the home, which began with a careful renovation of the carriage house and the associated slave quarters—discovered in a surprisingly intact state, including the original "haint blue" paint. The carriage house, where all tours begin, is now the home's gift shop.

Telfair Square

One of the few Savannah squares to show consistency in nomenclature, Telfair Square was indeed named for Mary Telfair, last heir of a family that was one of the most important in Savannah history. A noted patron of the arts, Mary bequeathed the family mansion to the Georgia Historical Society upon her death in 1875 to serve as a museum. Originally called St. James Square after a similar square in London, Telfair is the last of Oglethorpe's original four squares.

◖ TELFAIR MUSEUMS

Also consistent with its name, Telfair Square indeed hosts two of the three buildings operated by the Telfair Museums (912/790-8800, www.telfair.org), an umbrella organization that relies on a combination of private and public funding and drives much of the arts agenda in Savannah.

The original part of the complex and the oldest art museum in the South, the **Telfair Academy of Arts and Sciences** (121 Barnard St.) was built in 1821 by the great William Jay for Alexander Telfair, scion of that famous Georgia family. The five statues in front are of Phidias, Raphael, Rubens, Michelangelo, and Rembrandt. Inside, the sculpture gallery and rotunda were added in 1885, the year before the building's official opening as a museum.

As well as displaying Sylvia Judson Shaw's now-famous "Bird Girl" sculpture originally in Bonaventure Cemetery (actually the third of four casts by the sculptor), the Telfair Academy features an outstanding collection of primarily 18th- and 20th-century works, most notably the largest public collection of visual art by

Kahlil Gibran. Major paintings include work by Childe Hassam, Frederick Frieseke, Gari Melchers, and the massive *Black Prince of Crécy* by Julian Story.

The latest and proudest addition to the Telfair brand is the striking, 64,000-square-foot **Jepson Center for the Arts** (207 W. York St.), whose ultramodern exterior sits catty-corner from the old Telfair. Promoting a massive, daringly designed new facility devoted to nothing but modern art was a hard sell in this traditional town, especially when renowned architect Moshe Safdie insisted on building a glassed-in flyover across a lane between two buildings. But no one regrets it now, as Safdie's vision has exceeded even his supporters' high expectations. After a few delays in construction, Jepson opened its doors to the public in March 2006 and has since wowed locals and visitors alike with its cutting-edge assortment of late 20th- and 21st-century modern art, including digital installation pieces.

The Telfair Academy is open Monday noon–5 P.M., Tuesday–Saturday 10 A.M.–5 P.M., and Sunday 1–5 P.M. The Jepson Center

Jepson Center for the Arts

© JIM MOREKIS

A CITY OF ART

© JIM MOREKIS

the Telfair Academy of Arts and Sciences

There are more art galleries per capita in Savannah than in New York City – one gallery for every 2,191 residents, to be exact.

The no-brainer package experience for the visitor is the combo of the **Telfair Academy of Arts and Sciences** (121 Barnard St., 912/790-8800, www.telfair.org) and the **Jepson Center** (207 W. York St., 912/790-8800, www.telfair.org). These two affiliated arms of the Telfair Museums run the gamut, from the Academy's impressive collection of Kahlil Gibran drawings to the 2008 installation by local favorite Marcus Kenney at the Jepson, comprising dozens of tiny heads arranged on the entrance stairs in the atrium.

Naturally, Savannah College of Art & Design (SCAD) galleries (912/525-5225, www.scad.edu) are in abundance all over town, displaying the handiwork of students, faculty, and alumni.

The SCAD outposts with the most consistently impressive exhibits are the **Pei Ling Chan Gallery** (324 MLK Jr. Blvd.), **Gutstein Gallery** (201 E. Broughton St.) and **Pinnacle Gallery** (320 E. Liberty St.). The college also runs its own museum, the **SCAD Museum of Art** (227 MLK Jr. Blvd., 912/525-7191, www.scad.edu), home of the Newton Center for British American Studies as well as a massive new wing devoted to the huge and won-

derful Walter O. Evans Collection of African American Art.

While they don't get as much press, Savannah also has plenty of non-Telfair, non-SCAD galleries as well, ranging from the cutting edge and avant-garde to pedestrian acrylics of seagulls.

The more adventurous indie galleries in town include: **Chroma Gallery** (31 Barnard St., 912/232-2787, www.chromaartgallery.com); **Desotorow Gallery** (2427 DeSoto Ave., 912/335-8204, www.desotorow.org); **Gallery Espresso** (234 Bull St., 912/233-5348, www.galleryespresso.com), actually a coffeehouse; and **Kim Iocovozzi Fine Art** (1 W. Jones St., 912/234-9424), pronounced "ike-a-vozy" and hosting contemporary masters and a collection of daguerrotypes (Kim's a guy, by the way).

An interesting, newish gallery on Broughton Street, **Liquid Sands Glass Gallery** (319 W. Broughton St., 912/232-3600), deals in intricate blown glass.

Possibly the most unique and avant-garde space in Savannah, the **Co-Lab** (631 E. Broad St., http://zecolab.tumblr.com) was founded by a collective of SCAD alumni and hosts visual art, performance art, and multimedia exhibits. Check the website for what's happening there when you're in town – it's guaranteed to be thought-provoking.

is closed Tuesdays, and is open Monday, Wednesday, Friday, and Saturday from 10 A.M.–5 P.M., Thursday 10 A.M.–8 P.M., and Sunday noon–5 P.M.

Admission to each one singly is $15 for adults and $5 for children, but I recommend the Telfair's three-site combination ticket, which at the bargain price of $15 ($5 students) allows you to visit both art museums as well as the must-see Owens-Thomas House.

TRINITY UNITED METHODIST CHURCH

Directly between the Telfair and the Jepson stands Trinity United Methodist Church (225 W. President St., 912/233-4766, www.trinity church1848.org, Sunday services 8:45 A.M. and 11 A.M., sanctuary open to public daily 9 A.M.–5 P.M.), Savannah's first Methodist church. Built in 1848 on the site of the Telfair's family garden, its masonry walls are of famous "Savannah Gray" bricks—a lighter, more porous, and elegant variety—under stucco. Virgin long-leaf pines were used for most of the interior, fully restored in 1969. Call ahead for a tour.

Chippewa Square

Named for a battle in the War of 1812, Chippewa Square has a large monument not to the battle, natch, but to James Oglethorpe, clad in full soldier's regalia. Notice the general is still facing south, toward the Spanish!

Yes, the bench on the square's north side is in the same location as the one Tom Hanks occupied in *Forrest Gump*, but it's not the same bench that hosted the two-time Oscar winner's backside—that one was donated by Paramount Pictures to be displayed in the Savannah History Museum on MLK Jr. Boulevard.

From Chippewa Square look south for the huge rectangular steel-and-glass structure dominating the skyline along Liberty Street. That's the infamous **Drayton Tower,** an outstanding, nearly pure example of the Internationalist architecture style nonetheless loathed by traditionalists since its construction in 1955. Until recently it served as low-cost housing for students and seniors. They've since been kicked out, as now the building is subdivided into high-end condos with retail on the ground floor.

HISTORIC SAVANNAH THEATRE

At the northeast corner is the Historic Savannah Theatre (222 Bull St., 912/233-7764, www .savannahtheatre.com), which claims to be the oldest continuously operating theater in America. Designed by William Jay, it opened in 1818 with a production of *The Soldier's Daughter*. In the glory days of gaslight theater in the 1800s, some of the nation's best actors, including Edwin Booth, brother to Lincoln's assassin, regularly trod the boards of its stage. Other notable visitors were Sarah Bernhardt, W. C. Fields, and Oscar Wilde. Due to a fire in 1948, little remains of Jay's original design except a small section of exterior wall. It's currently home to a semi-professional revue company specializing in oldies shows.

INDEPENDENT PRESBYTERIAN CHURCH

Built in 1818, possibly by William Jay—scholars are unsure of the scope of his involvement—Independent Presbyterian Church (207 Bull St., 912/236-3346, www.ipcsav.org, Sunday service 11 A.M., Wednesday service noon) is called the "mother of Georgia Presbyterianism." A fire destroyed most of Independent Presbyterian's original structure in 1889, but the subsequent rebuilding was a very faithful rendering of the original design, based on London's St. Martin in the Fields. The marble baptism font survived the fire and is still used today. Note also the huge mahogany pulpit, another original feature. The church's steeple made a cameo appearance in *Forrest Gump* as a white feather floated by.

Lowell Mason, composer of the hymn "Nearer My God to Thee," was organist at Independent Presbyterian. In 1885 President Woodrow Wilson married local parishioner Ellen Louise Axson in the manse to the rear of the church. Presiding was her grandfather, minister at the time. During the Great Awakening in 1896, almost 3,000 people jammed the sanctuary to hear famous evangelist D. L. Moody preach. Call ahead for a tour.

© JOSH HALLETT

the Independent Presbyterian Church

FIRST BAPTIST CHURCH
The nearby First Baptist Church (223 Bull St., 912/234-2671, Sunday service 11 A.M.) claims to be the oldest original church building in Savannah, with a cornerstone dating from 1830. Services were held here throughout the Civil War, with Union troops attending during the occupation. The church was renovated by renowned local architect Henrik Wallin in 1922. Call ahead for a tour.

COLONIAL CEMETERY
Just north of Chippewa Square is Oglethorpe Avenue, originally called South Broad and the southern boundary of the original colony. At Oglethorpe and Abercorn Streets is Colonial Cemetery, first active in 1750. You'd be forgiven for assuming it's the "D.A.R." cemetery; the Daughters of the American Revolution contributed the ornate iron entranceway in 1913, thoughtfully dedicating it to themselves instead of the cemetery itself.

Unlike the picturesque beauty of Bonaventure and Laurel Grove cemeteries, Colonial Cemetery has a morbid feel. The fact that burials stopped here in 1853 plays into that desolation, but maybe another reason is because it's the final resting ground of many of Savannah's yellow fever victims.

Famous people buried here include Button Gwinnett, one of Georgia's three signers of the Declaration of Independence. The man who reluctantly killed Gwinnett in a duel, General Lachlan McIntosh, is also buried here. The original burial vault of Nathanael Greene is in the cemetery, though the Revolutionary War hero's remains were moved to Johnson Square over a century ago.

Vandalism through the years, mostly by Union troops, has taken its toll on the old gravestones. Many remain lined up along the east wall of the cemetery, with no one alive being able to remember where they originally stood.

Madison Square
Though named for the nation's fourth president, Madison Square memorializes a local hero who gave his life for his city during the American Revolution. Irish immigrant Sergeant William Jasper, hero of the Battle of Fort Moultrie in Charleston three years earlier, was killed leading the American charge during the Siege of Savannah, when an allied army failed to retake the city from the British.

Though the monument in the square honors Jasper, he isn't buried there. His body was interred in a mass grave near the battlefield along with other colonists and soldier-immigrants killed in the one-sided battle.

Though suitably warlike, the two small cannons in the square have nothing to do with the Siege of Savannah. They commemorate the first two highways in Georgia, today known as Augusta Road and Ogeechee Road.

GREEN-MELDRIM HOUSE
Given the house's beauty and history, visitors will be forgiven for not immediately realizing that the Green-Meldrim House (1 W. Macon St., 912/232-1251, tours every half-hour Tues.-Fri. 10 A.M.–3:30 P.M., Sat. 10 A.M.–12:30 P.M.,

the Green-Meldrim House

$7 adults, $2 children) is also the rectory of the adjacent St. John's Episcopal Church, which acquired it in 1892. Though known primarily for serving as General William T. Sherman's headquarters during his occupation of Savannah, visitors find the Green-Meldrim House a remarkably calming, serene location in and of itself, quite apart from its role as the place where Sherman formulated his ill-fated "40 acres and a mule" Field Order Number 15, giving most of the Sea Islands of Georgia and South Carolina to freed blacks.

A remarkably tasteful example of Gothic Revival architecture, this 1850 design by John Norris features a beautiful external gallery of filigree ironwork. The interior is decorated with a keen and rare eye for elegant minimalism in this sometimes *rococo*-minded town.

Nearby, the old **Scottish Rite Temple** at Charlton and Bull Streets was designed by Hyman Witcover, who also designed City Hall. A popular drugstore with a soda fountain for many years, it currently houses the Gryphon Tea Room, run by the Savannah College of Art and Design.

Directly across from that is SCAD's first building, **Poetter Hall,** known to old-timers as the Savannah Volunteer Guards Armory. With its imposing but somewhat whimsical facade right out of a Harry Potter movie, this brick and terra-cotta gem of a Romanesque Revival building was built in 1893 by William Gibbons Preston. It housed National Guard units (as well as a high school) until World War II, when the USO occupied the building during its tenant unit's service in Europe.

At the north side of Madison Square is the **Hilton Savannah DeSoto.** Imagine occupying that same space the most glorious, opulent, regal building you can think of, a paradise of brick, mortar, and buff-colored terra-cotta. That would have been the old DeSoto Hotel, which from its opening in 1890 was known as one of the world's most beautiful hotels and the clear masterpiece in Boston architect William Gibbons Preston's already-impressive Savannah portfolio. Alas, it didn't have air conditioning, so the Hilton chain demolished it in 1968 to build the current nondescript box.

Lafayette Square

Truly one of Savannah's favorite squares,

especially on St. Patrick's Day, verdant Lafayette Square boasts a number of important sights and attractions.

◖ CATHEDRAL OF ST. JOHN THE BAPTIST

Spiritual home to Savannah's Irish community and the oldest Catholic church in Georgia, the Cathedral of St. John the Baptist (222. E. Harris St., 912/233-4709, www.savannah cathedral.org, daily 9 A.M.–5 P.M. with a break for mass noon–12:30 P.M., Sunday services 8 A.M., 10 A.M., 11:30 A.M., Latin mass 1 P.M.) was initially known as Our Lady of Perpetual Help. It's the place to be for mass at 8 A.M. the morning of March 17, as the clans gather in their green jackets and white dresses to take a sip of communion wine before moving on to harder stuff in honor of St. Patrick.

Despite its overt Celtic character today, the parish was originally founded by Haitian émigrés who arrived after an uprising in their native country in the late 1700s. They were joined by other Gallic Catholics when some nobles fled from the French Revolution.

The first sanctuary on the site was built in 1873, after the diocese traded a lot at Taylor and Lincoln Streets to the Sisters of Mercy in exchange for this locale. In a distressingly common event back then in Savannah, fire swept the edifice in 1898, leaving only two spires and the external walls. In an amazing story of determination and skill, the cathedral was completely rebuilt within a year and a half.

In the years since, many renovations have been undertaken, including an interior renovation following the Vatican Council II to incorporate some of its sweeping reforms, for example, a new altar allowing the celebrant to face the congregation. The most recent renovation, from 1998 to 2000, involved the intricate removal, cleaning, and re-leading of more than 50 of the cathedral's stained-glass windows, a roof replacement, and an interior makeover.

When inside the magnificent interior, look for the new 9,000-pound altar and the 8,000-pound baptismal font, both made of Italian marble. The stained-glass window of the Virgin Mary is the largest of the three windows that survived the great fire of 1898.

In 2003, an armed man entered the Cathedral and set the pulpit and bishop's chair on fire, resulting in nearly $400,000 of damage. The pulpit you see now is an exact replica carved in Italy. The arsonist claimed he did it as a statement against organized religion.

ANDREW LOW HOUSE MUSEUM

Another major landmark on Lafayette Square is the Andrew Low House Museum (329 Abercorn St., 912/233-6854, www.andrew-lowhouse.com, Mon.–Wed. and Fri.–Sat. 10 A.M.–4:30 P.M., Sun. noon–4:30 P.M., last tour at 4 P.M., $8 adults, $4.50 children), once the home of Juliette "Daisy" Gordon Low, the founder of the Girl Scouts of the USA, who was married to cotton heir William "Billow" Low, Andrew Low's son. Despite their happy-go-lucky nicknames, the union of Daisy and Billow was a notably unhappy one. Still, divorce was out of the question, so the couple

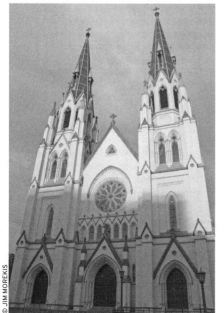

© JIM MOREKIS

the Cathedral of St. John the Baptist

lived separate lives until William's death in 1905. The one good thing that came out of the marriage was the germ for the idea for the Girl Scouts, which Juliette got from England's "Girl Guides" while living with her husband there, Savannah being the couple's winter residence.

Designed by the great New York architect John Norris, the Low House is a magnificent example of the Italianate style. Check out the cast-iron balconies on the long porch, a fairly rare feature in historic Savannah homes. Antiques junkies will go nuts over the furnishings, especially the massive secretary in the parlor, one of only four such in existence (a sibling is in the Metropolitan Museum of Art).

Author William Makepeace Thackeray ate in the dining room, now sporting full French porcelain service, and slept in an upstairs room (he also wrote at the desk by the bed). Also on the second floor you'll see the room where Robert E. Lee stayed during his visit, and the bed where Juliette Gordon Low died.

FLANNERY O'CONNOR CHILDHOOD HOME

On the other corner of Lafayette Square stands the rather Spartan facade of the Flannery O'Connor Childhood Home (207 E. Charlton St., 912/233-6014, www.flannery oconnorhome.org, Fri.–Wed. 1–4 P.M., closed

THE STORY OF "JINGLE BELLS"

Long after the Civil War, a North/South feud of a more harmless kind still simmers, as Boston and Savannah vie over bragging rights as to where the classic Christmas song "Jingle Bells" was written.

The song's composer, James L. Pierpont, led a life at times as carefree as his song itself. Born in Boston as the son of an abolitionist Unitarian minister, Pierpont's wanderlust manifested early, when he ventured from his new wife and young children to follow the Gold Rush to San Francisco, coming back east after one of that city's periodic enormous fires.

When his brother John was named minister of the new Unitarian congregation in Savannah in 1853 – a novelty down south at the time – Pierpont followed him, becoming music director and organist, again leaving behind his wife and children in Boston. During this time Pierpont became a prolific composer of secular tunes, including polkas, ballads, and minstrel songs.

Pierpont's first wife died of tuberculosis in 1856. By August 1857, he had remarried the daughter of the mayor of Savannah. That same month, a Boston-based publisher, Oliver Ditson and Co., published his song "One Horse Open Sleigh." Two years later it was re-released under the current title, "Jingle Bells." However, at neither time was the song a popular hit.

In 1859, with slavery tearing the country apart, the Unitarian Church in Savannah closed due to its abolitionist stance. By the outbreak of war, Pierpont's brother John had gone back up north. James Pierpont, however, opted to stay in Savannah with his second wife Eliza Jane, going so far as to sign up with the Isle of Hope Volunteers (he served as a company clerk) of the Confederate Army.

It took action by his son Juriah in 1880 to renew the copyright to what would become one of the most famous songs of all time. Pierpont died in 1883 in Winter Haven, Florida, and by his own request was buried in Savannah's Laurel Grove Cemetery.

The provenance of his now-famous song is more in doubt. In Massachusetts, they swear Pierpont wrote the song while at the home of one Mrs. Otis Waterman. In Georgia, scholars assure us a homesick Pierpont wrote the tune during a winter at a house at Oglethorpe and Whitaker streets, long since demolished.

The Savannah contingent's ace in the hole is the fact that "Jingle Bells" was first performed in public at a Thanksgiving program at the local Unitarian Universalist Church in 1857. And despite persistent claims in Massachusetts that he wrote the song in that state in 1850, southern scholars point out that Pierpont was actually in California in 1850.

Thursdays, $5). The Savannah-born novelist lived in this three-story townhome from her birth in 1925 until 1938 and attended church at the Cathedral across the square. Once a fairly nondescript attraction for so favorite a native daughter, a just-concluded round of renovations has returned the main two floors to the state Flannery would have known, including an extensive library. A nonprofit association sponsors O'Connor-related readings and signings.

While the current backyard garden is circa 1993, it is the place where five-year-old Flannery is said to have taught a chicken to walk backwards, foreshadowing the eccentric, gothic flavor of her writing.

Across from the O'Connor house is the **Hamilton-Turner Inn** (330 Abercorn St., 912/233-1833, www.hamilton-turnerinn.com). Now a privately owned bed-and-breakfast, this 1873 Second Empire mansion is best known for the showmanship of its over-the-top Victorian appointments and its role in "The Book" as the home of Joe Odom's girlfriend "Mandy Nichols" (real name Nancy Hillis). In 1883 it was reportedly the first house in Savannah to have electricity.

Troup Square

This low-key square boasts the most modern-looking monument downtown, the **Armillary Sphere.** Essentially an elaborate sundial, the

So in this case at least, it appears the South can claim victory over the Yankees.

In one of those delightful happenstances of serendipity, Pierpont's old church – moved to Troup Square from its original site on Oglethorpe Square – went on the market in the 1990s and the local Unitarian Universalist congregation was able to raise enough money to buy it. It remains there to this day.

the Unitarian Universalist Church of Savannah, where "Jingle Bells" was first performed in public

© JIM MOREKIS

sphere is a series of astrologically themed rings with an arrow that marks the time by shadow. It's supported by six tortoises.

Troup Square is also the home of the historic **Unitarian Universalist Church of Savannah** (313 E. Harris St., 912/234-0980, www.jingle bellschurch.org, Sunday service 11 A.M.). This original home of Savannah's Unitarians, who sold the church when the Civil War came, was recently re-acquired by the congregation. It is where James L. Pierpont first performed his immortal tune "Jingle Bells." However, when he did so the church was actually on Oglethorpe Square. The entire building was moved to Troup Square in the mid-1800s.

Just east of Troup Square, near the intersection of Harris and Price Streets, is the **Beach Institute** (502 E. Harris St., 912/234-8000, www.kingtisdell.org, Tues.–Sun. noon–5 P.M., $4). Built as a school by the Freedmen's Bureau soon after the Civil War, it was named after its prime benefactor, Alfred Beach, editor of *Scientific American,* and served as an African American school through 1919. Restored by SCAD and given back to the city to serve as a museum, the Beach Institute houses the permanent Ulysses Davis collection and a rotating calendar of art with a connection to black history.

JONES STREET

There aren't a lot of individual attractions on Jones Street, the east–west avenue between Taylor and Charlton Streets just north of Monterey Square. Rather, it's the small-scale, throwback feel of the place and its tasteful, dignified homes, including the former home of Joe Odom at 16 East Jones Street, that are the attraction.

The **Eliza Thompson House** (5 W. Jones St.), now a bed-and-breakfast, was in fact the first home on Jones Street. Cotton factor Joseph Thompson built the house for his wife Eliza in 1847. The carriage house is not original to the structure, having been built almost from scratch in 1980.

◖ Monterey Square

For many, this is the ultimate Savannah square.

Originally named "Monterrey Square" to commemorate the local Irish Jasper Greens' participation in a victorious Mexican-American War battle in 1846, the spelling morphed into its current version somewhere along the way. But Monterey Square remains one of the most visually beautiful and serene spots in all of Savannah.

At the center of the square is a monument not to the victory for which it's named but to Count Casimir Pulaski, killed while attempting to retake the city from the British, and whose remains supposedly lie under the 55-foot monument. As early as 1912, people began noticing the disintegration of the monument due to substandard marble used in some key parts, but it wasn't until the 1990s that a full restoration was accomplished.

(The restoration company discovered that one of the monument's 34 sections had been accidentally installed upside-down. So in the true spirit of preservation, they dutifully put the section back—upside down!)

The "Goddess of Liberty" atop the monument, however, is not original; you can see her in the Savannah History Museum.

Fans of ironwork will enjoy the ornate masterpieces in wrought iron featured at many houses on the periphery of the square.

MERCER-WILLIAMS HOUSE MUSEUM

Many tourists come to see the Mercer-Williams House Museum (429 Bull St., 912/236-6352, www.mercerhouse.com, Mon.–Sat. 10:30 A.M.–3:40 P.M., Sun. 12:30–4 P.M., $12.50 adults, $8 students). While locals never begrudge the business Savannah's enjoyed since "The Book," it's a shame that this grand John Norris building is now primarily known as a crime scene involving antiques dealer Jim Williams and his lover. Therefore it might come as no surprise that if you take a tour of the home, you might hear less about "The Book" than you may have expected.

Now proudly owned by Jim Williams' sister Dorothy Kingery, an established academic in her own right, the Mercer-Williams House deliberately concentrates on the early history of the home and her brother's prodigious talent as

© JIM MOREKIS

the Mercer-Williams House on Monterey Square

a collector and conservator of fine art and antiques. That said, Dr. Kingery's mama didn't raise no fool, as we say down here. The house was known to generations of Savannahians as simply the Mercer House until *Midnight* took off, at which time the eponymous nod to the late Mr. Williams was added.

Built for General Hugh W. Mercer, Johnny Mercer's great-grandfather, in 1860, the war interrupted construction. General Mercer—descendant of the Revolutionary War general and George Washington's close friend Hugh Mercer—survived the war, in which he was charged with the defense of Savannah. But he soon fell into hard times and was forced to sell the house to John Wilder, who moved in after completion in 1868.

(Just so you know, and despite what any tour guide might tell you, the great Johnny Mercer himself never lived in the house. Technically, no member of his family ever did, either.)

Tours of the home's main four rooms begin in the carriage house to the rear of the mansion. They're worth it for art aficionados even though the upstairs, Dr. Kingery's residence, is off-limits. Be forewarned that if you're coming just to see things about the book or movie, you might be disappointed.

TEMPLE MICKVE ISRAEL

Directly across Monterey Square from the Mercer House is Temple Mickve Israel (20 E. Gordon St., 912/233-1547, www.mickveisrael.org), a notable structure for many reasons: It's Georgia's first synagogue; it's the only Gothic synagogue in the country; and it's the third-oldest Jewish congregation in North America (following New York and Newport, R.I.). Notable congregants have included Dr. Samuel Nunes Ribiero, who helped stop an epidemic in 1733; his descendant Raphael Moses, considered the father of the peach industry in the Peach State; and current Mickve Israel Rabbi Arnold Mark Belzer, one of Savannah's most beloved community leaders. A specialist in the study of small, often-persecuted Jewish communities around the world, Belzer met Pope John Paul II in 2005 as a part of that Pontiff's historic rapprochement between the Catholic Church and Judaism.

Mickve Israel offers 30–45 minute tours of the sanctuary and museum, which are open daily 10 A.M.–1 P.M. and 2–4 P.M. It's closed weekends and on Jewish holidays.

Calhoun Square

The last of the 24 squares in Savannah's original grid, Calhoun Square is also the only square with all its original buildings intact—a rarity indeed in a city ravaged by fire so many times in its history.

Dominating the south side of the square is Savannah's first public elementary school and spiritual home of Savannah educators, the **Massie Heritage Center** (207 E. Gordon St., 912/201-5070, www.massieschool.com, Mon.–Fri. 9 A.M.–4 P.M., self-guided tour $5 adults, $3 children, guided tour $8 adults, $3 children). In 1841, Peter Massie, a Scots planter with a populist streak, endowed the school to give poor children as good an education as the children of rich families, like Massie's own, received.

Temple Mickve Israel

Another of Savannah's masterpieces by John Norris—whose impressive oeuvre includes the Low House, the Mercer House, and the Green-Meldrim House—the central portion of the tri-fold building was completed in 1856 and is a great example of Greek Revival architecture (the two large wings on each side were added later by different architects).

After the Civil War, the "Massie school," as it's locally known, was designated as the area's African American public school. Classes ceased in 1974 and it now operates as a living history museum, centering on the period-appointed one-room "heritage classroom."

Catty-corner to the Massie School is the **Wesley Monumental United Methodist Church** (429 Abercorn St., 912/232-0191, www.wesleymonumental.org, Sunday services 8:45 A.M. and 11 A.M., sanctuary open to public daily 9 A.M.–5 P.M.). This home of Savannah's first Methodist parish was named not only for movement founder John Wesley but for his musical younger brother Charles. Built in 1875 on the model of Queen's Kirk in Amsterdam and

the old Massie school

the fourth incarnation of the parish home, this is another great example of Savannah's Gothic churches. Its acoustically wonderful sanctuary features a magnificent Noack Organ, which would no doubt please the picky ears of Charles Wesley himself, author of the lyrics to "Hark! The Herald Angels Sing."

Martin Luther King Jr. Boulevard

Originally known as West Broad Street (you'll still hear old-timers refer to it that way), Martin Luther King Jr. Boulevard is the spiritual home of Savannah's African American community, though it has gone through several transformations. In the early 1800s, West Broad was a fashionable address, but during the middle of that century its north end got a bad reputation for crime and blight, as thousands of Irish immigrants packed in right beside the area's poor black population.

West Broad's glory days as a center of black culture happened in the first half of the 20th century, beginning and ending with the late, great Union Station terminal. Built in 1902, the terminal was the main gateway to the city and ushered in a heyday on West Broad that saw thriving black movie theaters like the Star. Here were packed venues on the "chitlin circuit" such as The Dunbar, hosting such legends as Little Richard. The great number of African American–owned banks on the street gave it the name "the Wall Street of black America."

The end came with the razing of the gorgeous Union Station in 1963 to make way for an on-ramp to I-16. The poorly planned project cut the historic boulevard in two, with several entire neighborhoods being destroyed to make way. While the hideous on-ramp remains, every now and then talk surfaces of moving it in an attempt to recreate the magic of old West Broad.

Renamed for the civil rights leader in 1990, MLK Jr. Boulevard currently is undergoing another renaissance. A city-sponsored face-lift of the median and a low-interest facade loan program, begun in 1996, have beautified some formerly run-down areas near the Historic District, while an increase in businesses servicing the SCAD student population brings a vibrant, edgy hustle to the area on into the night.

During his visit for the 2007 Savannah Music Festival, jazz great Wynton Marsalis dedicated a plaque to Louis Armstrong's mentor King Oliver in front of the building at 514 MLK Jr. Boulevard where Oliver spent his last days.

RALPH MARK GILBERT CIVIL RIGHTS MUSEUM

One of the former black-owned bank buildings on MLK Jr. Boulevard is now home to the Ralph Mark Gilbert Civil Rights Museum (460 MLK Jr. Blvd., 912/231-8900, www.savcivilrights.com, Mon.–Sat. 9 A.M.–5 P.M., $8 adults, $4 children). Named for the pastor of the First African Baptist Church and a key early civil rights organizer, the building was also the local NAACP headquarters for a time.

Three floors of exhibits here include photos and interactive exhibits, the highlight for historians being a fiber optic map of nearly 100 significant civil rights sites. The first floor features a re-creation of the Azalea Room of the local Levy's department store, an early boycott diner where blacks were not allowed to eat, though they could buy goods from the store. The second floor is more for hands-on education, with classrooms, a computer room, and a video/reading room. A film chronicles mass-meetings, voter registration drives, boycotts, sit-ins, kneel-ins (integration of churches), and wade-ins (integration of beaches).

SHIPS OF THE SEA MARITIME MUSEUM

One of Savannah's more unique museums is the quirky Ships of the Sea Maritime Museum (41 MLK Jr. Blvd., 912/232-1511, http://shipsofthesea.org, Tues.–Sun. 10 A.M.–5 P.M., $8 adults, $6 students). The stunning Greek Revival building in which it resides is known as the Scarbrough House because it was initially built in 1819 by the great William Jay for local shipping merchant William Scarbrough, owner of the SS *Savannah,* the first steamship to cross the Atlantic. After the Scarbroughs sold the

SAVANNAH

property, it became the West Broad School for African Americans from Reconstruction through integration.

One of the Historic Savannah Foundation's key restoration projects in the 1970s, the museum recently got another major facelift in 1998, including a roof based on the original Jay design and a delightful enlargement of the mansion's garden out back. Inside, children, maritime buffs, and crafts connoisseurs can find intricate and detailed scale models of various historic vessels, such as Oglethorpe's *Anne,* the SS *Savannah,* and the NS *Savannah,* the world's first nuclear-powered surface vessel. There's even a model of the *Titanic.*

BATTLEFIELD PARK

Under this name, three important sites are clustered together on MLK Jr. Boulevard under the auspices of the Coastal Heritage Society: the Savannah History Museum, the Roundhouse Museum, and the Siege of Savannah battlefield.

The **Savannah History Museum** (303 MLK Jr. Blvd., 912/651-6825, www.chs georgia.org, Mon.–Fri. 8:30 A.M.–5 P.M., Sat.–Sun. 9 A.M.–5 P.M., $5 adults, $3.75 students),

first stop for many a visitor to town because it's in the same restored Central of Georgia passenger shed as the Visitors Center, contains many interesting exhibits on local history, concentrating mostly on colonial times. Towards the rear of the museum is a room for rotating exhibits, as well as one of Johnny Mercer's two Oscars and of course the historic "*Forrest Gump* bench" that Tom Hanks sat on during his scenes in Chippewa Square.

The **Roundhouse Railroad Museum** (601 W. Harris St., 912/651-6823, www.chs georgia.org, daily 9 A.M.–5 P.M., $10 adults, $4 students) is an ongoing homage to the deep and strangely underreported influence of the railroad industry on Savannah. Constructed in 1830 for the brand-new Central of Georgia line, the Roundhouse's design was cutting-edge for the time, the first facility to put all the railroad's key facilities in one place. Spared by Sherman, the site saw its real heyday after the Civil War. But as technology changed, so did the Roundhouse, which gradually fell further into neglect until the 1960s, when preservation-minded buffs banded together to raise enough money to save it.

There's a large collection of various period

Battle Memorial Park off Martin Luther King Jr. Boulevard

© JIM MOREKIS

the Roundhouse Railroad Museum

locomotives and rail cars. Some of Savannah's greatest artisans have contributed their preservation skills to bring back much of the facility's muscular splendor. The real highlight of the Roundhouse is the thing in the middle that gave it its name, a huge central turntable for positioning rolling stock for repair and maintenance. Frequent demonstrations occur with an actual steam locomotive firing up and taking a turn on the turntable.

Right off MLK Jr. Boulevard is the new **Battle Memorial Park** (dawn–dusk, free), a.k.a. the Spring Hill Redoubt, a reconstruction of the British fortifications at the Siege of Savannah with an interpretive site. Note the redoubt is not at the actual location of the original fort; that lies underneath the nearby Sons of the Revolution marker. Eight hundred granite markers signify the battle's casualties, most of whom were buried in mass graves soon afterward. To Savannah's everlasting shame, most of the remains of these brave men were simply bulldozed up and discarded without ceremony during later construction projects.

VICTORIAN DISTRICT

Boasting 50 blocks of fine Victorian and Queen Anne frame houses, Savannah's Victorian district gets nowhere near the media attention as the older, more stately homes closer to the river. But it is truly magnificent in its own right, and nearly as expansive. The city's first suburb, built between 1870 and 1910, it runs from roughly Gwinnett Street south to Anderson Street, with Montgomery and Price Streets as east/west boundaries.

In addition to the glories of Forsyth Park, some key areas for connoisseurs of truly grand Victorian architecture are the residential blocks of East Hall Street between Lincoln and Price Streets—one of the few street sections in town with the original paving. Some other nice examples are in the 1900-2000 blocks of Bull Street near the large Bull Street Public Library, including the famous "Gingerbread House" at 1917 Bull St., now a private bridal design studio.

◖ Forsyth Park

A favorite with locals and tourists alike, the

vast, lush expanse of Forsyth Park is a center of local life, abuzz with activity and events year-round. The park owes its existence to William B. Hodgson, who donated its core 10 acres to the city for use as a park. Deeply influenced by the then-trendy design of greenspace areas in France, Forsyth Park's landscape design by William Bischoff dates to 1851. Named for Georgia Governor John Forsyth, the park comprises 30 acres and its perimeter is about a mile.

Near the center of the park is the "fort," actually a revitalized version of an old dummy fort used for military drills in the early 20th century. Now managed by the nearby Mansion on Forsyth hotel, it's a good

FORSYTH PARK WALKING TOUR

Here's a walking tour of Savannah's backyard, the one-of-a-kind Forsyth Park, beginning at the north end at Gaston and Bull Streets:

As you approach the park, don't miss the ornate ironwork on the west side of Bull street marking the **Armstrong House,** designed by Henrik Wallin. Featured in the 1962 film *Cape Fear* as well as 1997's *Midnight in the Garden of Good and Evil,* this Italianate mansion was once home to Armstrong Junior College before its move to the south side. When he's not practicing law in this building, Sonny Seiler, one of the characters in "The Book," still raises the University of Georgia's signature bulldog mascots. Directly across Bull Street is another site of *Midnight* fame, the Oglethorpe Club, one of the many brick and terra-cotta designs by local architect Alfred Eichberg.

It's easy to miss, but as you enter the park's north side, you encounter the **Marine Memorial,** erected in 1947 to honor the 24 Chatham County Marines killed in World War II. Subsequently, the names of Marines killed in Korea and Vietnam were added.

Look west at the corner of Whitaker and Gaston Streets. That's **Hodgson Hall,** home of the Georgia Historical Society. This 1876 building was commissioned by Margaret Telfair to honor her late husband William Hodgson, chief benefactor of the park the house overlooks. The Georgia Historical Society (912/651-2125, www.georgiahistory.com) administers a treasure of books, documents, maps, photos, and prints that has been a boon to writers and researchers since it was chartered by the state legislature in 1839.

Looking east at the corner of Drayton and Gaston Streets, you'll see the old **Poor House**

and Hospital, in use until 1854 when it was converted to serve as the headquarters for the Medical College of Georgia. During the Civil War, General Sherman used the hospital to treat wounded Federal soldiers. From 1930 to 1980 the building was the site of Candler Hospital.

Behind Candler Hospital's cast-iron fence you can soak in the venerable beauty of Savannah's most famous tree, the 300-year-old **Candler Oak.** During Sherman's occupation, wounded Confederate prisoners were treated within a barricade around the oak. The tree is on the National Register of Historic Trees and was the maiden preservation project of the Savannah Tree Foundation, which secured America's first-ever conservation easement on a single tree.

Walking south into the park proper you can't miss the world-famous **Forsyth Fountain,** an iconic Savannah sight if there ever was one. Cast in iron on a French model, the fountain was dedicated in 1858. Its water is typically dyed green a few days before St. Patrick's Day. Interestingly, two other versions of this fountain exist – one in Poughkeepsie, New York, and the other in, of all places, the central plaza in Cusco, Peru. Various acts of vandalism and natural disaster took its toll on the fountain until a major restoration in 1988 brought it to its present level of beauty.

Continuing south, you'll encounter two low buildings in the center of the park. The one on the east side is the so-called "Dummy Fort," circa 1909, formerly a training ground for local militia. Now it's the **Forsyth Park Café** (daily 7 A.M.-dusk, later on festival evenings) managed by the hotel Mansion on Forsyth Park just across Drayton Street.

place to stop in and get a snack or use the public restroom.

The park is a center of activities all year long, from free festivals to concerts to Ultimate Frisbee games to the constant circuit around the periphery of walkers, joggers, dog owners, and bicyclists. The only time you shouldn't venture into the park is after midnight. Otherwise, enjoy.

Carnegie Branch Library

Looking like Frank Lloyd Wright parachuted one of his buildings into Victorian Savannah, the Carnegie Branch Library (537 E. Henry St., 912/652-3600, Mon. 10 A.M.–8 P.M., Tues.–Thurs. 10 A.M.–6 P.M., Fri.–Sat. 2–6 P.M.) is the only example of Prairie-style architecture in town, designed by Savannah architect Julian

To the west is the charming **Fragrant Garden for the Blind.** One of those precious little Savannah gems that is too often overlooked in favor of other attractions, the Fragrant Garden was sponsored by the local Garden Club and based on others of its type throughout the United States.

The tall monument dominating Forsyth Park's central mall area is the **Confederate Memorial,** which recently received a major facelift. Dedicated in 1875, it wasn't finished in its final form until several years later. A New York sculptor carved the Confederate soldier atop the monument. A copy of it is in Poughkeepsie, New York, as a memorial to Federal dead – with the "C.S.A." on the soldier's rucksack changed to "U.S.A." The Bartow and McLaws monuments surrounding the Confederate Memorial were originally in Chippewa Square.

We'll close the walking tour with my favorite Forsyth Park landmark, at the extreme southern end. It's the Memorial to Georgia Veterans of the Spanish-American War, more commonly known as **"The Hiker"** because of the subject's almost casual demeanor and confident stride. Savannah was a major staging area for that conflict, and many troops were bivouacked in the park. Sculpted in 1902 by Alice Ruggles Kitson, more than 50 replicas of "The Hiker" were made and put up all over the United States; because the same bronze formula was used for all 50 of them, the statues are used by scientists today to gauge the effects of acid rain across the nation.

© JIM MOREKIS

the Forsyth Fountain

de Bruyn Kops and built, as the name implies, with funding from tycoon/philanthropist Andrew Carnegie in 1914. But much more importantly, the Carnegie Library was for decades the only public library for African Americans in Savannah. One of its patrons was a young Clarence Thomas, who would grow up to be a Supreme Court justice.

EASTSIDE
Old Fort Jackson

The oldest standing brick fort in Georgia, Old Fort Jackson (912/232-3945, http://chsgeorgia. org, daily 9 A.M.–5 P.M., $6 adults, $5.50 students, free for children six and under), named for Georgia Governor James Jackson, is also one of eight remaining examples of the so-called Second System of American forts built prior to the War of 1812. Its main claim to fame is its supporting role in the saga of the CSS *Georgia,* a Confederate ironclad now resting under 40 feet of water directly in front of the fort.

Built with $115,000 in funds raised by the Ladies Gunboat Society, the *Georgia*—wrapped in an armor girdle of railroad ties—proved too heavy for its engine. So it was simply anchored in the channel opposite Fort Jackson as a floating battery. With General Sherman's arrival in 1864, Confederate forces evacuating to South Carolina scuttled the vessel where she lay to keep her out of Yankee hands.

Maritime archaeology on the *Georgia* continues apace, with dive teams bringing up cannons, ammunition, and other artifacts. (Unlike Charleston's CSS *Hunley* submarine, no lives were lost in the *Georgia* incident, therefore there are no concerns about disrupting a gravesite.) Every now and then, talk surfaces of raising the ironclad—both for research and because the port views it as an impediment to dredging the channel even deeper—but most experts say it's unlikely to survive the stress.

Operated by the nonprofit Coastal Heritage Society, Fort Jackson is in an excellent state of preservation and provides loads of information for history buffs as well as for kids, who will enjoy climbing the parapets and running on the large parade ground (this area was once a rice field). Inside the fort's casemates underneath the ramparts you'll find well-organized exhibits on the fort's construction and history.

Most visitors especially love the daily cannon firings during the summer. If you're really lucky, you'll be around when Fort Jackson fires a salute to passing military vessels on the river—the only historic fort in America that does so.

To get to Fort Jackson, take President Street Extension (Islands Expressway) east out of downtown. The entrance is several miles down on your left.

Oatland Island Wildlife Center

The closest thing Savannah has to a zoo is the vast, multipurpose Oatland Island Wildlife Center (711 Sandtown Rd., 912/898-3980, www.oatlandisland.org, Mon.–Fri. 9 A.M.–4 P.M., Sat.–Sun. 10 A.M.–4 P.M., $5 adults, $3 children). Set on a former Centers for Disease Control site, it's undergone an extensive environmental cleanup and is now owned by the local school system, though supported purely by donation. Families by the hundreds come here for a number of special Saturdays throughout the year, including an old-fashioned cane-grinding in November and a day of sheep-shearing in April.

The main attractions here are the critters, located at various points along a meandering two-mile nature trail through the woods and along the marsh. All animals at Oatland are there because they're somehow unable to return to the wild, usually because of injury (often at the hands of humans). Highlights include a tight-knit pack of Eastern wolves, a pair of bison, some really cute foxes, and an extensive raptor aviary. Kids will love the petting zoo of farm animals, some of which are free to roam the grounds at will. But the crown jewel in Oatland's menagerie is no doubt the magnificent Florida panther, a rare cousin to the American cougar.

The massive central building was designed by noted local architect Henrik Wallin as a retirement home for railroad conductors. Inside, check out the display of a huge set of whalebones, the remains of a 50-foot-long endangered fin whale that washed ashore on Tybee Island in 1989.

To get there from downtown, take President Street Extension (Islands Expressway) about five miles. Begin looking for the Oatland Island sign on your right. You'll go through part of a residential neighborhood until you take a bend to the right; Oatland's gate is then on the left.

To get there from Bonaventure Cemetery, go straight out the gate on Bonaventure Road and take a right on Pennsylvania Avenue. As you dead-end on Islands Expressway, take a right and look for the entrance further along on the right.

◖ Bonaventure Cemetery

On the banks of the Wilmington River just east of town lies one of Savannah's most unique sights, Bonaventure Cemetery (330 Bonaventure Rd., 912/651-6843, daily 8 A.M.–5 P.M.). John Muir, who went on to found the Sierra Club, wrote of Bonaventure's Spanish moss–bedecked beauty in his 1867 book *A Thousand-Mile Walk to the Gulf,* marveling at the screaming bald eagles that then frequented the area. The bald eagles are long gone, but, like Muir, Savannahians to this day reserve a special place for Bonaventure in their hearts.

While its pedigree as Savannah's premier public cemetery goes back 100 years, it was used as a burial ground as early as 1794. In the years since, this achingly poignant vista of live oaks and azaleas has been the final resting place of such local and national luminaries as Johnny Mercer, Conrad Aiken, Wormsloe founder Noble Jones, and, of course, the Trosdal plot, former home of the famous "Bird Girl" statue (the original is now in the Telfair Academy of Arts and Sciences). Fittingly, the late, great Jack Leigh, who took the "Bird Girl" photo for the cover of *Midnight in the Garden of Good and Evil,* is interred here as well.

Go to Section K and see the Greek cemetery, a veritable stone chronicle of that local community's history from the late 1800s. Section K also holds many memorials to Spanish-

memorial to "Gracie" in Bonaventure Cemetery

© JIM MOREKIS

American War veterans, commemorated by a special cross. Close by is the Jewish section, established by congregants of Temple Mickve Israel, with many evocative inscriptions on the tombs of the many Holocaust survivors buried here. Closer to the river is an interesting plot set aside for railroad conductors.

While strolling through Bonaventure, you might see some burial sites lined with reddish-brown tiles, their tops studded with half-circles. Mistakenly known as "slave tiles," these are actually a rare type of Victorian garden tile that has nothing whatsoever to do with slaves.

Several local tour companies offer options that include a visit to Bonaventure. If you're doing a self-guided tour, go by the small visitors center at the entrance and pick up one of the free guides to the cemetery, assembled by the local volunteer Bonaventure Historical Society. By all means, do the tourist thing and pay your respects at Johnny Mercer's final resting place and go visit beautiful little "Gracie" in Section E, lot 99. But I also suggest doing as the locals do: Bring a picnic lunch and a

JOHNNY MERCER'S BLACK MAGIC

Visitors might be forgiven for thinking Paula Deen is Savannah's most famous native, but the Food Network star, born 200 miles away in Albany, Georgia, technically cannot claim that title.

The great Johnny Mercer is not only without a doubt Savannah's most noteworthy progeny, he is also one of the greatest lyricists music has ever known.

He grew up in southside Savannah on a small river then called the Back River but since renamed Moon River in honor of his best-known song. Armed with an innate talent for rhythm and a curious ear for dialogue – both qualities honed by his frequent boyhood contact with Savannah African American culture and musicians during the Jazz Age – Mercer moved away from Savannah to New York when he was only 19 to try his hand in Tin Pan Alley, then the world center of popular music.

There he met the woman who would be his wife, Ginger Meehan (real name Elizabeth Meltzer). This Brooklyn Jewish chorus girl – once Bing Crosby's lover – would be both muse and foil for Mercer in the decades to follow. Mutual infidelity and a partying lifestyle combined for a stormy marriage, yet both remained together until Mercer's death from a brain tumor in 1976 (Ginger passed away in 1994).

In a few years he was an established success in New York. By 1935, however, the show business center of gravity was moving towards Hollywood, and Mercer – ahead of his time as usual – sensed the shift early and moved to the West Coast to write musicals for RKO.

The advent of high-quality microphones was tailor-made for Mercer's nuanced lyrics. During his long and productive Hollywood career in the 1930s and 1940s, he wrote such classics as "Jeepers Creepers," "That Old Black Magic," "Come Rain or Come Shine," "Skylark," and "Ac-Cent-Tchu-Ate the Positive."

Mercer embarked on an affair with the young Judy Garland in 1941, a dalliance which he later said inspired the song "I Remember You."

While the advent of rock 'n' roll in the postwar era signaled the decline of Mercer's career, he wrote what is arguably his greatest song, "Moon River," in 1961. The song, debuted by Audrey Hepburn in the film *Breakfast at Tiffany's*, won an Academy Award for Best Original Song.

In addition to "Moon River," Mercer won three other Oscars, for "On the Atchinson, Topeka and the Santa Fe" (1946), "In the Cool Cool Cool of the Evening" (1951), and "Days of Wine and Roses" (1962).

Today you can pay your respects to Mercer in three places: his boyhood home at 509 E. Gwinnett St. (look for the historical marker in front of this private residence); the bronze sculpture of Mercer in the newly revitalized Ellis Square near City Market, erected in 2009 in honor of the centennial of his birth; and of course at his gravesite in beautiful Bonaventure Cemetery.

(Regardless of what anyone tells you, neither Johnny Mercer nor any member of his family ever lived in the Mercer-Williams House on Monterey Square, of *Midnight in the Garden of Good and Evil* fame. Though built for his great-grandfather, the home was sold to someone else before it was completed.)

Susie Chisholm's statue of Johnny Mercer in Ellis Square

© JIM MOREKIS

blanket and set yourself beside the breezy banks of the Wilmington River, taking in all the lazy beauty and evocative bygone history surrounding you.

To get there from downtown, take President Street Extension east and take a right on Pennsylvania Avenue, then a left on Bonaventure Road. Alternately, go east on Victory Drive (Hwy. 80) and take a left on Whatley Road in the town of Thunderbolt. Veer left onto Bonaventure Road. The cemetery is a mile ahead on the right.

Thunderbolt

Take a left out of Bonaventure Cemetery and continue on Bonaventure Road to find yourself in the little fishing village of Thunderbolt, almost as old as Savannah itself. According to Oglethorpe, the town was named after "a rock which was here shattered by a thunderbolt, causing a spring to gush from the ground, which continued ever afterward to emit the odor of brimstone."

Just off Victory Drive is the **Thunderbolt Museum** (at the corner of Victory Dr. and Mechanics Ave., Wed.–Thurs. 9:30 A.M.–2:30 P.M., Sat. 1–5 P.M., free) housed in the humble former town hall. Cross Victory onto River Road and notice how the road is built around the live oak tree in the middle of it. Though most of the nice views of the river have been obscured by high-rise condos, there's a cute public fishing pier.

Continue on River Road and you'll soon be at the entrance to **Savannah State University** (3219 College St., 912/356-2186, www.savstate.edu). This historically black university began life in 1890 as the Georgia State Industrial College for Colored Youth. Famous graduates include NFL great Shannon Sharpe. The main landmark is the newly restored Hill Hall, a 1901 building featured in the film *The General's Daughter*.

Daffin Park

A century spent in Forsyth Park's more genteel shadow doesn't diminish the importance of Daffin Park (1500 E. Victory Dr.) as Savannah's second major greenspace. Designed by John Nolen in 1907 and named for a former local parks commissioner, Daffin not only hosts a large variety of local athletes on its fields and courts, it's home to Historic Grayson Stadium on the park's east end. Recently given a serious face-lift, Grayson Stadium hosts the minor league Savannah Sand Gnats. One of the great old ballparks of America, this venue dates from 1941 and has hosted greats such as Babe Ruth, Jackie Robinson, and Mickey Mantle.

Most picturesque for the visitor, however, is the massive fountain set in the middle of the expansive central pond on the park's west side. Originally built in the shape of the continental United States, the pond was the backdrop for a presidential visit by Franklin D. Roosevelt in 1933, which included a speech to an African American crowd. On the far west end of Daffin Park along Waters Avenue is a marker commemorating the site of the Grandstand for the Great Savannah Races of 1911.

WESTSIDE
Laurel Grove Cemetery

Its natural vista isn't as alluring as Bonaventure's, but Laurel Grove Cemetery boasts its own exquisitely carved memorials and a distinctly Victorian type of surreal beauty that not even Bonaventure can match. In keeping with the racial apartheid of Savannah's early days, there are actually two cemeteries: **Laurel Grove North** (802 W. Anderson St., daily 8 A.M.–5 P.M.) for whites, and **Laurel Grove South** (2101 Kollock St., daily 8 A.M.–5 P.M.) for blacks. Both are well worth visiting.

By far the most high-profile site in the North Cemetery is that of Juliette Gordon Low, founder of the Girl Scouts of the USA. Other historically significant sites there include the graves of 8th Air Force founder Frank O. Hunter, Central of Georgia founder William Gordon, and "Jingle Bells" composer James Pierpont.

But it's the graves of the anonymous and near-anonymous that are the most poignant sights here. The various sections for infants, known as "Babylands," cannot fail to move. "Mr. Bones," a former Savannah Police dog,

© SONJA WALLEN

a Victorian gravesite in Laurel Grove Cemetery

is the only animal buried at Laurel Grove. There's an entire site reserved for victims of the great yellow fever epidemic. And don't blink or you'll miss the small rock pile, or cairn, near Governor James Jackson's tomb, the origin and purpose of which remains a mystery.

Make sure to view the otherworldly display of Victorian statuary, originally from the grand Greenwich Plantation which burned in the early 20th century. As with Bonaventure, throughout Laurel Grove you'll find examples of so-called "slave tiles," actually Victorian garden tiles, lining gravesites.

Laurel Grove South features the graves of Savannah's early black Baptist ministers, such as Andrew Bryan and Andrew Cox Marshall. Some of the most evocative sites are those of African Americans who obtained their freedom and built prosperous lives for themselves and their families. The vast majority of local firefighters in the 1800s were African Americans, and their simple graves are among the most touching, such as the headstone for one known simply as "August," who died fighting a fire.

To get to Laurel Grove North, take MLK Jr. Boulevard to Anderson Street and turn west. To get to Laurel Grove South, take Victory Drive (Hwy. 80) west to Ogeechee Road. Take a right onto Ogeechee, then a right onto West 36th Street. Continue on to Kollock Street.

Mighty Eighth Air Force Museum

Military and aviation buffs mustn't miss the Mighty Eighth Air Force Museum (175 Bourne Ave., 912/748-8888, www.mightyeighth.org, daily 9 A.M.–5 P.M., $10 adults, $6 children) in Pooler, Georgia, right off I-95. The 8th Air Force was born at Hunter Field, Savannah as the 8th Bomber Command in 1942, becoming the 8th Air Force in 1944 (it's now based in Louisiana).

A moving testament to the men and machines who conducted those strategic bombing campaigns over Europe in World War II, the museum also features later 8th Air Force history such as the Korean War, the Linebacker II bombing campaigns over North Vietnam, and the Persian Gulf. Inside you'll find not only airplanes like the P-51 Mustang and the German ME-109, there's also a restored B-17 bomber, the newest jewel of the collection.

Outside are several more aircraft, including a MIG-17, an F4 Phantom, and a B-47 Stratojet bomber like the one that dropped the fabled "Tybee Bomb" in 1958. A nearby "Chapel of the Fallen Eagles" is a fully functioning sanctuary to honor the more than 26,000 members of the Mighty Eighth that died during World War II.

To get to the Mighty Eighth Museum from downtown, take I-16 west until it intersects I-95. Take I-95 north and take Exit 102. Follow the signs.

Savannah-Ogeechee River Canal

A relic of the pre-railroad days, the Savannah-Ogeechee River Canal (681 Ft. Argyle Rd., 912/748-8068, www.savannahogeecheecanal .com, daily 9 A.M.–5 P.M., $2 adults, $1 students) is a 17-mile barge route joining the two rivers. Finished in 1830, it saw three decades of prosperous trade in cotton, rice, bricks, guano, naval stores, and agriculture before the coming of the railroads finished it off.

You can walk some of its length today near the Ogeechee River terminus, admiring the impressive engineering of its multiple locks to stabilize the water level. Back in the day, the canal would continue through four lift locks as it traversed 16 miles, before reaching the Savannah River.

Naturalists will enjoy the built-in nature trail that walking along the canal provides. Be sure to check out the unique sand hills nearby, a vestige of a bygone geological era when this area was an offshore sandbar. Kids will enjoy the impromptu menagerie of gopher turtles near the site's entrance.

To get there, get on I-95 south and take Exit 94. The canal is a little over two miles west.

Bamboo Farm and Coastal Garden

A joint project of the University of Georgia and Chatham County, the Bamboo Farm and Coastal Garden (2 Canebrake Rd., 912/921-5460, www.bamboo.caes.uga.edu,

Mon.–Fri. 8 A.M.–5 P.M., Sat. 10 A.M.–5 P.M., Sun. noon–5 P.M., free) is an education and demonstration center featuring a wide array of native species in addition to the eponymous Asian wonder weed, which has its roots in a private collection dating from the late 1800s. Many of the mature trees were planted in the 1930s. They also periodically hold you-pick-'em harvest days for berries. To get there, take Exit 94 off of I-95 and take U.S. 204 east towards Savannah. Turn right on East Gateway Boulevard, then left on Canebrake Road. Enter at the Canebrake gate.

SOUTHSIDE
Wormsloe State Historic Site

The one-of-a-kind Wormsloe State Historic Site (7601 Skidaway Rd., 912/353-3023, www .gastateparks.org/info/wormsloe, Tues.–Sun. 9 A.M.–5 P.M., $5 adults, $3.50 children) was first settled by Noble Jones, who landed with Oglethorpe on the *Anne* and fought beside him in the War of Jenkin's Ear. One of the great renaissance men of history, this soldier was also an accomplished carpenter, surveyor, forester, botanist, and physician. Wormsloe became famous for its bountiful gardens, so much so that the famed naturalist William Bartram mentioned them in his diary after a visit in 1765 with father John Bartram.

After his death, Noble Jones was originally buried in the family plot on the waterfront, but now his remains are at Bonaventure Cemetery. Jones' descendants donated 822 acres to The Nature Conservancy, which transferred the property to the state. The house, dating from 1828, and 65.5 acres of land are still owned by his family, and no, you can't visit them.

The stunning entrance canopy of 400 live oaks, Spanish moss dripping down the entire length, is one of those iconic images of Savannah that will stay with you the rest of your life. A small interpretive museum, one-mile nature walk, and occasional living history demonstrations make this a great site for the entire family.

Walk all the way to the Jones Narrows to see the ruins of the original 1739 fortification, one of the oldest and finest examples of tabby construction in the United States. No doubt the area's abundance of Native American shell middens, where early inhabitants discarded their oyster shells, came in handy for its construction. You can see one nearby.

To get to Wormsloe, take Victory Drive (U.S. 80) to Skidaway Road. Go south on Skidaway Road for about 10 miles and follow the signs; you'll see the grand entrance on your right.

Isle of Hope

A charming, friendly seaside community and National Historic District, Isle of Hope is one of a dwindling number of places where parents still let their kids ride around all day on bikes, calling them in at dinnertime. It doesn't boast many shops or restaurants—indeed, the marina is the only real business—but the row of waterfront cottages on Bluff Drive should not be missed. You might recognize some of them from movies such as *Forrest Gump* and *Glory*. Built from 1880 to 1920, they reflect Isle of Hope's reputation as a healing area and serene Wilmington River getaway from Savannah's age-old capitalist hustle.

To get to Isle of Hope, take Victory Drive (U.S. 80) east and take a right on Skidaway Road. Continue south on Skidaway and take a left on Laroche Avenue. Continue until you hit Bluff Drive.

Pin Point

Off Whitfield Avenue/Diamond Causeway on the route to Skidaway Island is tiny **Pin Point, Georgia,** a predominantly African American township better known as the boyhood home of Supreme Court Justice Clarence Thomas. Pin Point traces its roots to a community of former slaves on Ossabaw Island. Displaced by a hurricane, they settled at this idyllic site, itself a former plantation. Many new residents made their living by shucking oysters at the Varn Oyster Company, the central shed of which still remains. Pin Point is small—about 500 people—and very tightly knit. The area is best experienced by taking a local tour focused on African American history.

Skidaway Island

Though locals primarily know Skidaway Island as the site of The Landings, the first gated community in Savannah, for our purposes Skidaway Island is notable for two beautiful and educational nature-oriented sites.

The first, the **University of Georgia Marine Educational Center and Aquarium** (30 Ocean Science Circle, 912/598-3474, www.uga.edu/aquarium, Mon.–Fri. 9 A.M.–4 P.M., Sat. 10 A.M.–5 P.M., $4 adults, $2 children) shares a gorgeous 700-acre campus on the scenic Skidaway River with the research-oriented **Skidaway Institute of Oceanography,** also UGA-affiliated. It hosts scientists and grad students from around the nation, often on trips on is research vessel, the RV *Sea Dawg.*

The main attraction of the Marine Center is the small but well-done aquarium featuring 14 tanks with 200 live animals. Don't expect Sea World here; remember you're essentially on a college campus and the emphasis here is on education, not flash.

The second site of interest to visitors is **Skidaway Island State Park** (52 Diamond Causeway, 912/598-2300, www.gastateparks.org/info/skidaway, daily 7 A.M.–10 P.M., $2 parking fee). Yeah, you can camp there, but the awesome nature trails leading out to the marsh—featuring an ancient Native American shell midden and an old whiskey still—are worth a trip just on their own, especially when combined with the Marine Education Center Aquarium. To get there, take Victory Drive (Hwy. 80) until you get to Waters Avenue and continue south as it turns into Whitfield Avenue and then the Diamond Causeway. The park is on your left after the drawbridge. An alternate route from downtown is to take the Truman Parkway all the way to its dead end at Whitfield Avenue; take a left and continue as it turns into Diamond Causeway into Skidaway.

TYBEE ISLAND

Its name means "salt" in the old Euchee tongue, indicative of the island's chief export in those days. And Tybee Island—"Tybee" to locals—is

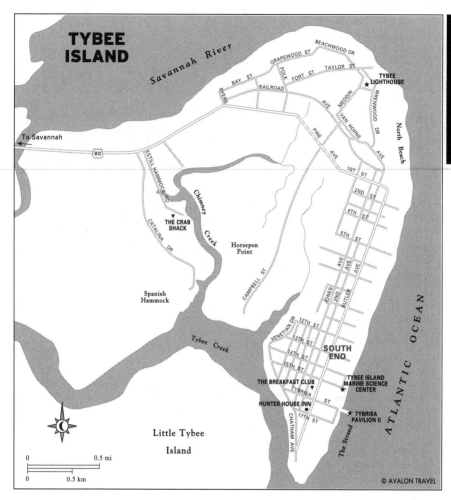

indeed one of the essential seasonings of life in Savannah. First incorporated as Ocean City and then Savannah Beach, the island has since reclaimed its original name.

While 18 miles from Savannah, in truth Tybee is part and parcel of the city's social and cultural fabric. Many of the island's 3,000 full-time residents, known for their boozy bonhomie and quirky personal style, commute to work in the city. And those living "in town" often reciprocate by visiting Tybee to dine in its few but excellent restaurants, drink in its casual and crazy watering holes, and frolic on its wide, beautiful beaches lined with rare sea oats waving in the Atlantic breeze.

(Fort Pulaski National Monument

There's one must-see before you get to Tybee Island proper. On Cockspur Island, you'll find Fort Pulaski National Monument (Hwy. 80 E., 912/786-5787, www.nps.gov/fopu, fort

© JIM MOREKIS

Fort Pulaski, on the way to Tybee Island

daily 8:30 A.M.–5:15 P.M., visitors center daily 9 A.M.–5 P.M., $3 per person 16 and up). Not only a delight for any history buff, the fort's also a fantastic place to take the kids. They can climb on the parapets, earthworks, and cannons, and burn off calories on the great nature trail nearby. Along the way they'll no doubt learn a few things as well.

Synchronicity and irony practically scream from every brick. Perhaps prophetically named for Count Casimir Pulaski, who died leading an ill-fated charge on the British in 1779, Fort Pulaski is also symbolic of a catastrophic defeat, this one in 1862 when Union forces using new rifled cannons reduced much of it to rubble in 30 hours. Robert E. Lee—yes, *that* Robert E. Lee—helped build the fort while a lieutenant with the U.S. Army Corps of Engineers. And the Union general who reduced the fort, Quincy A. Gillmore, was in the Corps of Engineers himself, helping to oversee the fort's construction.

By all means, visit the visitors center a few hundred yards from the fort itself—but the palpable pleasure starts when you cross the drawbridge over the moat and see a cannon pointed at you from a narrow gunport. Enter the inside of the fort itself and take in just how big it is—Union occupiers regularly played baseball on the huge, grassy parade ground. Take a walk around the perimeter, underneath the ramparts. This is where the soldiers lived and worked, and you'll see re-creations of officer's quarters, meeting areas, sick rooms, and prisoners' bunks among the cannons, where Confederate prisoners-of-war were held after the fort's surrender. Cannon firings happen most Saturdays.

And now for the pièce de résistance: Take the steep corkscrew staircase up to the ramparts themselves and take in the jaw-droppingly beautiful view of the lush marsh around the fort, the Savannah River and Tybee Island spreading out in the distance. Stop and sit near one of the several remaining cannons and contemplate what went on here a century and a half ago. (Warning: There's no railing of any kind on the inboard side of the ramparts. Keep the kids well back from the edge, because it's a lethal fall to the fort interior.)

Afterwards take a stroll all the way around the walls and see for yourself the power of those Yankee guns. Though much of the devastation was soon repaired, some sections of the wall remain in their damaged state. You can even pick out a few cannonballs still stuck in the masonry, like blueberries in a pie.

Save some time and energy for the extensive palmetto-lined nature trail through the sandy upland of Cockspur Island on which the fort is located. There are informative markers, a picnic area, and, as a bonus, there's a coastal defense facility from the Spanish-American War, Battery Hambright.

Cockspur Beacon

Continue east on Highway 80, passing over Lazaretto Creek, named for the quarantine or "lazaretto" built in the late 1700s to make sure

THE TYBEE BOMB

On a dark February night in 1958 at the height of the Cold War, a USAF B-47 Stratojet bomber based at Homestead, Florida, made a simulated nuclear bombing run somewhere over southeast Georgia. A Charleston-based F-86 fighter on a mock intercept came too close, clipping the big bomber's wing.

Before bringing down the wounded B-47 at Savannah's Hunter Airfield – then a Strategic Air Command base – Commander Howard Richardson decided he first had to jettison his lethal cargo: a 7,000-pound Mark 15 hydrogen bomb, serial number 47782.

We know for sure that he jettisoned it over water. Richardson, who won the Distinguished Flying Cross for his efforts that night, said so himself. What no one knows is exactly where.

And thus began the legend of "the Tybee bomb." Go in any Tybee watering hole and ask 10 people where they think it is and you'll get 10 different answers. Some say it's in the north side of Wassaw Sound, some the south. Some say it's in the shallows, some in deepwater.

Many local shrimpers, crabbers, and fishermen have claimed at various times to have ripped their nets on the bomb. Or on something...

Speculation ran wild, with some locals fearing nuclear explosion, radioactive contamination, or even that a team of scuba-diving terrorists would secretly retrieve the ancient weapon.

Former Army colonel and present-day raconteur and soldier-of-fortune Derek Duke took it as his personal mission to find the bomb. He says the Air Force could easily find it, but won't do so either because they don't want to go to the expense of finding it or they don't want to admit they lost a thermonuclear weapon for half a century. Duke claims to have found a radiation-emitting object off Little Tybee Island during a search in 2004.

Commander Richardson, now retired and living in Jackson, Mississippi, says the point is moot because the bomb wasn't armed when he jettisoned it. Environmentalists say that doesn't matter, because the enriched uranium the Air Force admits was in the bomb is toxic whether or not there's the risk of a nuclear detonation. Tybee fishermen say the fact that the bomb also had 400 pounds of high explosive "nuclear trigger" is reason enough to get it out of these waterways, which hosted the 1996 Olympic yachting competition.

And what of the owners of the Tybee Bomb, the Air Force? In 2000, they sent a team to Savannah to find the bomb, concluding it was buried somewhere off the coast in 5–15 feet of mud. In 2005, in another attempt to find the weapon – and also to shut down the rampant conspiracy theories, most of them propagated by Duke – they sent down another team of experts to look one last time.

Their verdict: The bomb's still lost.

That won't stop local speculation about its whereabouts, however. Who can resist a real-life cloak-and-dagger story? Certainly few people around here.

Postscript: No one was injured that night in 1958, except for some frostbite the F-86 pilot suffered as a result of ejecting from his damaged plane. In an interesting bit of synchronicity, the fighter pilot, Clarence Wilson, and the B-47 commander Howard Richardson grew up miles away from each other in Winston County, Mississippi.

newcomers, mostly slaves, were free of disease. As you cross, look to your left over the river's wide south channel. On a tiny oyster shell islet find the little Cockspur Beacon lighthouse, in use from 1848 to 1909, when major shipping was routed through the deeper north channel of the river. The site is now preserved by the National Park Service, and is accessible only by boat.

Tybee Lighthouse

Reaching Tybee proper on Highway 80, you'll soon arrive at the intersection with North Campbell Avenue. This is the entrance to the less-populated, more historically significant north end of the island, once almost entirely taken up by Fort Screven, a coastal defense fortification of the early 1900s. Take a left onto North Campbell Avenue then left again on Van Horne. Once on Van Horne, take an immediate right onto Meddin Drive. Continue until you see a lighthouse on your left and a parking lot on the right.

Rebuilt several times in its history, the Tybee Lighthouse (30 Meddin Ave., 912/786-5801, www.tybeelighthouse.org, Wed.–Mon. 9 A.M.–5:30 P.M., last ticket sold 4:30 P.M., $7 adults, $5 children) traces its construction to the first year of the colony, based on a design by the multitalented Noble Jones. At its completion in 1736, it was the tallest structure in America. One of a handful of working 18th-century lighthouses today, the facility has been restored to its 1916–1964 incarnation, featuring a nine-foot-tall first order Fresnel lens installed in 1867.

The entrance fee gives you admission to the lighthouse, the lighthouse museum, and the nearby Tybee Island Museum. All the outbuildings on the lighthouse grounds are original, including the residence of current lighthouse keeper and Tybee Island Historical Society Director Cullen Chambers, which is also the oldest building on the island. If you've got the legs and the lungs, definitely take all 178 steps up to the top of the lighthouse for a stunning view of Tybee, the Atlantic, and Hilton Head Island.

Old Fort Screven

All around the area of the north end around the Lighthouse complex, you'll see low-lying concrete bunkers. Though many are in private hands, these are remains of Fort Screven's coastal defense batteries. Battery Garland is open to tours, and also houses the aforementioned **Tybee Island Museum** (30 Meddin Ave., 912/786-5801), a charming, almost whimsical little collection of exhibits from various eras of local history.

On nearby Van Horne Avenue is a key part of Fort Screven, the **Tybee Post Theater** (912/323/7727, www.tybeeposttheater.org). Once a site for Army entertainment such as movies, concerts, and theatrical productions, the Post Theater is currently undergoing extensive renovation. It occasionally hosts events; check the website for details.

Continue on Van Horne around the delightful Jaycee Park to the row of ornate mansions with expansive porches facing the Atlantic. This is **Officer's Row,** former home of Fort Screven's commanding officers and now a mix of private residences, vacation rentals, and B&Bs.

South End

Now scoot out Van Horne to Butler Avenue and take a left. This is Tybee's main drag, the beach fully public and accessible from any of the numbered side streets on your left.

Go all the way down to **Tybrisa** (formerly 16th St.) to get a flavor of old Tybee. Here's where you'll find the old five-and-dimes like T. S. Chu's, still a staple of local life, and little diners, ice cream spots, and taverns. The new pride of the island is the large, long pier structure called the **Tybrisa Pavilion II,** built in 1996 in an attempt to recreate the lost glory of the Tybrisa Pavilion, social and spiritual center of the island's gregarious resort days. Built in 1891 by the Central of Georgia railroad, the Tybrisa hosted name entertainers and big bands on its expansive dance floor. Sadly, fire destroyed it in 1967, an enormous blow to area morale.

Literally at the foot of the Pavilion you'll find the **Tybee Island Marine Science Center** (1510 Strand, 912/786-5917, www.tybee marinescience.org, daily 10 A.M.–5 P.M., $4

© JIM MOREKIS

Tybee Island Marine Science Center

adults, $3 children), an outstanding resource with nine aquariums and a touch tank featuring native species. Here is the nerve center for the Tybee Island Sea Turtle Project, an ongoing effort to document and preserve the local comings-and-goings of the island's most beloved inhabitant and unofficial mascot, the endangered sea turtle. A very kid-friendly facility despite the seriousness of its mission, the Center holds summer Sea Camps for area children, and indeed one of its goals is to bring a hands-on aspect to educating the public about the area's rich variety of ocean, dune, and marsh life—only steps away.

TOURS

Savannah's tourist boom has resulted in a similar explosion of well over 50 separate tour services, ranging from simple guided trolley journeys to horse-drawn carriage rides to specialty tours to eco-tourism adventures. There's even an iPod walking tour. Here's a listing of the key categories with the most notable offerings in each (don't forget to tip your guide if you were satisfied with the tour):

Trolley Tours

The vehicle of choice for the bulk of the tourist masses visiting Savannah, trolley tours allow you to sit back and enjoy the views in a reasonably comfortable. As in other cities, the guides provide commentary while attempting, with various degrees of success, to navigate the cramped downtown traffic environment.

The main trolley companies in town are **Old Savannah Tours** (912/234-8128, www.old savannahtours.com, basic on-off tour $25 adults, $11 children), **Old Town Trolleys** (800/213-2474, www.trolleytours.com, basic on-off tour $23 adults, $10 children), **Oglethorpe Trolley Tours** (912/233-8380, www.oglethorpetours .com, basic on-off tour $22.50 adults, $10 children), and **Gray Line Tours** (912/234-8687, www.graylineofsavannah.com, basic on-off tour $15). All embark from the Savannah Visitors Center on Martin Luther King Jr. Boulevard about every 20–30 minutes on the same schedule, 9 A.M.–4:30 P.M.

Frankly there's not much difference between them, as they all offer a very similar range of services for similar prices, with most offering pickup at your downtown hotel. While the common "on-off privileges" allow trolley riders to disembark for awhile and pick up another of the same company's trolleys at marked stops, be aware there's no guarantee the next trolley will have enough room to take you onboard. Or the one after that.

Specialty Tours

Besides the standard narrated Historic District tours, all the above companies also offer a number of spin-off tours. Samples include the Pirate's House Dinner & Ghost Tour, Belles of Savannah, the Evening Haunted Trolley, and multiple Paula Deen tours.

The copious ghost tours, offered by all the companies, can be fun for the casual visitor. But students of the paranormal are likely to be disappointed by the cartoonish, Halloween aspect of some of them.

A standout in the ghost field is the **Hearse Ghost Tours** (912/695-1578, www.hearse ghosttours.com), a unique company that also operates tours in New Orleans and St. Augustine, Florida. Up to eight guests at a time ride around in the open top of a converted hearse, painted all black of course, and get a 90-minute, suitably over-the-top narration from the driver/guide. Still pretty cheesy, but a hip kind of cheesy.

For those who take their paranormal activity *very* seriously, there's Shannon Scott's **Sixth Sense Savannah Ghost Tour** (866/666-3323, www.sixthsensesavannah.com, $20, $38.50 midnight tour), an uncensored, straightforward look at Savannah's poltergeist population.

Longtime tour guide and raconteur Greg Proffit and his staff offer fun walking "pub crawls," **Savannah Tours by Foot** (912/238-3843, www.savannahtours.com), wherein the point is to meet your guide at some local tavern, ramble around, learn a little bit, and imbibe a lot, though not necessarily in that order. The adult tour is the "Creepy Crawl" ($18) whereas the kid-and-Girl Scout-appropriate tour is the "Creepy Stroll" ($10 adults, $5 Girl Scouts). You may not want to believe everything you hear, but you're sure to have a lot of fun. The tours book up early, so make arrangements in advance.

To learn about Savannah's history of filmmaking and to enjoy the best of local cuisine, try a **Savannah Movie Tour** (912/234-3440, www.savannahmovietours.net, $25 adults, $15 children), taking you to various film locations in town, and a newer **Savannah Foody Tour** (912/234-3440, www.savannahmovietours .net, $48) featuring 6–9 local eateries.

Storyteller and author Ted Eldridge leads **A Walk Through Savannah Tours** (912/921-4455, www.awalkthroughsavannah.brave host.com, $15 adults, $5 children 6–12, free for children under 6) and offers all kinds of specialty walking tours, such as a garden tour, a ghost tour, a historic churches tour, and of course a *Midnight* tour.

For a more enlightened take than you'll usually get on a local tour, contact licensed guide **Orlando Montoya** (912/308-2952, $20) for a personalized walking tour. His regular job is as a journalist with Georgia Public Radio, so expect a higher level of taste and information with this journey.

Truly independent travelers might want to use Phil Sellers' **Citytrex** (912/228-5608, www.citytrex.com, $12–15), Savannah's only podcast-based self-guided walking tour. Just go to the website and download a tour offered directly to your iPod or cell phone. Some downloads offer enhanced content such as photos.

To see downtown Savannah by bicycle—quite a refreshing experience—try **Savannah Bike Tours** (803/760-3143, www.savannahbike tours.com, $15 adults, $10 under 12), two-hour trips through all 19 squares and Forsyth Park with your "rolling concierge" guide. They leave every day at 10 A.M. and 2 P.M. from a spot near the corner of Whitaker and West Hall streets. Rent bikes from them or ride your own.

The unique **Negro Heritage Trail Tour** (912/234-8000, $19 adults, $10 children) takes you on a 90-minute air-conditioned bus tour of over 30 of Savannah's key African American history sites. Pick up the Negro Heritage Tour at the Visitors Center downtown (301 MLK Jr. Blvd.) at 10 A.M. and noon Tuesday–Saturday.

Carriage Tours

Ah, yes—what could be more romantic and more traditional than enjoying downtown Savannah the way it was originally intended to be traveled, by horse-drawn carriage? Indeed, this is one of the most fun ways to see the city, for couples as well as for those with horse-enamored children. Yes, the horses sometimes look tired, but the tour operators generally take great care to keep the horses hydrated and out of the worst of the heat.

There are three main purveyors of equine tourism in town: **Carriage Tours of Savannah** (912/236-6756, www.carriage toursofsavannah.com, pick up in City Market), **Historic Savannah Carriage Tours** (888/837-1011, www.savannahcarriage.com, pick up at the Hampton Inn), and **Plantation Carriage Company** (912/201-0001, pick up in City Market).

As with the trolleys, the length of the basic tour and the price is about the same for all—45–60 minutes, about $20 for adults and $10 for children. All offer specialty tours as well, from ghost tours to evening romantic rides with champagne. Some will pick you up at your hotel.

Water Tours

The heavy industrial buildup on the Savannah River means that the main river tours for tourists, all departing from the docks in front of the Hyatt Regency hotel, tend to be disappointing in their unrelenting views of cranes, docks, storage tanks, and smokestacks. Still, for those into that kind of thing, narrated trips up and down the river on the *Georgia Queen* and the *Savannah River Queen* are offered by **Savannah Riverboat Cruises** (912/232-6404, www.savannahriverboat.com, $18.95 adults, $9.95 children 4–12).

If you've just *got* to get out on the river for a short time, by far the best bargain is to take one of the two little **Savannah Belles** (daily 7:30 a.m.–10:30 p.m., free) water ferries, which shuttle passengers from River Street to Hutchinson Island and back every 15–20 minutes. Pick up either the *Juliette Gordon Low* or the *Susie King Taylor* on River Street in front of City Hall or at the Waving Girl landing a few blocks east.

WWW.SAVANNAHVISIT.COM

Take one of the Savannah Belle ferries across the Savannah River.

Ecotours

The most complete eco-tourism operator in the Savannah area is the 35-year-old nonprofit **Wilderness Southeast** (912/897-5108, www.wilderness-southeast.org, $10–35). Guided trips include paddles to historic Mulberry Grove, birding trips, and beach explorations. Regularly scheduled "Walks on the Wild Side" run the gamut from "Alligators to Anhingas" to the "Urban Forest" to "Explore the Night Sky" to the "Blackwater River Float." Custom tours are also available.

On Highway 80 just as you get on Tybee Island is another quality tour service, **Sea Kayak Georgia** (1102 Hwy. 80, 888/529-2542, www.seakayakgeorgia.com, $55 for half-day tour). Run by locals Marsha Henson and Ronnie Kemp, both certified kayak and canoe instructors, Sea Kayak offers many different types of kayak tours of the coast, and can even customize one to your tastes. Instruction classes are also offered.

Run by Capt. Mike Neal, an experienced local boatsman and conservationist, **Moon River Kayak Tours** (912/898-1800, www.moonriverkayak.com, $50) focuses on 2.5-hour tours of the Skidaway Narrows and scenic Moon River, departing from the public boat ramp at the foot of the main bridge to Skidaway Island. No kayaking experience is required.

Entertainment and Events

If you like to have a good time, you're in the right place. Savannah is known for its heavy year-round schedule of festivals, many of them outdoors, as well as its copious variety of watering holes hosting a diverse range of local residents and adventurous tourists.

NIGHTLIFE

Let's face it: Savannah is a hard-drinking town, and not just on St. Patrick's Day. Visitors expecting a Bible Belt atmosphere are sometimes surprised—often, it must be said, pleasantly so—at Savannah's high tolerance for intoxication and its associated behavior patterns. (A few years ago a city councilman decided he'd had a few too many and simply got a ride home from an on-duty cop.) The ability to legally walk downtown streets with beer, wine, or a cocktail in hand also contributes to the overall joie de vivre.

A party here is never far away, any night of the week, so it makes sense to begin this section with a close, loving look at the bars, pubs, and taverns that are the heart of Savannah's social scene and really make it tick. Bars close in Savannah at 3 A.M., a full hour later than in Charleston.

One catch though: Due to Georgia's notorious blue laws, establishments that serve alcohol that do not derive at least 50 percent of their revenue from food may not open on Sundays. Supermarkets and convenience stores cannot sell alcoholic beverages of any kind on Sundays, and liquor stores are closed all day Sunday.

Bars and Pubs

Savannah's best dive—and I mean that in the nicest way—is without a doubt **Pinkie Masters** (318 Drayton St., 912/238-0447, Mon.–Fri. 4 P.M.–3 A.M., Sat. 5 P.M.–3 A.M.). Small, dark, crowded, and dusty, but oh-so alive, Pinkie's, named for a legendary local political king-maker, is a favorite not only with students, artists, and professors, but also with lawyers, journalists, and grizzled war vets. Traditionally the watering hole for local political types, the bar sports walls plastered over with signed photos of a diverse range of politicos and entertainers from the 1970s through today, from all sides of the spectrum. This is where Jimmy Carter, ironically a teetotaler, stood on the bar and announced his candidacy for Georgia governor. The service is friendly but casual; bartenders often finish their shift and simply take their place on a barstool with the customers.

THE TO-GO CUP TRADITION

Arguably the single most civilized trait of Savannah and certainly one of the things that most sets it apart, is the glorious old tradition of the "to-go cup." True to its history of hard-partying and general open-mindedness, Savannah, like New Orleans, allows you to legally walk the streets downtown with an open container of your favorite adult beverage.

Of course, you have to be 21 and over, and the cup must be Styrofoam or plastic, never glass or metal, and no more than 16 ounces. While there are boundaries to where to-go cups are legal, in practice this includes most all areas of the Historic District frequented by tourists. The quick and easy rule of thumb is keep your to-go cups north of Jones Street.

Every other election year, some local politician tries to get the church folk all riled up and proposes doing away with to-go cups in the interest of public safety. And he or she is inevitably shouted down by the outcry from the tourist-conscious Chamber of Commerce and from patriotic Savannahians defending their way of life.

Every downtown watering hole has stacks of cups at the bar for patrons to use. You can either ask the bartender for a to-go cup – alternately a "go cup" – or just reach out and grab one yourself. Don't be shy – it's the Savannah way.

Think of **Hang Fire** (27 Whitaker St., 912/443-9956, Mon.–Sat. 5 P.M.–3 A.M.) as Pinkie's, the new generation. Though only a few years old, this Whitaker Street haunt, occupying the site of downtown's last strip bar, is already one of the most popular bars in town, and, like Pinkie's, caters to a wide range of people who seem to get along in more or less perfect harmony. Trivia nights on Tuesdays are a hoot.

One of the hottest hangouts downtown is **The Distillery** (416 W. Liberty St., 912/236-1772, www.distillerysavannah.com), located in, yes, a former distillery. As such, the atmosphere isn't exactly dark and romantic—it's sort of one big open room—but the excellent location at the corner of MLK Jr. Boulevard and Liberty Street, the long, vintage bar, and the great selection of beers on tap combine to make this a happening spot.

Long known as Savannah's premier place for young hotties to meet other young hotties, the **Bar-Bar** (219 W. Julian St. in City Market, 912/231-1910, www.thebarbar.com, Mon.–Sat. 7 P.M.–3 A.M.) is a sprawling underground den underneath an old warehouse. The low-ceilinged but spacious spot boasts a great little dance floor, pool tables, and plenty of places to sit and relax in privacy. And oh, yeah, plenty of hotties.

Also a decent restaurant, the bar at **1790** (307 E. President St., 912/236-7122, lunch Mon.–Fri. 11:30 A.M.–2 P.M., dinner daily 6–10 P.M., bar Mon.–Fri. 11 A.M.–3 A.M., Sat.–Sun. 6 P.M.–3 A.M.) has long been a gathering place for some of Savannah's most well-connected businesspeople to let their hair down and gossip about each other until last call. You can order from the restaurant menu until 10 P.M.

The main landmark on the west end of River Street is the famous (or infamous, depending on which side of "The Troubles" you're on) **Kevin Barry's Irish Pub** (117 W. River St., 912/233-9626, www.kevinbarrys.com, daily 11 A.M.–3 A.M.), one of Savannah's most beloved establishments. K.B.'s keeps alive the spirit of Irish independence, so don't be alarmed when you see a tribute on the wall to some martyr or other, killed fighting the English. It's open seven days a week, with evenings seeing performances by a number of Irish troubadours, all veterans of the East Coast trad circuit. An eclectic mix of tourists, local Irish, military, and sailors keeps this place always interesting and alive. While no one in their right mind goes to an Irish pub for the food, Kevin Barry's offers a good, solid range of typical fare, including a serviceable corned beef and cabbage.

Don't get too excited about the "rooftop dining" advertised at **Churchill's Pub & Restaurant** (13–17 W. Bay St., 912/232-8501, www.the britishpub.com, Mon.–Fri. 5 P.M.– 3 A.M., Sat.

Kevin Barry's Irish Pub on River Street

© JIM MOREKIS

10 A.M.–3 A.M., kitchen closes 10 P.M. Sun.–Thurs., 11 P.M. Fri.–Sat.), unless you enjoy looking at the sides of other buildings. The real attractions at Churchill's are threefold: the great selection of beer; the great company; and perhaps most of all, the fish and chips, which are hands-down the best in town. Don't forget to be liberal with the malt vinegar; it's key.

The "other" English pub in town, **Six Pence Pub** (245 Bull St., 912/233-3151, daily 11:30 A.M.–midnight) is centrally located off Chippewa Square downtown, and is a good place to stop in for a pint on a rainy day. Look for the big red London telephone booth out front.

The only brewpub in Savannah, **Moon River Brewing Company** (21 W. Bay St., 912/447-0943, www.moonriverbrewing .com, Mon.–Thurs. 11 A.M.–11 P.M., Fri.–Sat. 11 A.M.–midnight, Sun. 11 A.M.–10 P.M.) directly across from the Hyatt Regency, offers half a dozen handcrafted beers—from a pale ale to a stout to all points in-between.

Live Music and Karaoke

Despite its high-volume offerings, the hardcore/heavy metal club **The Jinx** (127 W. Congress St., 912/236-2281, www.thejinx.net,

Mon.–Sat. 4 P.M.–3 A.M.) is a friendly watering hole and probably the closest thing Savannah has to a full-on Athens, Georgia, music club. Shows start *very* late here, never before 11 P.M. and often later than that. If you're here for the show, bring earplugs.

The other live rock club of note in Savannah is **Live Wire Music Hall** (307 W. River St., 912/233-1192, www.livewiremusichall .com, Mon.–Thurs. 4 P.M.–3 A.M., Fri.–Sat. 11 A.M.–3 A.M.). The music—which is every bit on par with what the Jinx offers—is on the ground floor, while the second floor has a bar and a few pool tables.

Savannah's undisputed karaoke champion is **McDonough's** (21 E. McDonough St., 912/233-6136, www.mcdonoughsof savannah.com, Mon.–Sat. 8 P.M.–3 A.M., Sun. 8 P.M.–2 A.M.), an advantage compounded by the fact that a lot more goes on here than karaoke. The kitchen at McDonough's is quite capable, and many locals swear you can get the best burger in town here. Despite the sports bar atmosphere, the emphasis here is on the karaoke, which ramps up every night at 9:30 P.M., and a very competent group of regulars never fails to entertain. The crowd here is surprisingly diverse, racially and socioeconomically mixed, featuring lawyers and students, rural folks and Rangers in equal numbers.

Gay and Lesbian

Any examination of gay and lesbian nightlife in Savannah must of course begin with **Club One Jefferson** (1 Jefferson St., 912/232-0200, www.clubone-online.com) of *Midnight* fame, with its famous drag shows, including the notorious Lady Chablis, upstairs in the cabaret, and its rockin' 1,000-square-foot dance floor downstairs. Cabaret showtimes are Thurs.–Sat. 10:30 P.M. and 12:30 A.M., Sunday 10:30 P.M. and Monday 11:30 P.M. Call for Chablis's showtimes. As with all local gay nightclubs, straights are more than welcome here.

A friendly, kitschy little tavern at the far west end of River Street near the Jefferson Street ramp, **Chuck's Bar** (301 W. River St., 912/232-1005, www.myspace.com/chucks_bar, Mon.–Wed. 8 P.M.–3 A.M., Thurs.–Sat. 7 P.M.–3 A.M.) is a great place to relax and see some interesting local characters. Karaoke at Chuck's is especially a hoot, and they keep the Christmas lights up all year.

Though technically it doesn't market itself as a gay and lesbian venue, **Venus de Milo** (38 MLK Jr. Blvd., 912/447-0901, Mon.–Sat. 4:30 P.M.–3 A.M.) is historically a favorite gathering place for the community. It's also by far the best wine bar in Savannah, with an excellent selection of all varietals.

Blaine's Back Door (13 E. Perry Lane, 912/233-6765, www.blainesbar.com, Mon.– Sat. 2 P.M.–3 A.M.) is the closest thing in Savannah to the classic East Village or West Coast gay bar, with lots of pictures of muscular men in various degrees of undress on the wall, and a small but active dance floor.

PERFORMING ARTS
Theater

While live theatre isn't what it used to be in Savannah, the multiuse venue **Muse Arts Warehouse** (703D Louisville Rd., 912/713-1137, www.musesavannah.org) hosts a variety of community-based plays and performances within a well-restored historic train depot. Get there by taking Liberty Street west from downtown, where it turns into Louisville Road.

The semi-pro troupe at the **Historic Savannah Theatre** (222 Bull St., 912/233-7764, www.savannahtheatre.com) performs a busy, rotating schedule of oldies revues (typical title: *Return to the '50s*), which make up for their lack of originality with the tightness and energy of their talented young cast of regulars.

For a fun evening of boozy, interactive theater, go down to the River Street docks on a Thursday night for **Murder Afloat** (boards next to the Hyatt Regency, cruise starts at 9:30 P.M., 912/232-6404, www.murderafloat.com, $26.95 adults, $18.95 children under 12). The mysterious fun happens during a 90-minute cruise on the Savannah River aboard one of two riverboats, during which you can talk to the actors and try to figure out "whodunit." Food is included and there's a cash bar onboard.

There are few things to recommend Savannah's southside to the visitor, but one of them is the **Armstrong Atlantic State University Masquers** (11935 Abercorn St., 912/927-5381, www.finearts.armstrong.edu), the second-oldest college theater group in the country (only Harvard's Hasty Pudding Theatricals is older). Now nearing their 75th anniversary, the Masquers boast a newly restored performance space at the Jenkins Theatre, and might surprise you with the high quality of their performances—despite being a student program. Parking is never a problem.

Music and Dance

The Savannah Symphony is no more, a victim of the same economic and demographic challenges facing orchestras in small-to-mid-sized cities all over the United States. But carrying on their proud tradition—and using many of the same musicians—is the **Savannah Philharmonic** (800/514-3849, www.thesavannahphil.org), a professional troupe that performs concertos and sonatas at various venues around town and is always worth checking out.

A prime dance company in town is **Savannah Danse Theatre** (912/897-2100,

SAVANNAH

CINEMA IN SAVANNAH

The first high-profile film to be made in Savannah was 1962's *Cape Fear,* starring Gregory Peck and Robert Mitchum (who years before filming was arrested and briefly jailed for public indecency while wandering in a drunken state through Savannah).

But 1975's *Gator,* directed by and starring Burt Reynolds, really put the city on the Hollywood map, due in no small part to the then-mega star power of Reynolds himself, whose personal filmmaking mission was, in his words, to "say some nice things about the South." Old-timers still tell stories of hanging out at the pool with Burt and crew at the old Oglethorpe Hotel on Wilmington Island, once owned by the Teamsters and rumored to be the final resting place of Jimmy Hoffa (it's now a condo development).

In short order, parts of the landmark 1970s TV miniseries *Roots* were filmed in and around Savannah, as were part of the follow-up *Roots: The Next Generation.*

Film aficionados fondly remember the sadly forgotten 1980 TV movie *The Ordeal of Dr. Mudd,* starring Dennis Weaver. In addition to the infamous story from "The Book" where Jim Williams unfurls a swastika banner to ruin a shot on Monterey Square, there are other reasons to remember the film. *Dr. Mudd* also expertly uses interiors of Fort Pulaski to tell this largely sympathetic account of the physician accused of aiding Abraham Lincoln's assassin John Wilkes Booth. In a chilling bit of synchronicity, Booth's brother Edwin, the most famous actor in America during the 1800s, played in Savannah often.

A key chapter in local filmography came with the filming of 1989's *Glory* in coastal Georgia. River Street was the set for the parade scenes, and as Colonel Shaw, Matthew Broderick delivered his stirring address to the troops one block west of Mrs. Wilkes' Boarding House on Jones Street. The railroad roundhouse off MLK Jr. Boulevard stood in for a Massachusetts training ground, but local preservationists were aghast when they discovered that some black paint the film crew had applied to the historic facility wouldn't come off. There were calls for Savannah never again to host another film crew, but luckily cooler heads prevailed.

Another brush with Hollywood came with the filming of 1994's *Forrest Gump* in and around Savannah. Look for the long-running series of shots of Tom Hanks sitting on a bench in Chippewa Square – and note how the traffic runs the wrong direction around the square! The famous bench itself now resides in the Savannah History Museum on MLK Jr. Boulevard. The steeple you see in the shot of the floating

www.savannahdansetheatre.org), known chiefly for its complete *Nutcracker* performance each December at the Lucas Theatre, with live accompaniment by a full symphony orchestra hired especially for the occasion—quite a rarity in a city this size.

CINEMA

The closest multiplex to downtown is the **Victory Square Stadium 9** (1901 E. Victory Dr., 912-355-5000, www.trademarkcinemas .com), which also hosts the screenings of **The Reel Savannah Group** (www.reelsavannah .org, reelsavanah@hotmail.com), a nonprofit that brings in foreign independent releases one Sunday a month.

The historic **Lucas Theatre for the Arts** (32 Abercorn St., 912/525-5040, www.lucas theatre.com) downtown is a great place to see a movie, and the Savannah Film Society hosts screenings there throughout the year. Check the website for scheduling.

The **Sentient Bean Coffeehouse** (13 E. Park Ave., 912-232-4447, www.sentientbean.com) hosts counterculture and political documentaries and kitsch classics at least two nights a week.

FESTIVALS AND EVENTS

Savannah's calendar fairly bursts with festivals, many outdoors. Dates shift from year to year, so it's best to consult the listed websites for details.

white feather is of nearby Independent Presbyterian Church.

Ben Affleck and Sandra Bullock filmed many scenes of 1999's *Forces of Nature* on Tybee Island and in Savannah (yours truly's house is in the final scene for about two seconds).

Longtime Hollywood producer and Savannah native Stratton Leopold, who also owns Leopold's Ice Cream on Broughton Street, helped Savannah land 1999's *The General's Daughter* starring John Travolta (look for the grand exterior of the main building at Oatland Island and shots of The Crab Shack seafood restaurant on Tybee, actually an old fishing camp).

Trotting out a serviceable Southern accent for a Brit, Kenneth Branagh came to town to play a disgruntled Savannah lawyer in Robert Altman's *Gingerbread Man*. Despite the late Altman's reputation as an actor's director, he's one of the few directors to grasp the extent of the Georgia coast's natural beauty; the views of the Tybee marsh are some of the best landscape shots of the area you'll ever see.

Though quite a few downtown art students had no idea what the fuss was about, Robert Redford still turned female heads of a certain age when he came to town to direct 2000's *The Legend of Bagger Vance*, with Will Smith as the eponymous caddie. In the film, watch for the facsimile of a Depression-era storefront specially built around City Market.

Redford returned to Savannah in late 2009 to film *The Conspirator*, yet another locally shot film about the Lincoln assassination. (Savannah stands in for Washington DC in the film.)

Cate Blanchett and Katie Holmes starred in 2000's *The Gift*, one of the few movies to take full advantage of the poignant and stunning natural beauty of Bonaventure Cemetery.

Ironically, considering the impact of "The Book" on Savannah, Clint Eastwood's *Midnight in the Garden of Good and Evil* (1997) is arguably the worst movie ever filmed here. Though now lionized as one of Hollywood's great directors, Eastwood's famously laissez-faire attitude toward filmmaking – reportedly there were no rehearsals before cameras rolled – did not serve the story or the setting well, perhaps because Savannah's already a pretty darn laissez-faire kind of place to begin with.

But the biggest stir of them all came in summer 2009, when Disney star Miley Cyrus of "Hannah Montana" fame came to Tybee Island to film *The Last Song*. Mobbed by crowds of young girls, Cyrus found a bit of fun afterhours at a Tybee club called Sting Rays, where she briefly sang and played guitar in an impromptu concert.

January

Floats and bands take part in the **Martin Luther King Jr. Day Parade** downtown to commemorate the civil rights leader and Georgia native. The bulk of the route consists of historic MLK Jr. Boulevard, formerly West Broad Street.

February

Definitely *not* to be confused with St. Patrick's Day, the **Savannah Irish Festival** (912/232-3448, www.savannahirish.org) focuses on Celtic music. A regular performer and Savannah's most popular "Irishman at large" is folk singer Harry O'Donoghue, a native of Ireland who regularly plays at Kevin Barry's Irish Pub on River Street and hosts his own Celtic music show, "The Green Island," on local public radio 91.1 FM Saturday evenings.

Hosted by the historically black Savannah State University at various venues around town, the monthlong **Black Heritage Festival** (912/691-6847) is tied into Black History Month and boasts name entertainers like the Alvin Ailey Dance Theatre (performing free!). This event also usually features plenty of historical lectures devoted to the very interesting and rich history of African Americans in Savannah.

Also in February is the **Savannah Book Festival** (www.savannahbookfestival.org), modeled after a similar event in Washington

DC and featuring many local and regional authors at various venues.

March

One of the most anticipated events for house-proud Savannahians, the **Tour of Homes and Gardens** (912/234-8054, www.savannah tourofhomes.org) offers guests the opportunity to visit six beautiful sites off the usual tourist-trod path. This is a great way to expand your understanding of local architecture and hospitality beyond the usual house museums.

More than just a day, the citywide **St. Patrick's Day** (www.savannahsaintpatricks day.com) celebration generally lasts at least half a week and temporarily triples the population. The nearly three-hour parade—second-biggest in the United States—always begins at 10 A.M. on St. Patrick's Day (unless that falls on a Sunday, in which case it's generally on the previous Saturday) and includes an interesting mix of marching bands, wacky floats, and sauntering local Irishmen in kelly green jackets.

The appeal of the event comes not only from the festive atmosphere and generally beautiful spring weather, but from Savannah's unique law allowing partiers to walk the streets with a plastic cup filled with the adult beverage of their choice. Because of this, however, there is inevitably going to be over-imbibing, which Savannahians generally think of as "local character." While you may disagree, there's no escaping the event if it's going on while you're here. Your best course of action is to simply put on a "Kiss Me I'm Irish" button, sample a beverage yourself, and live and let live if possible.

While the parade itself is very family-friendly, afterwards hardcore partiers generally head en masse to River Street, which is blocked off for the occasion and definitely *not* where you want to take small children. Five bucks will buy those 21 and over a bracelet allowing them to drink alcohol. For information on this aspect of the celebration, go to www .riverstreetsavannah.com. If you want to hear traditional Celtic music on St. Patrick's Day in Savannah, River Street isn't the place to go,

with the exception of Kevin Barry's on the west end. Outdoor entertainment on River Street during the celebration is generally a lame assortment of cover bands. For authentic Irish music on St. Paddy's Day, wander around the pubs in the City Market area.

Savannah's answer to Charleston's Spoleto, the three-week **Savannah Music Festival** (912/234-3378, www.savannahmusicfestival .org) is held at various historic venues around town and begins right after St. Patrick's Day. Past festivals have featured Wynton Marsalis, the Beaux Arts Trio, and Diane Reeves. The jazz portion is locked down tight, thanks to the efforts of festival director Rob Gibson, a Georgia native who cut his teeth as the founding director of Jazz at Lincoln Center. The classical side is equally impressive, helmed by one of the world's great young violinists, Daniel Hope, acting as associate director. Other genres are featured in abundance as well, from gospel to bluegrass to zydeco to world music to the always-popular American Traditions vocal competition.

The most economical way to enjoy the Music Festival is to purchase tickets online before December of the previous year at a 10 percent discount. However, if you just want to take in a few events, individual tickets are available at a tiered pricing system that allows everyone to enjoy this popular event. You can buy tickets to individual events in town at the walk-up box office beside the Trustees Theatre on Broughton Street.

April

Short for "North of Gaston Street," the **NOGS Tour of Hidden Gardens** (912/961-4805, www.gcofsavnogstour.org, $30) is available two days in April and focuses on Savannah's amazing selection of private gardens selected for excellence of design, historical interest, and beauty.

Everyone loves the annual free **Sidewalk Arts Festival** (912/525-5865, www.scad.edu) presented by the Savannah College of Art and Design in Forsyth Park. Contestants claim a rectangular section of sidewalk on which to display their chalk art talent. There's a non-contest section with chalk provided.

May

The SCAD-sponsored **Sand Arts Festival** (www.scad.edu) on Tybee Island's North Beach centers on a competition of sand castle design, sand sculpture, sand relief, and wind sculpture. You might be amazed at the level of artistry lavished on the sometimes-wondrous creations, only for them to wash away with the tide.

If you don't want to get wet, don't show up at the **Tybee Beach Bum Parade,** an uproarious Memorial Day event with a distinctly boozy overtone. This unique 20-year-old event features homemade floats filled with partiers who squirt the assembled crowds with various water pistols. The crowds, of course, pack their own heat and squirt back.

July

Two key events happen around **Fourth of July,** primarily the large fireworks show on River Street, always on July 4, and also an impressive fireworks display from the Tybee Pier and Pavilion, which sometimes is on a different night. A nice bonus of the Tybee event is that sometimes you can look out over the Atlantic and see a similar fireworks display held on nearby Hilton Head Island, South Carolina, a few minutes away by boat (but nearly an hour by car).

September

The second-largest gay and lesbian event in Georgia (only Atlanta's version is larger), the **Savannah Pride Festival** (www.savannah pride.org, various venues, free) happens every September. Crowds get pretty big for this festive, fun event, which usually features lots of dance acts and political booths.

Though the quality of the acts has been overshadowed lately by the Savannah Music Festival in the spring, the **Savannah Jazz Festival** (www.savannahjazzfestival.org) has two key things going for it: It's free, and it's outside in the glorious green expanse of Forsyth Park. Generally spread out over several nights,

the volunteer-run festival draws a good crowd regardless of the lineup, and concessions are available.

October

The Savannah Symphony Orchestra is now-defunct, but area musicians unite to play a free evening at **Picnic in the Park** (www .savannahga.gov), a concert in Forsyth Park that draws thousands of noshers. Arrive early to check out the ostentatious, whimsical picnic displays, which compete for prizes. Then set out your blanket, pop open a bottle of wine, and enjoy the sweet sounds.

The combined aroma of beer, sauerkraut, and sausage that you smell coming from the waterfront is the annual **Oktoberfest on the River** (www.riverstreetsavannah.com), which has evolved to be Savannah's second-largest celebration (behind only St. Patrick's Day). Live entertainment of varying quality is featured, though of course the attraction is the aforementioned beer and German food. A highlight is the Saturday morning "Weiner Dog races" involving, you guessed it, competing dachshunds.

If pickin' and grinnin' is your thing, don't miss the low-key but always entertaining **Savannah Folk Music Festival** (www.savannah folk.org). The main event of the weekend is held on a Sunday night in the historic Grayson Stadium in Daffin Park, but a popular Old-Time Country Dance is usually held the Saturday prior. Members of the Savannah Folk Music Society will help you learn how to do the dance, so don't be shy!

Sponsored by St. Paul's Greek Orthodox Church, the popular **Savannah Greek Festival** (www.stpaul.ga.goarch.org) features food, music, and Greek souvenirs. The weekend event is held across the street from the church at the parish center—in the gym, to be exact, right on the basketball court. Despite the pedestrian location, the food is authentic and delicious, and the atmosphere convivial and friendly.

Despite its generic-sounding name, the **Fall Festival** (www.bamboo.caes.uga.edu) is actually quite interesting, given its location in the unique Bamboo Farm and Coastal Garden. A joint project of the University of Georgia and Chatham County, the Bamboo Farm features a wide array of native species, all lovingly tended. The festival features tours, displays, arts and crafts, food, and lots of kids' activities. The event is free, but you'll pay $1 to park. To get there, take Exit 94 off of I-95 and take U.S. 204 east towards Savannah. Turn right on East Gateway Boulevard, then left on Canebrake Road. Enter at the Canebrake gate.

Hosted by the Savannah College of Art and Design, the weeklong **Savannah Film Festival** (www.scad.edu) beginning in late October is rapidly growing not only in size but in prestige. Lots of older, more established Hollywood names appear as honored guests for the evening events, while buzz-worthy, up-and-coming actors, directors, producers, writers, and animators give excellent workshops during the day. Many of these usually jaded show-biz types really let their hair down for this festival, because, as you'll see, Savannah is the real star.

The best way to enjoy this excellent event is to buy a pass, which enables you to walk from event to event. Most importantly, the passes gain you admission to what many locals consider the best part of the festival: the afterparties, where you'll often find yourself face to face with some famous star or director. But whatever you do, don't ask for an autograph. The thing at these parties is to be cool—and if you can't *be* cool, at least act that way!

One of Savannah's most unique events is October's **"Shalom Y'all" Jewish Food Festival** (912/233-1547, www.mickveisrael .org), held in Forsyth Park and sponsored by the historic Temple Mickve Israel. Latkes, matzo, and other nibbles are all featured along with entertainment.

November

Generally kicking off the month is the popular **Telfair Art Fair** (www.telfair.org), a multiday annual art show and sale under a huge tent in Telfair Square between the two museums there, the Telfair Academy and the Jepson Center. Browse or buy, either way it's a culturally enlightening good time.

The name says it all. The **Savannah Seafood Festival** (www.riverstreetsavannah .com) on River Street offers mouthwatering fare from a variety of local vendors, plus live entertainment.

December

Arts and crafts and holiday entertainment highlight the **Christmas on the River and Lighted Parade** (www.riverstreetsavannah .com) that happens on River Street.

Another beloved local tour, the annual **Holiday Tour of Homes** (912/236-8362, www.dnaholidaytour.net) sponsored by the Downtown Neighborhood Association is a great way to get up close with a half-dozen or so of some of Savannah's best private homes, all dolled up in their finest for the holidays. There's an afternoon tour and a candlelight tour by trolley.

Shopping

Downtown Savannah's main shopping district is Broughton Street, which is included here along with several other key shopping areas of note.

BROUGHTON STREET

The historic center of downtown shopping has recently seen a major renaissance, and is once again home to the most vibrant shopping scene in Savannah, just like it was in the 1940s and '50s. While several chain stores have made inroads onto the avenue, here are some of the most notable independent shops.

Art Supply

A great art town needs a great art supply store,

and in Savannah that would be **Primary Art Supply** (14 E. Broughton St., 912/233-7624, http://primaryartsupply.com, Mon.–Fri. 8 A.M.–8 P.M., Sat.–Sun. 10 A.M.–6 P.M.), which has two full floors of equipment and tools for the serious artist—priced to be affordable for students. But casual shoppers will enjoy it as well for its collection of hip magazines and offbeat gift items.

Clothes and Fashion

Perhaps Broughton's most beloved shop is **Globe Shoe Co.** (17 E. Broughton St., 912/232-8161), a Savannah institution and a real throwback to a time of personalized retail service. They have no website and no Facebook page—they're all about simple one-to-one service like in the old days.

The clothing store for Savannah's hippest, up-and-coming women, **Bleu Belle** (205 W. Broughton St., 912/443-0011, www.bleubelle.com, Mon.–Sat. 10 A.M.–6 P.M., Sun. noon–5 P.M.) stays on top of the trends with a wide selection, from casual chic to drop-dead evening wear.

Gaucho is another popular choice for women, with an emphasis on accessories, jewelry, and shoes. There are two locations: 18 East Broughton Street (912/234-7414, Mon.–Sat. 10 A.M.–6 P.M.) and the original location at 250 Bull Street (912/232-7414, Mon.–Sat. 10 A.M.–6 P.M., Sun. 1–5 P.M.).

Vintage shoppers will enjoy **Civvies** (22 E. Broughton St., 912/236-1551), a second-floor shop with a nice selection of previously owned clothing.

Popular Georgia/South Carolina chain **Loose Lucy's** (212 W. Broughton St., 912/201-2131, www.looselucys.com, Mon.–Fri. 10 A.M.–7 P.M., Sat. 10 A.M.–9 P.M., Sun. 11 A.M.–6 P.M.) features cool clothes and shoes heavy on 1960s psychedelic chic.

Home Goods

While Savannah is an Anglophile's dream, Francophiles will enjoy **The Paris Market & Brocante** (36 W. Broughton St., 912/232-1500, www.theparismarket.com, Mon.–Sat.

10 A.M.–6 P.M., Sun. 11 A.M.–4 P.M.) on a beautifully restored corner of Broughton Street. Home and garden goods, bed and bath accoutrements, and a great selection of antique and vintage items combine for a rather opulent shopping experience. Plus there's a "café" inside where you can enjoy a coffee, tea, or hot chocolate.

Those looking for great home decorating ideas with inspiration from both global and Southern aesthetics should check out **24e Furnishings at Broughton** (24 E. Broughton St., 912/233-2274, www.twentyfoure.com, Mon.–Thurs. 10 A.M.–6 P.M., Fri.–Sat. 10 A.M.–7 P.M., Sun. noon–5 P.M.), located in an excellent restored 1921 storefront.

One of the most unique Savannah retail shops is the **Savannah Bee Company** (104 W. Broughton St., 912/233-7873, www.savannahbee.com, Mon.–Sat. 10 A.M.–7 P.M., Sun. 11 A.M.–5 P.M.), which as the name implies carries an extensive line of honey-based merchandise, from foot lotion to lip balm. All the honey comes from area hives owned by company founder and owner Ted Dennard. The company now has a sizeable national presence since being picked up for the Williams-Sonoma catalogue in 2003.

Outdoor Outfitters

Outdoor lovers should make themselves acquainted with **Half Moon Outfitters** (15 E. Broughton St., 912/201-9313, www.halfmoonoutfitters.com, Mon.–Sat. 10 A.M.–7 P.M., Sun. noon–6 P.M.), a full-service camping, hiking, skiing, and kayaking store. Half Moon is part of a regional chain that also has two locations in Charleston.

WATERFRONT

Amid the T-shirt shops, candy stores, and tchotchke places, Savannah's waterfront area does have a few worthy shopping options.

Antiques

One of the coolest antique shops in town is **Jere's Antiques** (9 N. Jefferson St., 912/236-2815, www.jeresantiques.com, Mon.–Sat.

9:30 A.M.–5 P.M.). It's in a huge historic warehouse on Factor's Walk, and has a concentration on fine European pieces.

Clothes

The river's most popular clothing store by far is the boutique **Jezebel Limited** (25 E. River St., 912/236-4333, Mon.–Sun. 10 A.M.–6 P.M.), which packs a lot of cute, wearable high fashion into a small place.

Clothe your inner biker at **Harley-Davidson** (503 E. River St., 912/231-8000, Mon.–Sat. 10 A.M.–6 P.M., Sun. noon–6 P.M.).

CITY MARKET

A borderline tourist trap, City Market strongly tends towards more touristy, less unique items. Here are a few exceptions:

An absolutely one-of-a-kind shopping experience can be had in City Market at **Universe Trading Company** (27 Montgomery St., 912/233-1585, Tues.–Sat. 10 A.M.–5 P.M.) on the southwest corner of Franklin Square. This mind-blowing collection of kitsch—including, at last check, an actual cigar-store Indian—is the real thing: a great old-fashioned junk shop, in the best sense of the term.

The whimsical **A. T. Hun Gallery** (302 W. St. Julian St., 912/233-2060, www.athun .com, Mon.–Thurs. 10 A.M.–6 P.M., Fri.–Sat. 10 A.M.–10 P.M., Sun. 11 A.M.–5 P.M.) is one of the first true art galleries in town and features a variety of adventurous art from local and regional favorites.

Another City Market favorite is **Chroma Gallery** (31 Barnard St., 912/232-2787, www.chromaartgallery.com, daily 10 A.M.–5:30 P.M.), run by two of Savannah's most beloved artists, Lori Keith Robinson and Jan Clayton Pagratis.

Check out some whimsical watches at **Time After Time** (305 W. Bryan St., 912/233-0568, daily 10 A.M.–6 P.M.).

If you're dying for a good smoke, try **Savannah Cigars** (308 W. Congress St., 912/233-2643, Mon.–Thurs. 11 A.M.–6 P.M., Fri.–Sat. 11 A.M.–11 P.M., Sun. noon–6 P.M.).

City Market

DOWNTOWN DESIGN DISTRICT

Focusing on upscale art and home goods, this small shopping area runs for three blocks on Whitaker Street downtown beginning at Charlton Lane and ending at the Mercer-Williams House on Monterey Square.

Antiques

Arcanum Antiques and Interiors (422 Whitaker St., 912/236-6000, Mon.–Sat. 10 A.M.–5 P.M.) deals in a tasteful range of vintage items with a chic twist.

For a more European take, try **The Corner Door** (417 Whitaker St., 912/238-5869, Tues.–Sat. 10 A.M.–5 P.M.).

Perhaps the most eclectic antique shop in the Downtown Design District is **Peridot Antiques and Interiors** (400 Whitaker St., 912/596-1117).

Clothes

Custard Boutique (414 Whitaker St., 912/232-4733) has a cute, fairly cutting-edge selection of women's clothes.

Mint Boutique (413 Whitaker St., 912/341-8961, Mon.–Fri. 10 A.M.–6 P.M.) right next door brings a similarly modern style to this often very conservative town.

Home Goods

An eclectic, European-style home goods store popular with locals and tourists alike is **One Fish Two Fish** (401 Whitaker St., 912/484-4600, Mon.–Sat. 10 A.M.–5 P.M., Sun. noon–5 P.M.). Owner Jennifer Beaufait Grayson, a St. Simons Island native, came to town a decade ago to set up shop in this delightfully restored old dairy building on the corner of Whitaker and Jones and has been getting rave reviews since.

Madame Chrysanthemum (101 W. Taylor St., 912/238-3355) is technically a florist, and a fine one at that, but they also deal with fun home items and gift ideas.

BOOKS

The fact that **E. Shaver Bookseller** (326 Bull St., 912/234-7257, Mon.–Sat. 9 A.M.–6 P.M.) is one of the few locally owned independent bookstores left in town should not diminish the fact that it is also one of the best bookstores in town. Esther Shaver and her friendly, well-read staff can help you around the rambling old interior of their ground-level store and its generous stock of regionally themed books. Don't miss the rare map room, with some gems from the 17th and 18th centuries.

Specializing in "gently used" books in good condition, **The Book Lady** (6 E. Liberty St., 912/233-3628, Mon.–Sat. 10 A.M.–5:30 P.M.) on Wright Square features many rare first editions. Enjoy a gourmet coffee while you browse the stacks.

The beautiful Monterey Square location and a mention in *Midnight in the Garden of Good and Evil* combine to make **V&J Duncan** (12 E. Taylor St., 912/232-0338, www.vjduncan.com, Mon.–Sat. 10:30 A.M.–4:30 P.M.) a Savannah "must-shop." Owner John Duncan and his wife Virginia ("Ginger" to friends) have collected an impressive array of prints, books, and maps over the past quarter-century, and are themselves a treasure trove of information.

OTHER UNIQUE STORES

Not only a valuable outlet for SCAD students and faculty to sell their artistic wares, **shopSCAD** (340 Bull St., 912/525-5180, www.shopscadonline.com, Mon.–Wed. 9 A.M.–5:30 P.M., Thurs.–Fri. 9 A.M.–8 P.M., Sat. 10 A.M.–8 P.M., Sun. noon–5 P.M.) is also one of Savannah's most unique boutiques. You never really know what you'll find, but whatever it is, it will be one-of-a-kind. The jewelry in particular is always cutting-edge in design and high-quality in craftsmanship. The designer T-shirts are a hoot, too.

A delightful little slice of Europe on Abercorn, **Fabrika** (140 Abercorn St., 912/236-1122, www.fabrikasavannah.com, Mon.–Sat. 10 A.M.–6 P.M., Sun. noon–4 P.M.) seems more like a store in Holland or France than one in Savannah. Tiny and personable, the store is jammed with high-quality, buzz-worthy bolts of fabric, oodles of beads, and lots of sewing paraphernalia. They even offer custom sewing and sewing lessons.

And in this town so enamored of all things Irish, a great little locally owned shop is **Saints and Shamrocks** (309 Bull St., 912/233-8858, www.saintsandshamrocks.org, Mon.–Sat. 9:30 A.M.–5:30 P.M., Sun. 11 A.M.–4 P.M.). Pick up your St. Patrick's-themed gear and gifts to celebrate Savannah's highest holiday, or high-quality Irish imports.

MALLS

The mall closest to downtown—though it's not that close at about 10 miles south—is **Oglethorpe Mall** (7804 Abercorn St., 912/354-7038, www.oglethorpemall.com, Mon.–Sat. 10 A.M.–9 P.M., Sun. noon–6 P.M.). Its anchor stores are Sears, Belk, J. C. Penney, and Macy's.

Much farther out on the southside is the **Savannah Mall** (14045 Abercorn St., 912/927-7467, www.savannahmall.com, Mon.–Sat. 10 A.M.–9 P.M., Sun. noon–6 P.M.). Its anchor stores are Dillard's, Target, and Bass Pro Shops Outdoor World.

GROCERIES AND MARKETS

Savannah's first and still premier health food market, **Brighter Day Natural Foods** (1102 Bull St., 912/236-4703, www.brighterday foods.com, Mon.–Sat. 10 A.M.–7 P.M., Sun. 12:30–5:30 P.M.) has been the labor of love of Janie and Peter Brodhead for 30 years, all of them in the same location at the southern tip of Forsyth Park. Boasting organic groceries, regional produce, a sandwich and smoothie bar in the back, and an extensive vitamin, supplement, and herb section, Brighter Day is an oasis in Savannah's sea of chain supermarkets.

A throwback to the South's old ways and a pleasant spot to pick up some fresh area produce downtown is **Polk's Fresh Market** (530 E. Liberty St., 912/238-3032, Mon.–Sat. 8 A.M.–6 P.M.).

If you need some good quality groceries downtown—especially after-hours—try **Parker's Market** (222 E. Drayton St., 912/231-1001, daily 24 hours). In addition to a pretty wide array of gourmet-style victuals inside, there are gas pumps outside to fuel your vehicle.

A local tradition for 20 years, **Keller's Flea Market** (5901 Ogeechee Rd., Exit 94 off I-95, 912/927-4848, www.ilovefleas.com, Sat.–Sun. 8 A.M.–6 P.M.) packs in about 10,000 shoppers over the course of a typical weekend, offering a range of bargains in antiques, home goods, produce, and general kitsch. Free admission, concessions on-site.

A short ways into southside Savannah is a **Fresh Market** (5525 Abercorn St., 912/354-6075, Mon.–Sat. 9 A.M.–9 P.M., Sun. 11 A.M.–8 P.M.).

Currently there's only one true supermarket in downtown Savannah, **Kroger** (311 E. Gwinnett St., 912/231-2260, daily 24 hours).

Sports and Recreation

Savannah more than makes up for its sad organized sports scene with copious outdoor options that take full advantage of its temperate climate and the natural beauty of its marshy environment next to the Atlantic Ocean.

ON THE WATER
Kayaking and Canoeing

Probably the single best kayak/canoe adventure in Savannah is the run across the Back River from Tybee to **Little Tybee Island,** an undeveloped State Heritage Site that despite its name is actually twice as big as Tybee, albeit mostly marsh. Many kayakers opt to camp on the island. You can even follow the shoreline out into the Atlantic, but be aware that wave action can get intense offshore.

Begin the paddle at the public boat ramp on the Back River. To get there, take Butler all the way to 18th Street and take a right, then another quick right onto Chatham Avenue. The parking lot for the landing is a short way up Chatham

© BRUCE TUTEN

Kayakers head to Little Tybee Island.

on your left. (Warning: Do not attempt to swim to Little Tybee no matter how strong a swimmer you think you are—the currents are exceptionally vicious. Also, do not be tempted to walk far out onto the Back River beach at low tide. The tide comes in very quickly and often strands people on the sandbar.)

Many local kayakers put in at the Lazaretto Creek landing, at the foot of the Lazaretto Creek bridge on the south side of U.S. Highway 80 on the way to Tybee Island. This is a peaceful, pretty paddle for novice and experienced kayakers alike.

One of the great overall natural experiences in the area is the massive **Savannah National Wildlife Refuge** (912/652-4415, www.fws .gov/savannah, daily dawn–dusk, no fee). This 30,000-acre reserve—half in Georgia, half in South Carolina—is on the Atlantic Flyway, so you'll be able to see birdlife in abundance, in addition to alligators and manatee. Earthen dikes crisscrossing the refuge are vestigial remnants of rice paddies from plantation days.

You can kayak on your own, but many opt to take guided tours offered by **Wilderness Southeast** (912/897-5108, www.wilderness-southeast.org, two-hour trips start at $37.50 for

two people), **Sea Kayak Georgia** (888/529-2542, www.seakayakgeorgia.com, $55 per person), and **Swamp Girls Kayak Tours** (843/784-2249, www.swampgirls.com, $45). To get there, take U.S. Highway 17 north over the big Talmadge Bridge, over the Savannah River into South Carolina. Turn left on South Carolina Highway 170 South and look for the entrance to Laurel Hill Wildlife Drive on the left.

Another pleasant kayaking route is the **Skidaway Narrows.** Begin this paddle at the public boat ramp, which you find by taking Waters Avenue all the way until it turns to Whitefield Avenue and then Diamond Causeway. Continue all the way over the Moon River to a drawbridge; park at the foot of the bridge. Once in the water, paddle northeast. Look for the osprey nests on top of the navigational markers in the Narrows as you approach Skidaway Island State Park. Continuing on you'll find scenic Isle of Hope high on a bluff to your left, with nearly guaranteed dolphin sightings around marker 62.

Farther out of town but worth the trip for any kayaker is the beautiful blackwater **Ebenezer Creek,** near the tiny township of New Ebenezer in Effingham County. Cypress trees lining this nationally designated Wild and Scenic River hang overhead and wildlife abounds in this peaceful paddle. Look for old wooden sluice gates, vestiges of the area's rice plantation past. To get there, take Exit 109 off I-95. Go north on Highway 21 to Rincon, Georgia, then east on Highway 275 (Ebenezer Rd.). Put in at the Ebenezer Landing ($5).

The one-stop shop for local kayaking information, tours, and equipment is **Sea Kayak Georgia** (1102 Hwy. 80, 888/529-2542, www.seakayakgeorgia.com), run by Tybee Islanders Marsha Henson and Ronnie Kemp.

Another popular tour operator is **Savannah Canoe & Kayak** (2169 Tennessee Ave., 912/341-9502, www.savannahcanoeandkayak.com).

Fishing

Savannah is a saltwater angler's paradise, rich in trout, flounder, and king and Spanish mackerel. Offshore there's a fair amount of deep-sea action, including large grouper, white and blue marlin, wahoo, snapper, sea bass, and big amberjack near some of the many offshore wrecks.

Perhaps the best-known local angler is Captain Judy Helmey, a.k.a. "Miss Judy." In addition to her frequent and entertaining newspaper columns, she runs a variety of well-regarded charters out of **Miss Judy Charters** (912/897-2478, www.missjudycharters.com). Four-hour trips start at $500. To get there, go west on U.S. 80, take a right onto Bryan Woods Road, a left onto Johnny Mercer Boulevard, a right onto Wilmington Island Way, and a right down the dirt lane at her sign.

Another highly regarded local fishing charter is the Tybee-based **Amick's Deep Sea Fishing** (912/897-6759, www.amicksdeepseafishing.com). Captain Steve Amick and crew run offshore charters starting at $110 per person daily. Go east on U.S. 80 and turn right just past the Lazaretto Creek Bridge; boats are behind Café Loco.

Another charter service is offered at **Lazaretto Creek Marina** (1 U.S. 80, 912/786-5848, www.tybeedolphins.com). Half- and full-day inshore and offshore fishing charters are available, starting at $250 for four hours. Go east on Highway 80 and turn right just past the Lazaretto Creek Bridge. Turn right at the dead end.

Shallow-water fly fishers might want to contact **Savannah Fly Fishing Charters** (56 Sassafras Trail, 912/308-3700, www.savannahfly.com). Captain Scott Wagner takes half- and full-day charters both day and night from Savannah all the way down to St. Simons Island. Half-day rate starts at $300. Book early.

Diving

Diving is a challenge off the Georgia coast because of the silty nature of the water and its mercurial currents. Though not particularly friendly to the novice, plenty of great offshore opportunities abound around the many artificial reefs created by the Georgia Department of Natural Resources. An excellent guidebook in PDF form with full GPS data is available at http://crd.dnr.state.ga.us/assets/documents/ReefBooklet.pdf.

Certainly no underwater adventure in the area would be complete without a dive at **Gray's Reef National Marine Sanctuary** (912/598-2345, www.graysreef.noaa.gov). Administered by the National Oceanic and Atmospheric Administration, this fully protected marine sanctuary 17 miles offshore is in deep enough water to provide divers good visibility of its live-bottom habitat. Not a classic living coral reef, but rather one built by sedimentary deposits, Gray's Reef's provides a look at a truly unique ecosystem.

Some key dive charter operators that can take you to Gray's Reef are Captain Walter Rhame's **Mako Dive Charter** (600 Priest Landing Dr., 912/604-6256) which leaves from the Landings Harbor Marina; **Georgia Offshore** (1191 Lake Dr., Midway, 912/658-3884); and **Fantasia Scuba** (3 E. Montgomery Cross Rd., 912/921-8933). The best all-around dive shop in town is **Diving Locker and Ski Chalet** (74 W. Montgomery Cross Rd., 912/927-6603, www.divinglockerskichalet.com) on the south side.

Surfing and Boarding

Other than some action around the pier,

the surfing is poor on Tybee Island, with its broad shelf, tepid wave action, and lethal rip currents. But board surfers and kiteboarders have a lot of fun on the south end of Tybee beginning at about 17th Street. The craziest surf is past the rock jetty, but be advised that the rip currents are especially treacherous there.

The best—and pretty much only—surf shop in town is **High Tides Surf Shop** (405 Hwy. 80, 912/786-6556, www.hightidesurfshop .com). You can get a good local surf report and forecasts at their website.

ON THE LAND
Golf
There are several strong public courses in Savannah that are also great bargains. Chief among these has to be the **Henderson Golf Club** (1 Al Henderson Blvd., 912/920-4653, www.hendersongolfclub.com), an excellent municipal course with reasonable green fees of $39 during the week and $48 on the weekend, both of which include a half-cart.

Another local favorite and unbeatable bargain is the circa-1926 **Bacon Park Golf Course** (Shorty Cooper Dr., 912/354-2625, www.bacon parkgolf.com), comprising three nine-hole courses with a choice of three 18-hole combinations and some very small, fast greens. Green fees hover around $30.

A relatively new course but not one you'd call a bargain is the **Club at Savannah Harbor** (2 Resort Dr., 912/201-2007, www .theclubatsavannahharbor.com) across the Savannah River on Hutchinson Island, adjacent to the Westin Savannah Harbor Resort. Home to the Liberty Mutual Legends of Golf Tournament each spring, the Club's tee times are 7:30 A.M.–3 P.M., with half-light play 2–5 P.M. Green fees are $135, or $70 for twilight fees.

The **Wilmington Island Club** (501 Wilmington Island Rd., 912/897-1612) has arguably the quickest greens in town and is unarguably the most beautiful local course, set close by the Wilmington River amid lots of mature pines and live oaks. Green fees are $69.

Tennis
The closest public courts to the downtown area are at the south end of **Forsyth Park** (912/351-3850), which features four free, lighted courts. As you might expect, they get serious use. Farther south in **Daffin Park** (1001 E. Victory Dr., 912/351-3850), there are nine courts ($3), three of which are available for night play. On the south side, **Bacon Park** (6262 Skidaway Rd., 912/351-3850) has 14 lighted courts ($3).

If you get the tennis jones on Tybee, there are two free courts at **Tybee Island Memorial Park** (912/786-4573, www.cityoftybee.org) at Butler Avenue and Fourth Street.

Hiking
Though hiking in Savannah and the Lowcountry is largely a 2-D experience given the flatness of the terrain, there are plenty of good nature trails from which to observe the area's rich flora and fauna up close. My favorite trails are at **Skidaway Island State Park** (52 Diamond Causeway, 912/598-2300, www.gastateparks.org, daily 7 A.M.–10 P.M., $2 per vehicle daily parking fee). The three-mile Big Ferry Trail is the best overall experience, taking you out to a wooden viewing tower from which you can see the vast expanse of the Skidaway Narrows. A detour takes you past a Native American shell midden, Confederate earthworks, and even a rusty old still—a nod to Skidaway Island's former notoriety as a bootlegger's sanctuary. The shorter but still fun Sandpiper Trail is wheelchair-accessible.

An interesting, if hardly challenging, trail is the **McQueen Island Trail,** more commonly known as "Rails to Trails." This paved, palm-lined walking trail along the Savannah River was built on the old bed of the Savannah-to-Tybee railroad, which operated during Tybee's heyday as a major East Coast vacation spot in the 1930s and '40s. To get there, cross the long, low, Bull River Bridge and take an *immediate* left into the small parking area, being very mindful of fast-moving inbound traffic on U.S. 80.

Biking

Most biking activity centers on Tybee Island, with the **McQueen Island Trail** being a popular and simple ride. Many locals like to load up their bikes and go to **Fort Pulaski** (912/786-5787, www.nps.gov, open every day except Christmas, fort hours 8:30 A.M.–5:15 P.M., visitors center 9 A.M.–5 P.M., $2 per person 17 and up). From the grounds you can ride all over scenic and historic Cockspur Island.

It's not a strenuous ride, but pedaling around the idyllic little neighborhoods of **Isle of Hope** is relaxing fun.

Bird-Watching

Birding in the Savannah area is excellent at two spots on the **Colonial Coast Birding Trail** (http://georgiawildlife.dnr.state.ga.us). Chief among them is **Skidaway Island State Park** (52 Diamond Causeway, 912/598-2300, www.gastateparks.org, daily 7 A.M.–10 P.M., $2 per vehicle daily parking fee). Spring and fall bring a lot of the usual warbler action, while spring and summer feature nesting osprey and painted bunting, always a delight.

The other trail spot is Tybee Island's **North Beach** area ($5 per day parking fee, meters available). You'll see a wide variety of shorebirds

---

SAVANNAH BASEBALL

Savannah has a long and important history with the national pastime. In fact, the first known photograph of a baseball game was taken in Fort Pulaski, of Union occupation troops at play on the parade ground.

A pivotal figure in baseball history also has a crucial association with Savannah. Long before gaining notoriety for his role on the infamous Chicago "Black Sox" that threw the 1919 World Series, baseball legend Shoeless Joe Jackson was a stalwart on the South Atlantic or "Sally" League circuit. Playing for the Savannah Indians in 1909, Joe played ball predominantly at Bolton Street Park, off what's now Henry Street. That year Jackson hit .358, a Sally League performance bested only twice that century.

The South Carolina native must have remembered his days in Savannah fondly, for after his career ended ignominiously Joe returned to town, began a thriving dry-cleaning business, and lived with his wife at 143 Abercorn Street and then on East 39th Street. No doubt tired of the jokes up north about his Southern accent and his alleged illiteracy – the degree of which is a matter of some dispute – Joe said he simply felt more at home here.

Another early great who played in Savannah was Georgia native Ty Cobb, who visited in 1905 with an Augusta team. He's remembered, typically enough, for getting into a fistfight with a teammate who voiced his displeasure at Cobb eating popcorn in the outfield and muffing an easy catch.

Savannah got a proper ballpark in 1926, named Municipal Stadium. After a hurricane destroyed it in 1940, rebuilding began but abruptly stopped when Pearl Harbor was attacked the next year and all the laborers rushed off to enlist. So abruptly did they drop their tools, in fact, that to this day behind third base you can still clearly see the jagged line indicating where construction halted. The stadium was renamed Grayson Stadium in honor of Spanish-American War hero William Grayson, who spearheaded the venue's eventual renovation.

The great Babe Ruth played in the stadium once in 1935 in his final year as a major leaguer, as his Boston Braves beat the South Georgia Teachers College (now Georgia Southern University) 15-1 in an exhibition game. Ruth, of course, hit a home run.

There's a common thread between Jackson and Babe Ruth, who wasn't known as a hitter until after he'd already established himself as a standout pitcher. Shoeless Joe – perhaps the game's most consummate hitter until Ted Williams' arrival on the scene 30 years later – tried to change Ruth's stance in the batter's box to improve his hitting. The rest, as they say, is history.

and gulls, as well as piping plover, northern gannets, and purple sandpiper (winter).

Wading birds in particular are in wide abundance at the **Savannah National Wildlife Refuge.** The views are excellent all along the Lauren Hill wildlife drive, which takes you through the heart of the old rice paddies that crisscrossed the entire area.

SPECTATOR SPORTS

Topping the list of local spectator sports—indeed, it's basically the entire list—is the **Savannah Sand Gnats** (1401 E. Victory Dr., 912/351-9150, www.sandgnats.com) baseball franchise, currently a single-A affiliate of the New York Mets. The attraction here is not the level of play but the venue itself, Grayson Stadium in Daffin Park in the city's midtown area, a historic venue that's hosted such greats as Babe Ruth, Jackie Robinson, and Mickey Mantle over the years. The Gnats' season runs April–September.

There's not a bad seat in the house, so your best bet by far is to just buy a $6 general admission ticket. The games never sell out, so there's no need to stress. Entertainment runs the usual gamut of minor league shenanigans, including frequent fireworks displays after the games.

Mickey Mantle and the defending world champion New York Yankees played the Cincinnati Reds in a 1959 exhibition game in Savannah. The switch-hitting slugger hit two of his trademark mammoth home run shots during the game – both left-handed and each over 500 feet, according to witnesses.

Atlanta Braves great Hank Aaron, then a skinny second baseman with a Jacksonville club, played in Grayson's first game with both black and white players in 1953. Frank Robinson played one of the first games of his storied career here with the Columbia Reds. He showed up late to the game and still hit two home runs. Jackie Robinson stole home base in an exhibition game.

But in a way, all these names pale in comparison to one Savannah player whose influence can be felt to this day, not only in sports but in the business world at large: Curt Flood gave the world free agency.

Flood, who played for the Savannah Redlegs in 1957, refused to report to the Phillies after the Cardinals traded him in 1969. Flood sued Major League Baseball the next year, saying the so-called "reserve clause" allowing the trade violated antitrust laws. While Flood would lose the lawsuit in the U.S. Supreme Court, the narrowly worded decision left the way open for collective bargaining and today's massive free agent salaries.

The Savannah minor league team has taken on various incarnations over the years. The 1962 Savannah White Sox was the most successful, contributing an amazing 14 players to the majors. But the taste of success was short-lived. That was the year local civil rights great W. W. Law, then a postman, called for African Americans to boycott Grayson Stadium to protest its segregated seating policy. (The concession stand off the third base line is a reminder of that shameful era. It was once the "colored" restroom.)

Rather than risk violence at the stadium, the White Sox disbanded. Grayson was dormant until the Savannah Braves, a double-A team, began a very successful run in 1971 (including a 12-game winning season by pitcher and controversial *Ball Four* writer Jim Bouton), followed in 1984 by the Savannah Cardinals.

The current single-A team, the Savannah Sand Gnats, had their name chosen by a poll of daily newspaper readers. While their level of play rarely conjures mental images of Shoeless Joe or the Babe, Grayson Stadium itself has just been given an impressive new facelift courtesy of the city, with a new scoreboard and upgraded seating. By far the Sand Gnats' most famous face so far has been Cy Young Award–winning pitcher Eric Gagne, who pitched his very first professional game with the local club.

Accommodations

The hotel scene in Savannah, once notorious for its absurdly high price-to-service ratio, has improved a great deal in the past couple of years. Perhaps ironically, several stylish new downtown hotels opened more or less concurrently with the recent economic downturn. Their addition means increased competition, and therefore marginally lower prices, across the board.

Savannah's many historic bed-and-breakfasts are competitive with the hotels on price, and often outperform them on service and ambience. If you don't need a swimming pool and don't mind climbing some stairs every now and then, a B&B is usually your best bet. And of course the breakfasts are great, too!

CITY MARKET
$150-300

A Days Inn property, the **Inn at Ellis Square** (201 W. Bay St., 912/236-4440, www.innat ellissquare.com, $189) is smack dab between City Market and Bay Street: in other words, the heart of the tourist action. Set in the renovated 1851 Guckenheimer Building, the Inn is one of the better-appointed chain hotels in town.

Over $300

Providing a suitably modernist decor to go with its somewhat atypical architecture for Savannah, the new **C AVIA Savannah** (14 Barnard St., 912/233-2116, www.aviahotels .com, $320) overlooks restored Ellis Square and abuts City Market with its shopping, restaurants, and nightlife. Named one of the top new U.S. hotels by *Condé Nast Traveler* magazine, the AVIA's guest rooms and suites feature top-of-the-line linens, extra large and well-equipped bathrooms, in-room snack bars, and technological features such as mp3 docking stations, free Wi-Fi, and of course the ubiquitous flatscreen TV. Customer service is a particular strong suit. Just off the lobby is a very hip lounge/wine bar that attracts locals as well as hotel guests. Keep in mind things can get a little noisy in this area at nighttime on weekends.

WATERFRONT
$150-300

A cut above the Holiday Inn chain, with which it's affiliated, the **C Mulberry Inn** (601 E. Bay St., 912/238-1200, www.holidayinn.com, $189) is a longtime favorite with travelers to Savannah, with a charming central courtyard and with peaceful little Washington Square on the back of the building. Don't miss the genuine English teatime, complete with jazz piano accompaniment, observed in the lobby each afternoon at 4 P.M. (as if there's another English teatime). Another nifty touch is a dedicated parking garage—an amenity only someone who's spent half an hour looking for a parking space in downtown Savannah will truly appreciate. Parking is free for Holiday Inn "priority members" (you can sign up for membership at check-in). The building formerly housed one of the first Coca-Cola bottling plants in the U.S.; look for the historical photos all around the building.

Over $300

Though very new, **C The Bohemian Hotel** (102 W. Bay St., 912/721-3800, www .bohemianhotelsavannah.com, $279–350) is already gaining a reputation as one of Savannah's premier hotels, both for the casual tourist as well as for visiting celebrities. Between busy River Street and bustling City Market, this isn't the place for peace and quiet, but its combination of boutique-style retro-hip decor and happening rooftop bar scene (swank and quite popular with local scenesters) make it a great place to go for a fun stay that's as much Manhattan as Savannah. Valet parking is available, which you will come to appreciate.

For years critics have called it an insult to architecture and to history. That said, one of the few name-brand hotels in Savannah worth the price and providing a consistent level of service is one of its original chain hotels, the **C Hyatt Regency Savannah** (2 E. Bay St., 912/238-1234, www.savannah.hyatt.com, $379). Though it's more than three decades

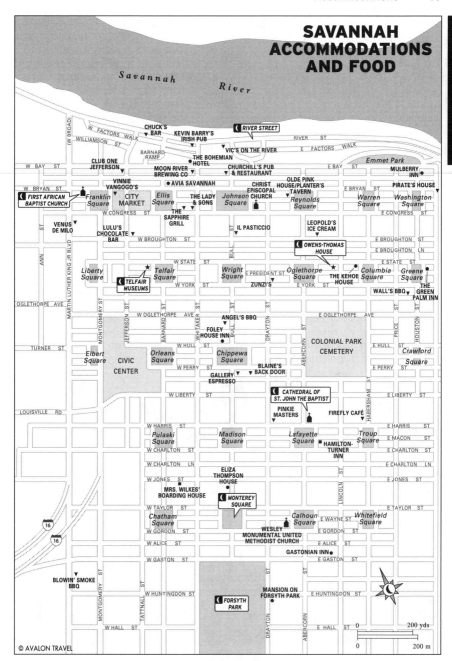

SAVANNAH ACCOMMODATIONS AND FOOD

Savannah   River

CHUCK'S BAR
KEVIN BARRY'S IRISH PUB
RIVER STREET
W FACTORS WALK
WILLIAMSON ST
RIVER ST
E FACTORS WALK
BARNARD RAMP
VIC'S ON THE RIVER
THE BOHEMIAN HOTEL
CLUB ONE JEFFERSON
MOON RIVER BREWING CO
CHURCHILL'S PUB & RESTAURANT
E BAY ST
Emmet Park
W BAY ST
AVIA SAVANNAH
OLDE PINK HOUSE/PLANTER'S TAVERN
MULBERRY INN
VINNIE VANGOGO'S
CHRIST EPISCOPAL CHURCH
PIRATE'S HOUSE
W BRYAN ST
E BRYAN ST
FIRST AFRICAN BAPTIST CHURCH
Franklin Square
CITY MARKET
Ellis Square
THE LADY & SONS
Johnson Square
Reynolds Square
Warren Square
Washington Square
VENUS DE MILO
W CONGRESS ST
THE SAPPHIRE GRILL
E CONGRESS ST
LULU'S CHOCOLATE BAR
IL PASTICCIO
LEOPOLD'S ICE CREAM
W BROUGHTON ST
E BROUGHTON ST
E BROUGHTON LN
OWENS-THOMAS HOUSE
E STATE ST
W STATE ST
Liberty Square
Telfair Square
Wright Square
E PRESIDENT ST
Oglethorpe Square
THE KEHOE HOUSE
Columbia Square
Greene Square
TELFAIR MUSEUMS
W YORK ST
ZUNZI'S
E YORK ST
WALL'S BBQ
THE GREEN PALM INN
OGLETHORPE AVE
W OGLETHORPE AVE
E OGLETHORPE AVE
TURNER ST
ANGEL'S BBQ
FOLEY HOUSE INN
E HULL ST
Elbert Square
Orleans Square
W HULL ST
Chippewa Square
COLONIAL PARK CEMETERY
Crawford Square
CIVIC CENTER
W PERRY ST
BLAINE'S BACK DOOR
E PERRY ST
LOUISVILLE RD
GALLERY ESPRESSO
W LIBERTY ST
CATHEDRAL OF ST. JOHN THE BAPTIST
E LIBERTY ST
PINKIE MASTERS
FIREFLY CAFÉ
W HARRIS ST
E HARRIS ST
Pulaski Square
Madison Square
Lafayette Square
Troup Square
E MACON ST
W CHARLTON ST
HAMILTON-TURNER INN
E CHARLTON ST
W CHARLTON LN
E CHARLTON LN
ELIZA THOMPSON HOUSE
W JONES ST
E JONES ST
MRS. WILKES' BOARDING HOUSE
MONTEREY SQUARE
W TAYLOR ST
E TAYLOR ST
Chatham Square
Calhoun Square
E WAYNE ST
Whitefield Square
W GORDON ST
WESLEY MONUMENTAL UNITED METHODIST CHURCH
E GORDON ST
W ALICE ST
E ALICE ST
GASTONIAN INN
W GASTON ST
E GASTON ST
BLOWIN' SMOKE BBQ
W HUNTINGDON ST
MANSION ON FORSYTH PARK
E HUNTINGDON ST
W HALL ST
FORSYTH PARK
E HALL ST

0   200 yds
0   200 m

© AVALON TRAVEL

old, a competent renovation means that the Hyatt—a sort of exercise in Cubism straddling an entire block of River Street—has avoided the neglect of many older chain properties downtown. While the price may seem daunting, consider the location: literally smack dab on top of River Street, mere blocks from the bulk of the important attractions downtown and some of its best restaurants. Three sides of the hotel offer views of the bustling Savannah waterfront, with its massive ships coming in from all over the world.

HISTORIC DISTRICT
$150-300

Easily the best bed-and-breakfast for the price in Savannah is **The Green Palm Inn** (546 E. President St., 912/447-8901, www.greenpalm inn.com, $159–189), a folksy and romantic little Victorian number with some neat gingerbread exterior stylings and four cute rooms, each named after a species of palm tree. It's situated on the very easternmost edge of the Historic District—hence it's reasonable rates—but let's face it, being right next to charming little Greene Square is far from the worst place you

could be. Delightful innkeeper Diane McCray provides a very good and generous breakfast plus a pretty-much-constant dessert bar.

One of Savannah's original historic B&Bs, the **(Eliza Thompson House** (5 W. Jones St., 912/236-3620, www.elizathompsonhouse .com, $180–225) is a bit out of the bustle on serene, beautiful Jones Street but still close enough to get involved whenever you feel the urge. You can enjoy the various culinary offerings—breakfast, wine and cheese, nighttime munchies—either in the parlor or on the patio overlooking the house's classic Savannah garden. One of the half-dozen lodging properties owned by the locally based HLC group, the Eliza Thompson House hews to their generally high standard of service.

Over $300

The circa-1896 **(Foley House Inn** (14 W. Hull St., 912/232-6622, www.foleyinn.com, $199–375) is a four-diamond B&B with some rooms available at a three-diamond price. Its 19 individualized, Victorian-decor rooms, in two townhouses, range from the smaller Newport overlooking the "grotto courtyard" to the four-

© JIM MOREKIS

The Kehoe House

poster, bay-windowed Essex room, complete with fireplace and whirlpool bath. The location on Chippewa Square is pretty much perfect: well off the busy east–west thoroughfares but in the heart of Savannah's active theater district and within walking distance of anywhere.

One of Savannah's favorite bed-and-breakfasts, **The Kehoe House** (123 Habersham St., 912/232-1020, www.kehoehouse.com, $215–315) is a great choice for its charm and attention to guests. Its historic location, on quiet little Columbia Square catty-corner to the Isaiah Davenport House, is within walking distance to all the downtown action, but far enough from the bustle to get some peace out on one of the rocking chairs on the veranda.

Once a bordello, the 1838 mansion that is home to the 16-room **Ballastone Inn** (14 E. Oglethorpe Ave., 912/236-1484, www.ballastone.com, $235–355) is one of Savannah's favorite inns. Highlights include an afternoon tea service and one of the better full breakfasts in town. Note that some rooms are at what Savannah calls the "garden level," i.e., sunken basement-level rooms with what amounts to a worm's-eye view.

VICTORIAN DISTRICT
$150-300

A short walk from Forsyth Park, the **Dresser-Palmer House** (211 E. Gaston St., 912/238-3294, www.dresserpalmerhouse.com, $189–319) features 15 rooms in two wings, but still manages to make things feel pretty cozy. Garden-level rooms go for a song (under $200).

Over $300

The 1868 (**Gastonian Inn** (220 E. Gaston St., 912/232-2869, www.gastonian.com, $245–455) got a major renovation in 2005 and remains a favorite choice for travelers to Savannah, mostly for its 17 sumptuously decorated rooms and suites (all with working fireplaces) and the always-outstanding full breakfast. They pile on the epicurean delights with teatime, evening nightcaps, and complimentary wine. This is one of the six properties owned by the local firm HLC, which seems to have consistently higher standards than most out-of-town chains here.

How ironic that a hotel built in a former mortuary would be one of the few Savannah hotels not to have a resident ghost story. But that's the case with **Mansion on Forsyth Park** (700 Drayton St., 912/238-5158, www.mansiononforsythpark.com, $339–419), which dominates an entire block alongside Forsyth Park, including partially within the high-Victorian former Fox & Weeks Mortuary building. Its sumptuous, big-bed, big-bath, big-screen-TV-equipped rooms scream "boutique hotel," as does the swank little bar and the alfresco patio area. The Mansion's Addams Family decor of thick velvet and vaguely Dadaist artwork isn't for everyone, but still, it certainly beats seagulls and pink flamingoes.

TYBEE ISLAND

Most of the hotels on Butler Avenue are what we describe in the South as "rode hard and put away wet," i.e., they see a lot of wear and tear from eager vacationers. That doesn't make them bad, just be aware. Also be aware that any place on Butler, even the substandard places, charge a premium during the high season of March–October.

For long-term stays, weekly rentals are the name of the game. Though not cheap—expect to pay roughly $1,000 a week in the summer—they provide a higher level of accommodation than some hotels on the island. For weekly rentals, try **Oceanfront Cottage Rentals** (800/786-5889, www.oceanfrontcottage.com), **Tybee Island Rentals** (912/786-4034, www.tybeeislandrentals.com), or **Tybee Vacation Rentals** (866/359-0297, www.tybeevacationrentals.com).

Here are a few places that are a cut above. All cluster at $200 or below.

On glorious Officer's Row on the North End, the sumptuous suites of the (**Savannah Beach Inn** (21 Officers Row, 800/844-1398, www.savannahbeachinn.com, $200) are tastefully restored, without a hint of Tybee kitsch. The breezy veranda boasts some of the island's most awesome views over the Atlantic. This is easily one of the most romantic spots in the area, with access to the dunes and total seclusion from the partying at the South End.

One of Tybee's most worthwhile lodging experiences for the money, the single-suite ◖ **Bluebird Bed and Breakfast** (1206 Venetian Dr., 912/786-0786, www.tybee bandb.com, $125) is tucked away on Horsepen Creek and the Back River, away from the general beach-town hubbub—but that's what makes it all the more romantic, in a whimsical sort of way. Its spacious and charming interior comprises a master bedroom, a large kitchen/den area, and a delightful breakfast nook overlooking the marsh. There's even a resident dock if you want to put in your kayak or canoe. Two-night minimum on weekends.

Available for daily or weekly rentals, the delightful and well-appointed upstairs apartment of **The Octopus Lair** (12th Street, 912/660-7164, www.octopuslair.com, $125) is tucked away on the south side of the island, equidistant from both the beach and the more active areas. There's even a propane grill on the porch so you can cook out.

Right around the corner from the bustling 16th Street corridor, the **Hunter House Inn** (1701 Butler Ave., 912/786-7515, $150) is still a relatively peaceful getaway. There are two ground-level suites for larger groups of people, each with a large living room with sleeper sofa in addition to a queen-size bed. Upstairs are two smaller rooms, also with queens. Whimsically appointed and more on the casual side, these are not ultra-plush accommodations, but are great for people who want a laid-back fun time at the beach.

CAMPING

The best overall campground in town is at the well-managed and never overcrowded **Skidaway Island State Park** (52 Diamond Causeway, 912/598-2300, www.gastate parks.org, $2 per vehicle daily parking fee, $24 per night tent and RV sites, $35 per night for group camping). There are 88 sites with 30-amp service. A two-night minimum stay is required on weekends and a three-night minimum for Memorial Day, Labor Day, Independence Day, and Thanksgiving. Despite these restrictions, the natural beauty of the park and its easy access to some great nature trails make it worth the price.

There's one campground on Tybee, the **River's End Campground and RV Park** (915 Polk St., 912/786-5518, www.cityoftybee.org). Owned by the city of Tybee Island itself, River's End on the north side of the island offers 100 full-service sites plus some primitive tent sites. During Tybee's sometimes-chilly off-season, you can relax and get warm inside the common "River Room." There's also a swimming pool and laundry facilities. Basic water and electric sites are $34 per night, while 50-amp full hook-ups with water and electric are $45.

Totally wilderness camping can be done on state-owned Little Tybee, accessible across the Back River by boat only. No facilities.

The best camping and wilderness resource locally is **Half Moon Outfitters** (15 E. Broughton St., 912/201-9393, www.half moonoutfitters.com).

Food

Though Charleston's cuisine scene is clearly a cut above Savannah's, the Georgia city is still a foodie's paradise, with a big-city selection of cuisine at competitive prices, concocted by a cast of executive chefs who despite their many personal idiosyncrasies tend to go with what works rather than experimenting for the sake of experimentation.

Here's a breakdown of the most notable offerings, by area and by type of cuisine. You'll note there's no separate "Seafood" section listed. That's because seafood is an intrinsic part of most restaurant fare in Savannah, whether through regular menu offerings or through specials.

CITY MARKET
Classic Southern

Every year, thousands of visitors come to Savannah for the privilege of waiting for hours outside in all weather, the line stretching a full city block, for a chance to eat at **The Lady & Sons** (102 W. Congress St., 912/233-2600, www.ladyandsons.com, lunch Mon.–Sat. 11 A.M.–3 P.M., dinner Mon.–Sat. begins at 5 P.M., Sunday buffets 11 A.M.–5 P.M., $17–25) and sample some of local celebrity Paula Deen's "home" cooking—actually a fairly typical Southern buffet with some decent fried chicken, collard greens, and mac and cheese. For the privilege, you must begin waiting in line as early as 9:30 A.M. for lunch and as early as 3:30 P.M. for dinner in order to be assigned a dining time. You almost assuredly will never see Paula, who has precious little to do with the restaurant these days.

Eating at this Savannah landmark provides a story that visitors will be able to tell friends and family for the rest of their lives, and far be it from me to look down upon them for doing so. That being said—if it were me, I'd take that four hours spent waiting in line and instead go to one of Savannah's many other excellent eating establishments, leaving lots of time left over for an afternoon beer or coffee or dessert, and leaving yet more time to see one of Savannah's many interesting and beautiful sights. A chef friend of mine puts it best: When food sits out under a heat lamp too long, it all tastes the same anyway.

Italian

One would never call Savannah a great pizza town, but the best pizza here is ([**Vinnie VanGoGo's** (317 W. Bryan St., 912/233-6394, www.vinnievangogos.com, Mon.–Thurs. 4–11:30 P.M., Fri. 4 P.M.–1 A.M., Sat. noon–1 A.M., Sun. noon–11:30 P.M., $3–13, cash only) at the west end of City Market on Franklin Square. Featuring some of the best local characters both in the dining area and behind the counter, Vinnie's is a classic Savannah hangout, due in no small part to its excellent beer selection and late hours on weekends. Their pizza is a thin-crust Neapolitan style—though the menu claims it to be New York style—with a delightful tangy sauce and fresh cheese. Individual slices are huge, so don't feel

obliged to order a whole pie. Personally I opt for Italian sausage and extra cheese to offset the richness of the sauce. Calzones are also massive and well stuffed. The waiting list for a table can get pretty long, but take heart: Vinnie's offers free delivery throughout downtown, delivered by bicycle courier. Remember, cash only!

Many Savannahians recall a time when the charmingly old-school **Garibaldi Café** (315 W. Congress St., 912/232-7118, daily 5–10 P.M., $11–33) was the only fine dining restaurant downtown. And you know what? It's still great. More like a spot you'd find in Little Italy than Savannah, Garibaldi features the over-the-top decor typical of the genre, from Roman busts to massive brocade curtains and the huge chandelier in the "Grand Ballroom." But longtime master chef Gerald Green's food is still the draw, a dependable Northern Italian menu known for its well-made veal dishes, its raw bar offerings, and the signature dish, the popular crispy scored flounder with apricot glaze (don't forget to flip the flounder over; there's more fish under there to enjoy). Reservations recommended.

New Southern

Accomplishing the difficult task of being achingly hip while also offering some of the best food in town, ([**Sapphire Grill** (110 W. Congress St., 912/443-9962, www.sapphire grill.com, Fri.–Sat. 5:30–11:30 P.M., Sun.–Thurs. 6–10:30 P.M., $25–40) comes closer than any other Savannah restaurant to replicating a high-class, trendy Manhattan eatery—at prices to match. With its bare stone walls, lean ambience, and romantically dark interior, you'd be tempted to think it's all sizzle and no steak. But executive chef Chris Nason, former exec at Charleston's Anson Restaurant, has a way with coastal cuisine, relying on the freshest local seafood. But his classic meat dishes like lamb, filet mignon, and veal are equally skillful. The lobster bisque is a must-have, and the benne-encrusted local black grouper is always a good choice. As you'd expect, the wine list is impressive, but a close look shows a refined taste for some of the lesser-known labels that other local places miss. Reservations are essential, and while there's no dress code per se, you don't want to go here looking unkempt.

Coffee, Tea, and Sweets

Combine a hip bar with outrageously tasty dessert items, and you get ◖ **Lulu's Chocolate Bar** (42 MLK Jr. Blvd., 912/238-2012, www.luluschocolatebar.net). While the whole family is welcome before 10 P.M. to enjoy chocolate chip cheesecake and the like, after that it's strictly 21-and-over. The late crowd is younger and trendier and there mostly for the unique specialty martinis like the Pineapple Upside Down Martini.

WATERFRONT
Classic Southern

Locals rarely eat at the Savannah institution called the **Pirate's House** (20 E. Broad St., 912/233-5757, www.thepirateshouse.com, lunch daily 11 A.M.–4 P.M., dinner Sun.–Thurs. 4–9:30 P.M., Fri.–Sat. 4–10 P.M., $17–26), known primarily for its delightfully kitschy pre–Jack Sparrow pirate decor and its dependably pedestrian food. Still, the history here is undeniable: One of America's oldest buildings, built in 1753, the Pirate's House hosted many a salty sea dog—though perhaps few actual pirates—in its day as a seamen's inn. And any place that rates a shout-out in Robert Louis Stevenson's *Treasure Island* has to be worth a visit.

The rambling interior of the old house, each of the 15 dining rooms with its own different nautical flavor, just adds to the general air of jaunty buccaneer insouciance. "The Captain's Room" is allegedly where shipmasters would shanghai unwary men to complete their chronically short-handed crews. Supposedly a tunnel from there goes all the way to the river, the better to transport the drugged kidnapping victims. The "Southern Buffet" each day 11 A.M.–3 P.M. features the Pirate House's signature honey pecan fried chicken.

Very few restaurants on River Street rise above tourist schlock, but a clear standout is **Vic's on the River** (16 E. River St., 912/721-

1000, www.vicsontheriver.com, Sun.–Thurs. 11 A.M.–10 P.M., Fri.–Sat. 11 A.M.–11 P.M., $22–40). Hewing more to Charleston-style fine dining than most Savannah restaurants—with dishes like wild Georgia shrimp, stone-ground grits, and blue crab cakes with a three-pepper relish—Vic's combines a romantic, old Savannah atmosphere with an adventurous take on Lowcountry cuisine. Note the entrance to the dining room is not on River Street, but on the Bay Street level on Upper Factor's Walk.

HISTORIC DISTRICT
Asian

Part of the renovation of the Martin Luther King Jr. Boulevard corridor, the relatively new **Wasabi's** (113 MLK Jr. Blvd., 912/233-8899, daily 11 A.M.–10:30 P.M., $8–20) is making a name for itself with its sushi, in a town with several very good sushi restaurants already. The à la carte tempura is also especially tasty and the Sapporo on draft is a real plus. There's an early-bird sushi boat for two offered 4–6:30 P.M., $29.95.

With an unprepossessing interior but an excellent, inexpensive menu that's a Vietnamese/Thai hybrid, **Saigon** (4 W. Broughton St., 912/232-5288, $7) is a good place to stop in for a quick, tasty lunch while shopping.

Barbecue

Purists may scoff at its attractive interior and awesome bottled beer selection, but the hottest BBQ joint in town is ◖ **Blowin' Smoke BBQ** (514 Martin Luther King Jr. Boulevard, 912/231-2385, www.blowinsmokebbq.com, Sun.–Thurs. 11 A.M.–9 P.M., Fri.–Sat. 11 A.M.–10 P.M., $7–12). It isn't necessarily the most authentic, but it's the most fun, with a large outdoor courtyard in addition to the roomy interior. The service is good, and the BBQ portions are vast and tasty, with a delicious sauce that avoids the overly sweet nature of many regional sauces.

A local legend, **Wall's BBQ** (515 E. York Lane, 912/232-9754, Thurs.–Sat., call for hours, $6–9) is one family's labor of love, tucked away in a back alley—they're called "lanes" in Savannah—that you'll miss if you blink.

Another great local barbecue joint tucked away in a lane is **Angel's BBQ** (21 W. Oglethorpe Lane, 912/495-0902, www .angels-bbq.com, Tues. 11:30 A.M.–3 P.M., Wed.–Sat. 11:30 A.M.–6 P.M., $5–9). Get there by finding Independent Presbyterian Church at the northwest corner of Chippewa Square and walking down the lane next to the church. They offer a particularly Memphis-style take on barbecue, but you might try the unique house specialty, the barbecued bologna. Don't miss the peanuts-and-greens on the side. Vegetarians can opt for the "Faux-Q," i.e., barbecue-flavored tofu.

Breakfast and Brunch

Downtowners swear by the low-key little **Firefly Café** (321 Habersham St., 912/234-1971, Tues.–Sun. 7:30 A.M.–9:30 P.M., $12–25) on quiet Troup Square, and not only for the excellent omelets (maybe the best in town), great sandwiches (one word: Reuben!), and fresh salads (try the spinach salad with goat cheese). It's also a neighborhood place to see old friends and catch up over coffee, with the charming interior only enhancing the general *bonhomie*. This is a particularly good choice for vegetarians and vegans for all meals of the day.

Classic Southern

The meteoric rise of Paula Deen and her Lady & Sons has only made local epicures even more exuberant in their praise for **C Mrs. Wilkes' Dining Room** (107 W. Jones St., 912/232-5997, www.mrswilkes.com, Mon.–Fri. 11 A.M.–2 P.M., $13), Savannah's original comfort food mecca. President Obama's impromptu lunchtime visit with the local mayor in 2010 has further raised the restaurant's already legendary profile.

Though the delightful Sema Wilkes herself has passed on, nothing has changed—not the communal dining room, the cheerful service, the care taken with take-out customers, and, most of all, not the food—a succulent mélange of the South's greatest hits, from the best fried chicken in town to snap beans to black-eyed peas to collard greens. While each day boasts a different set menu, most all the classics are on the table each meal.

Once the home of General James Habersham and the first place the Declaration of Independence was read aloud in Savannah, the **C Olde Pink House** (23 Abercorn St., 912/232-4286, Sun.–Thurs. 5:30–10:30 P.M., Fri.–Sat. 5:30–11 P.M., $15–30) is still a hub of activity in Savannah, as tourists and locals alike frequent the classic interior of the dining room and the downstairs Planter's Tavern. Regularly voted "Most Romantic Restaurant in Savannah"—though make no mistake, they pack you in pretty tight here—the Pink House is known for its savvy (and often sassy!) service and the uniquely regional flair it adds to traditional dishes, with liberal doses of pecans, Vidalia onions, shrimp, and crab. The she-crab soup and lamb chops in particular are crowd-pleasers, and the scored crispy flounder stacks up to similar versions of this dish at several other spots in town. Reservations recommended.

the **Olde Pink House** on Reynolds Square

© JIM MOREKIS

Some writers would be tempted to put **Cha Bella** (102 E. Broad St., 912/790-7888, www.cha-bella.com, Tues.–Sun. 5:30–10 P.M., $17–35) in the "New Southern" category, but I prefer to think that this restaurant's forte—savory dishes using only the freshest locally grown organic ingredients—makes it a classic throwback to the way food was always intended to be. This new spot is getting a large local following eager to enjoy its concise menu from Chef Matthew Roher, featuring fresh salads like grilled eggplant and plum tomatoes topped with local artisan goat cheese, and entrées like the Georgia white shrimp risotto. The patio bar is a favorite hangout for downtown's hip movers and shakers.

Cuban

For years, Savannahians with good taste have patronized the location of this restaurant in the city's ugly southside sprawl. Now, there's a new downtown location of **Rancho Alegre** (402 MLK Blvd., 912/292-1656, $8–20) at the fringe of the Historic District bringing the same dedication to authentic Cuban cuisine. Try the tamal with roasted pork on the side, or perhaps the *chicharrones de pollo*. If you have a large party, call ahead so Chef Juan Manuel Rodriguez can prepare his signature seafood paella. In any case, save room for dark, delicious Cuban coffee.

Italian

Though the dining room stays busy, the entrées at **Il Pasticcio** (2 E. Broughton St., 912/231-8888, www.ilpasticciosavannah.com, Mon.–Thurs. 5:30–10 P.M., Fri. and Sat. 5:30–11:30 P.M., Sun. 5:30–9:30 P.M., $20–36) take a back seat to its atmosphere: dark, sexy, and Euro-trendy—think Florence or Milan. Take a seat at the cozy, ornate circular bar and order an appetizer while you enjoy the cosmopolitan crowd of beautiful people and the spacious views.

The hot new Italian place in town is **Leoci's Trattoria** (606 Abercorn St., 912/335-7027, www.leocis.com, daily 11 A.M.–10 P.M., $10–20), named for its executive chef, Italian-American Roberto Leoci. His compact but

diverse menu offers delights such as a crispy delicious pizza, excellent paninis, and a wild mushroom risotto. The room is small and intimate and the restaurant is quite popular, so a wait is not unusual.

Mexican

A new addition to the Broughton Street restaurant mix is the storefront spot **T-Rex Mex** (217 W. Broughton St., 912/232-3466), which serves its own unique version of typical Tex-Mex food, with a particular focus on excellent burritos. My favorite is the jerk chicken burrito.

Moroccan

Savannah's single most unique dining experience happens at **Casbah** (118 E. Broughton St., 912/234-6168, daily 5:30–10:30 P.M., $10–20). This Moroccan restaurant features nightly belly dancing shows, with the dancers doing their thing from table to table to pre-recorded (and loud) music beginning at 6:30 or 7 P.M., with continuing shows through the evening. Beware—sometimes they grab a guest for a quick "lesson"! But don't let the over-the-top floor show or the "market" of authentic but overpriced Moroccan goods take away from the incredible food. Served in communal Moroccan style, these dishes hew to the deceptively simple cuisine of North Africa, with an emphasis on expertly grilled and seasoned meats and saffron rice. The lamb kabobs are to die for—best I've had anywhere.

South African

Look for the long lunchtime line outside the tiny storefront that is **Zunzi's** (108 E. York St., 912/443-9555, Mon.–Sat. 11 A.M.–6 P.M., $5–10). This takeout joint is one of Savannah's favorite lunch spots, the labor of love of South African expatriates Gabby and Johnny DeBeer. Try the exquisite South African–style sausage.

Coffee, Tea, and Sweets

He helped produce *Mission Impossible III* and other Hollywood productions, but Savannah native Stratton Leopold's other claim to fame art exhibits by well-known local artists, all curated by owner Jessica Barnhill.

For a more upscale take on sweets, check out the chocolate goodies at **Wright Square Cafe** (21 W. York St., 912/238-1150). While they do offer tasty wraps and sandwiches, let's not kid ourselves. The draw here is the outrageous assortment of high-quality, European-style brownies, cookies, cakes, and other sweet treats.

Starbucks has a location downtown at 1 E. Broughton St. (912/447-6742).

VICTORIAN DISTRICT

For our purposes, this area spans Forsyth Park south to Victory Drive (U.S. Hwy 80).

Middle Eastern

For a falafel fix, travel well off the beaten path to **Al Salaam Deli** (2311 Habersham St., 912/447-0400, $5–10). The signature falafel at this humble little storefront is big-city quality, and the gyros are almost as good. While it's not in the most elegant of neighborhoods, Al Salaam—run by a family of Jordanian expatriates—has a devoted local following, and deservedly so.

New Southern

Before there was Paula Deen, there was Elizabeth Terry, Savannah's first well-known high-profile chef and founder of this most elegant of all Savannah restaurants, **(Elizabeth on 37th** (105 E. 37th St., 912/236-5547, daily 6–10 P.M., $25 and up). Terry has since sold the place to two of her former waiters, Greg and Gary Butch, but this restaurant has for the most part continued to maintain her high standards—though, frankly, there have been a few complaints from those who think its heyday has past. In a beautifully restored Victorian mansion just outside the historic district, with its own lovingly tended herb garden and emphasis on local suppliers, Elizabeth on 37th continues to be—a quarter-century after its founding—where many Savannahians go when the evening calls for something really memorable. Executive chef Kelly Yambor uses eclectic, seasonally shifting ingredients that blend

© JIM MOREKIS

Leopold's Ice Cream is in the heart of the theater district.

is running the 100-year-old family business at **(Leopold's Ice Cream** (212 E. Broughton St., 912/234-4442, www.leopoldsicecream.com, Sun.–Thurs. 11 A.M.–10 P.M., Fri.–Sat. 11 A.M.–11 P.M.). Now in a new location but with the same delicious family ice cream recipe, Leopold's also offers soup and sandwiches to go with its delicious sweet treats. Memorabilia from Stratton's various movies is all around the shop, which always stays open after every evening performance at the Lucas Theatre around the corner. You can occasionally find Stratton himself behind the counter doling out scoops.

A coffeehouse before coffeehouses were cool, Savannah's original java joint, **Gallery Espresso** (234 Bull St., 912/233-5348, www.galleryespresso.com, Mon.–Fri. 7:30 A.M.–10 P.M., Sat.–Sun. 8 A.M.–11 P.M.), currently occupies a prime corner lot on beautiful Chippewa Square. Of course there's the requisite free Wi-Fi, and while you sip and surf you can also enjoy the regular rotating modern the South with the South of France. Along with generally attentive service, it makes for a wonderfully old-school fine dining experience. Reservations recommended.

A fairly new darling of local foodies is the aptly named **Local 11 Ten** (1110 Bull St., 912/790-9000, www.local11ten.com, Tues.–Thurs. 6–10 P.M., Fri.–Sat. 6–10:30 P.M., $22–39), just off the south end of Forsyth Park. Its wide-open dining room has a great view of the streetscape, adventurous cuisine (the handiwork of Memphis-born Keith Latture), and a cute bar—each proven big attractions. Try the hanger steak with a side of Vidalia onion rings.

Coffee, Tea, and Sweets

The coffee at **The Sentient Bean** (13 E. Park Ave., 912/232-4447, www.sentientbean.com, daily 7:30 A.M.–10 P.M.) is all fair-trade and organic, and the all-vegetarian fare is a major upgrade above the usual coffeehouse offering. But "The Bean" is more than a coffeehouse—it's a community. Probably the best indie film venue in town, the Bean regularly hosts screenings of cutting-edge, left-of-center documentary and kitsch films, as well as rotating art exhibits. When there's no movie, there's usually some low-key live entertainment or spoken word open mic action.

Though it's primarily known for its sublime sweet treats, **⟨ Back in the Day Bakery** (2403 Bull St., 912/495-9292, www.backinthedaybakery.com, Tues.–Fri. 9 A.M.–5 P.M., Sat. 8 A.M.–3 P.M., $7) in the Starland Design District at the southern edge of the Victorian District also offers a small but delightfully tasty (and tasteful) range of lunch soups, salads, and sandwiches 11 A.M.–2 P.M. Lunch highlights are the baguette with camembert, roasted red peppers, and lettuce; and the *caprese,* the classic tomato/mozzarella/basil trifecta on a perfect *ciabatta.* But whatever you do, save room for dessert, which runs the full sugar spectrum from red velvet cupcakes, lemon bars, macaroons, carrot cake, Cosmopolitan Cake, Nana's Pudding, and my favorite, Omar's Mystic Espresso Cheesecake.

For a quick Starbucks coffee or a panini, stop by the **Forsyth Park Café** (912/233-7848, daily 7 A.M.–dusk, later on festival evenings) located in what was once the circa-1920 "dummy fort."

EASTSIDE
Classic Southern

Located just across the Wilmington River from the fishing village of Thunderbolt, **⟨ Desposito's** (187 Old Tybee Rd., 912/897-9963, www.despositosseafood.com, Tues.–Fri. 5–10 P.M., Sat. noon–10 P.M., $15–25) is a big hit with locals and visitors alike, though it's not in all the guidebooks. The focus here is on fresh seafood and lots of it, served humbly on tables covered with newspapers. The shrimp is not to be missed—all perfectly fresh, caught wild in local waters.

If you're checking out a Savannah Sand Gnats minor league baseball game at Historic Grayson Stadium, right across the street is one of Savannah's best soul food places, **Geneva Geneva's Home Plate** (2812 Bee Rd., 912/356-9976, Tues.–Thurs. and Sun. 11 A.M.–8:30 P.M., Fri.–Sat. 11 A.M.–9 P.M., $10–15). Think incredible fried chicken, moist cornbread, and homemade veggies.

SOUTHSIDE
Asian

Also opposite the Oglethorpe Mall across busy Abercorn is **Chiriya's** (7805 Abercorn St., 912/303-0555, Mon.–Sat. 11 A.M.–3 P.M. and 5–10 P.M., Sun. 5–10 P.M., $15–20), an excellent Thai place with some Hawaiian touches sprinkled into the mix. The kitchen will gladly spice up your food to your personal comfort level.

It's not pretty and it's not fancy. But hands-down the best Vietnamese cuisine in town is at **⟨ Saigon Flavors** (6604 Waters Ave., 912/352-4182, daily 11 A.M.–9 P.M.), a humble little place in a nondescript storefront. But the food is anything but nondescript—excellent, authentic, inexpensive, and tasty. I usually get the pork and noodles dish with a side order of their delicious fried spring rolls, but any of their shrimp dishes are great, too.

Southwestern

Should you find yourself shopping at Oglethorpe

Mall on Savannah's ugly, paved-over southside, take a quick jaunt across Abercorn to **Moe's Southwestern Grill** (7801 Abercorn St., 912/303-6688, daily 11 A.M.–10 P.M., $5–10) in the Chatham Plaza shopping center. This regional franchise offers made-to-order Southwestern fare—or a Southeastern version of it, anyway—in a boisterous atmosphere. Local vegetarians and vegans love this spot, since you tell the counter staff exactly what you want in your burrito and you can always substitute tofu for any meat.

WHITEMARSH ISLAND

Pronounced "wit marsh," this overwhelmingly residential area is on the way from the city of Savannah to Tybee Island's beaches. For our purposes here, it's notable for the presence of two outstanding barbecue joints, right across U.S. Highway 80 from each other.

Barbecue

Though relatively new, **Wiley's Championship BBQ** (4700 U.S. Hwy. 80 E., 912/201-3259, www.wileyschampionshipbbq .com, lunch Mon.–Sat. 11 A.M.–3 P.M., dinner Wed.–Thurs. 5–8 P.M., Fri.–Sat. 5–9 P.M., $8–25) has what is already widely considered the best pulled pork in Savannah. In addition—and unusually for this area—they smoke a mean brisket, too. Save room for the great sides, such as mac & cheese and sweet potato casserole.

Papa's Bar-B-Q (4700 U.S. Hwy. 80, 912/897-0236, www.papasbar-b-que.com, Mon.–Wed. 11 A.M.–9 P.M., Thurs.–Sat. 11 A.M.–10 P.M., Sun. noon–9 P.M., $6–15) has a very wide-ranging menu in addition to its signature pulled pork sandwiches, including shrimp, tilapia, and flounder cooked in a variety of ways, and cold plates including chef, shrimp, and chicken salads. Their house barbecue sauce is very smooth and a clear cut above the generally poor quality sauce in this area.

TYBEE ISLAND
Breakfast and Brunch

Considered the best breakfast in the Savannah area for 30 years and counting, **The Breakfast Club** (1500 Butler Ave., 912/786-5984, www.tybeeisland.com/dining/brclub/ Default.htm, daily 6:30 A.M.–1 P.M., $5–15), with its brisk diner atmosphere and hearty, Polish sausage–filled omelets, is like a little bit of Chicago in the South. Lines start early for a chance to enjoy such house specialties as Helen's Solidarity, the Athena Omelet, and the Chicago Bear Burger, but don't worry—you'll inevitably strike up a conversation with someone interesting while you wait.

Casual Dining

Set in a large former fishing camp overlooking Chimney Creek, **The Crab Shack** (40 Estill Hammock Rd., 912/786-9857, www.thecrab shack.com, Mon.–Thurs. 11:30 A.M.–10 P.M., Fri.–Sun. 11:30 A.M.–11 P.M., $6–30) is a favorite local seafood place and also something of an attraction in itself. Don't expect gourmet fare or quiet seaside dining; the emphasis is on mounds of fresh, tasty seafood, heavy on the raw bar action, all in a casual and boisterous outdoor atmosphere.

Getting there is a little tricky: Take U.S. 80 to Tybee, cross the bridge over Lazaretto Creek, and begin looking for Estill Hammock Road to Chimney Creek on your right. Take Estill Hammock and veer right. After that, it's hard to miss.

If you're hanging out on the south end near the Pier, you can't miss the three-story pink building with the open decks and the words "Time to Eat" in six-foot letters across the top of the facade. That's not the name of the restaurant—it's actually **Fannie's on the Beach** (1613 Strand Ave., 912/786-6109, www.fannieson thebeach.com, Mon.–Thurs. 11 A.M.–10 P.M. Fri.–Sun. 11 A.M.–11 P.M., $8–24) a great-for-all-ages restaurant and bar with a menu that's a cut above the usual tavern fare. You can't go wrong with any of their fine, rich, cheese-heavy pizzas; my favorite is the spinach and feta with sun-dried tomatoes. Sunday brunches noon–3 P.M. are a local favorite.

Classic Southern

One of my favorite restaurants anywhere, the **Hunter House** (1701 Butler Ave., 912/786-

7515, www.hunterhouseinn.com, Mon.–Sat. from 6 P.M., $20–30), boasts the one-of-a-kind talents of legendary local chef Espy Geissler. With equal mastery of continental cuisine and Southern classics alike, Espy never fails to amaze with his perfectly textured sauces, delightful presentation, and attention to detail. In fact, the story goes that Espy got his job at the Hunter House, also a small inn, because owner John Hunter got tired of hearing him complain about the food. So he hired him, and the rest is culinary history. The dining room is elegant without being overwhelming, romantic without being cloying, keeping just enough seaside touches to remind you that you are, after all, on Tybee. The tiny but perfect bar, off in a side dining room, is often cheerfully manned by John Hunter himself, who makes a point of visiting each table. Start with the seafood bisque or the succulent fried green tomatoes. Listen closely to the specials, but know that any seafood entrée is a good bet. To get here, take U.S. 80 onto Tybee until you veer right at the Atlantic Ocean. Now called Butler Avenue, this road takes you all the way past Tybrisa (16th Street). Look for the Hunter House on your right.

Information and Services

VISITORS CENTERS

The main clearinghouse for tourist information is the downtown **Savannah Visitors Center** (301 MLK Jr. Blvd., 912/944-0455, Mon.–Fri. 8:30 A.M.–5 P.M., Sat., Sun., and holidays 9 A.M.–5 P.M.).

The newly revitalized Ellis Square features a small visitors kiosk at the northwest corner (Mon.–Fri. 8 A.M.–6 P.M.), with public restrooms and elevators to the underground parking garage beneath the square.

Other visitors centers in the area include the **River Street Hospitality Center** (1 River St., 912/651-6662, daily 10 A.M.–10 P.M.), the **Tybee Island Visitor Center** (S. Campbell Ave. and Hwy. 80, 912/786-5444, daily 9 A.M.–5:30 P.M.), and the **Savannah Airport Visitor Center** (464 Airways Ave., 912/964-1109, daily 10 A.M.–6 P.M.).

The **Savannah Convention and Visitors Bureau** (101 E. Bay St.) keeps a list of lodgings at its website at www.savcvb.com and can be reached at 877/SAVANNAH (877/728-2662).

HOSPITALS

Savannah has two very good hospital systems. Centrally located near midtown, **Memorial Health University Hospital** (4700 Waters Ave., 912/350-8000, www.memorialhealth.com) is the region's only Level-1 Trauma Center and is one of the best in the nation. The St. Joseph's/Candler Hospital System (www.sjchs.org) has two units, **St. Joseph's Hospital** (11705 Mercy Blvd., 912/819-4100) on the extreme south side and **Candler Hospital** (5401 Paulsen St., 912/819-6000) closer to midtown.

POLICE

The city and county police forces recently merged to form the **Savannah/Chatham County Metropolitan Police Department.** For non-emergencies, call 912/651-6675. For emergencies, call 911.

MEDIA
Newspapers

The daily newspaper of record is the *Savannah Morning News* (912/525-0796, www.savannahnow.com). It puts out an entertainment insert, called "Do," on Thursdays.

The free weekly newspaper in town is *Connect Savannah* (912/721-4350, www.connectsavannah.com), hitting stands each Wednesday. Look to it for culture and music coverage, as well as an alternative take on local politics and issues.

Two glossy magazines compete, the hipper *The South* magazine (912/236-5501, www.thesouthmag.com) and the more establishment *Savannah* magazine (912/652-0293, www.savannahmagazine.com).

Radio and Television

The National Public Radio affiliate is the Georgia Public Broadcasting station WSVH 91.1 FM. Savannah State University offers jazz, reggae, and Latin music at WHCJ 90.3 FM.

Georgia Public Broadcasting is on WVAN. The local NBC affilate is WSAV, the CBS affiliate is WTOC, the ABC affiliate is WJCL, and the Fox affiliate is WTGS.

LIBRARIES

The **Live Oak Public Library** (www.live oakpl.org) is the umbrella organization for the libraries of Chatham, Effingham, and Liberty counties. By far the largest branch is south of downtown Savannah, the **Bull Street Branch** (222 Bull St., 912/652-3600, Mon.–Thurs. 9 A.M.–9 P.M., Fri.–Sat. 9 A.M.–6 P.M., Sun. 2–6 P.M.). Farthest downtown and tucked away on Upper Factor's Walk is the charming little **Ola Wyeth Branch** (4 E. Bay St., 912/232-5488, Mon.–Fri. noon–3 P.M.). In midtown Savannah is the **Carnegie Branch** (537 E. Henry St., 912/231-9921, Mon. 10 A.M.–8 P.M., Tues.–Thurs. 10 A.M.–6 P.M., Fri.–Sat. 2–6 P.M.). The beach has its own **Tybee Island Branch** (405 Butler Ave., 912/786-7733, open Mon. and Fri.–Sat. 2–6 P.M., Tues. 10 A.M.–8 P.M., Wed. 10 A.M.–6 P.M.).

The **Georgia Historical Society** (501 Whitaker St., 912/651-2128, www.georgia history.com, Tues.–Sat. 10 A.M.–5 P.M.) has an extensive collection of clippings, photos, maps, and other archived material at its headquarters at the corner of Forsyth Park in Hodgson Hall. Their website has been extensively revamped and is now one of the Southeast's best online resources for Georgia history information.

The SCAD-run **Jen Library** (201 E. Broughton St., 912/525-4700, www.scad .edu) features 3,000 Internet connections in its cavernous 85,000-square-foot space. Its main claim to fame is the remarkable variety of art periodicals to which it subscribes, nearly 1,000 at last count. Though built for the school's 7,000-plus art students, the public can enter and use it as well with photo ID (you just can't check anything out). It's open Monday–Friday 7:30 A.M.–1 A.M., Saturday 10 A.M.–1 A.M., Sunday 11 A.M.–1 A.M., with shorter hours when class is out of session.

POST OFFICES

There are two post offices of note for most visitors to Savannah. The largest with the longest hours is the **Main Branch** (2 N. Fahm St., open Mon.–Fri. 8 A.M.–5:30 P.M., Sat. 9 A.M.–1 P.M.). It's off Bay Street just past the western edge of the Historic District. A smaller but more convenient branch downtown is the **Telfair Square Station** (118 Barnard St., open Mon.–Fri. 8 A.M.–5 P.M.).

GAY AND LESBIAN RESOURCES

Visitors often find Savannah to be surprisingly cosmopolitan and diverse for a Deep South city, and nowhere is this more true than in its sizeable and influential gay and lesbian community. In line with typical Southern protocol, the community is largely apolitical and more concerned with integration than provocation. But they're still very much aware of their growing impact on the local economy and are major players in art and commerce.

The **Savannah Pride Festival** is held every September at various venues in town. Top-flight, dance-oriented musical acts perform, restaurants show off their creativity, and activists staff information booths.

The chief resource for local gay and lesbian information and concerns is the First City Network, whose main website (www .firstcitynetwork.org) features many useful links, though many might find its MySpace page (www.myspace.com/firstcitynetwork) useful as well. Another great Internet networking resource is Gay Savannah (www.gay savannah.com).

For specifically gay-friendly accommodations, try the **Under the Rainbow Inn** (104–106 W. 38th St., 912/790-1005, www .under-the-rainbow.com, $109–155), a great B&B in the historic Thomas Square district, a former streetcar suburb of Savannah.

Getting There and Around

BY AIR

Savannah is served by the fairly new and efficient **Savannah/Hilton Head International Airport** (400 Airways Ave., 912/964-0514, airport code SAV, www.savannahairport.com) directly off I-95 at exit 104. The airport is about 20 minutes from downtown Savannah and an hour from Hilton Head Island. Airlines with routes into and out of SAV include AirTran (www.airtran.com), American Eagle (www.aa.com), Continental (www.continental.com), Delta (www.delta.com), United Express (www.ual.com), and US Airways (www.usairways.com).

Taxi stands are available for transportation to Savannah at the following regulated fares and conditions: The cost is $2 for the first sixth of a mile and $0.32 per sixth of a mile thereafter, not to exceed $3.60 for the first mile and $1.92 per mile thereafter. Waiting charge is $21 per hour. No charge for baggage. The maximum fare for destinations in the Historic District is $25.

BY CAR

Savannah is the eastern terminus of I-16, and that Interstate is the most common entrance to the city. However, most travelers get to I-16 via I-95, taking the exit for downtown Savannah (Historic District). Once on I-16, the most common entry points into Savannah proper are via the Gwinnett Street exit, which puts you near the southern edge of the Historic District near Forsyth Park, or, more commonly, the Montgomery Street exit farther into the heart of downtown.

Paralleling I-95 is the old coastal highway, now U.S. 17, which goes through Savannah. U.S. 80 is Victory Drive for most of its length through town; however, after you pass through Thunderbolt on your way to the islands area, including Tybee, it reverts to U.S. 80.

BY TRAIN

Savannah is on the north–south "Silver Service" of Amtrak (2611 Seaboard Coastline Dr., 912/234-2611, www.amtrak.com). To get to the station on the west side of town, take I-16 west and get off on I-516 north. Immediately take the Gwinnett Street/Railroad Station exit and follow the Amtrak signs.

BY BUS

Chatham Area Transit (www.catchacat.org), Savannah's publicly supported bus system, is quite thorough and efficient considering Savannah's relatively small size. Plenty of routes crisscross the entire area, with one-way fares of $1 per person, exact change only, which includes one connecting route. Service runs weekdays and Saturdays 5:30 A.M.–11:30 P.M., Sundays 7 A.M.–9 P.M. Children under 41 inches tall ride free. A weekly pass is $12. Buy advance tickets at two locations: 900 East Gwinnett Street and 124 Bull Street.

Of primary interest to visitors is the completely free **CAT Shuttle,** which travels a continuous circuit route throughout the Historic District, keyed around hotels, historic sites, and the Savannah Visitors Center. The Shuttle is wheelchair-accessible and runs weekdays and Saturdays 7 A.M.–7 P.M., Sundays 9:30 A.M.–5 P.M.

BY RENTAL CAR

The vast bulk of rental car facilities are at the Savannah/Hilton Head International Airport, including Avis (800/831-2847), Budget (800/527-0700), Dollar (912/964-9001), Enterprise (800/736-8222), Hertz (800/654-3131), National (800/227-7368), and Thrifty (800/367-2277).

Rental locations away from the airport are Avis (7810 Abercorn St., 912/354-4718), Budget (7070 Abercorn St., 912/355-0805), Enterprise (3028 Skidaway Rd., 912/352-1424; 9505 Abercorn St., 912/925-0060; 11506-A Abercorn Expy., 912/920-1093; 7510 White Bluff Rd., 912/355-6622).

BY TAXI

Taxi services in Georgia tend to be less regulated than other states, but services are plentiful

© JOSH HALLETT

The bus stops here.

in Savannah and are generally reasonable. The chief local service is **Yellow Cab** (866/319-9646, www.savannahyellowcab.com). For wheelchair accessibility, request cab #14. Other services include **Adam Cab** (912/927-7466), **Magikal Taxi Service** (912/897-8294), and **Sunshine Cab** (912/272-0971).

If you like some local flavor to go with your cab ride, call **Concierge Taxi Services** (912/604-8466), the one-man show of local author Robert S. Mickles. He's very friendly and always has a great Savannah story to tell.

If you're not in a super hurry, it's always fun to take a **Savannah Pedicab** (912/232-7900, www.savannahpedicab.com) for quick trips around downtown. Your friendly driver will pedal one or two passengers anywhere within the Historic District for a reasonable price.

PARKING

Parking is at a premium in downtown Savannah. The city's Parking Services Department is extremely vigilant about parking violations, ostensibly to encourage "turnover" of the valuable spaces, but also of course to generate revenue. Traditional coin-operated metered parking is available throughout the city, ranging from 15 minutes to a precious few 10-hour meters. More and more, the city is going to self-pay kiosks where you purchase a stamped receipt to display inside your dashboard.

Bottom line: Be sure to pay for all parking weekdays 8:30 A.M.–5 P.M. No matter what the printed information on the meter tells you, there is *no* enforcement of parking meters at all on weekends or after 5 P.M. any day. That information has been on the meters for years and almost seems intended to bilk tourists. That being said, you should also know that illegally parking and parking in sweep zones will get you ticketed and/or towed any time of day.

Tybee Island is even more strict about parking regulations than Savannah. If the meter says to feed it until 8 P.M. on the weekend, then feed the meter until 8 P.M. on the weekend!

The city operates several parking garages at various costs and hours: The **Bryan Street Garage** (100 E. Bryan St.) is open 24/7 and costs $1 per hour Monday–Friday. Evenings 6 P.M.–7 A.M. are a $2 fee and anytime Saturday and Sunday is a $3 fee. The **Robinson Garage** (132 Montgomery St.) is open 24/7 and costs $1 per hour Monday–Friday. Evenings 6 P.M.–7 A.M. are $2 flat rate and weekends are $3 flat rate. The **State Street Garage** (100 E. State St.) is open Sunday–Friday 5 A.M.–1 A.M., Saturday 5 A.M.–5 A.M., and costs $1 per hour.

Evenings 6 P.M.–1 A.M. are $2, and weekends are $3 flat rate. The **Liberty Street Garage** (401 W. Liberty St.) is open Monday–Friday 5 A.M.–6 P.M. for $1 per hour and flat rate of $2 for 6 P.M.–1 A.M. Weekends are $1 flat rate. The new **Whitaker Street Garage** underneath revitalized Ellis Square is open 24 hours and is $2 per hour. Special events sometimes occur and are $5–20.

Outside Savannah

As is the case with Charleston, Savannah's outlying areas still bear the indelible marks of the plantation era. The marsh still retains traces of the old rice paddies, and the economics of the area still retain a similar sense of class and racial stratification.

While history is no less prominent, it is more subtle in these largely semi-rural areas, and the tourist infrastructure is much less well-developed than Savannah proper. This area contains some of the most impoverished communities in Georgia, so keep in mind that the locals may have more on their minds than keeping you entertained—though certainly at no point will their Southern manners fail them.

And also keep in mind that you are traveling in one of the most unique ecosystems in the country and natural beauty is never far away.

MIDWAY AND LIBERTY COUNTY

Locals will tell you that Midway is named because it's equidistant from the Savannah and Altamaha Rivers on Oglethorpe's old "river road," which it certainly is. But others say the small but very historic town is actually named after the Medway River in England.

In any case, we know that in seeking to pacify the local Creek tribe, the Council of Georgia in 1752 granted a group of Massachusetts Puritans then residing in Dorchester, S.C., a 32,000-acre land grant as incentive to move south. After moving into Georgia and establishing New Dorchester, they soon founded a

nearby settlement that would later take on the modern spelling of Midway.

Midway's citizens were very aggressive early on in the cause for American independence. That's the very reason the area's three original parishes were combined and named Liberty County in 1777—the only Georgia county named for a concept rather than a person. Two of Georgia's three signers of the Declaration of Independence, Lyman Hall and Button Gwinnett, resided primarily in Midway and both attended the historic Midway Church. But a key part of Liberty County history is no more: the once-thriving seaport of Sunbury, which formerly challenged Savannah for economic supremacy in the region but is now nonexistent.

The main highways in Midway are I-95, U.S. 17, and U.S. 84 (also called "Oglethorpe Highway," which becomes GA 38 or "Islands Highway" east of I-95).

Sights

Tourism in this area has been made much more user-friendly by the liberal addition of signage for the "Liberty Trail," a collection of key attractions. When in doubt follow the signs.

In Midway proper is the charming **Midway Museum** (Hwy. 17, 912/884-5837, Tues.–Sat. 10 A.M.–4 P.M., Sun. 2–4 P.M., $3 per person) and the adjacent **Midway Church,** sometimes called the "Midway meetinghouse." The museum contains a variety of artifacts, most from the 18th and 19th centuries, and

© JIM MOREKIS

the historic Midway Church

an extensive genealogy collection. The Midway Church, built in 1756, was burned during the Revolution but rebuilt in 1792. Both Button Gwinnett and Lyman Hall attended services here, and during the Civil War some of Sherman's cavalry set up camp. The cemetery across the street is wonderfully poignant and is the final resting place of two Revolutionary War generals; Union cavalry kept horses within its walls. The museum, church, and cemetery are easy to find: take Exit 76 off I-95 South, and take a right on U.S. 84 (Oglethorpe Highway). Turn right on U.S. 17 and they're just ahead on your right.

One of the most interesting eco-tourism and cultural sites in the region is the **Melon Bluff Nature and Heritage Preserve** (2999 Islands Hwy., 912/884-5779, www.melonbluff.com, Sept.–May, call for further details, $3 day use, $15 riding fee). Melon Bluff is a key part of the Colonial Birding Trail. Its 20 miles of trails, on 2,200 acres, wind through virtually every type of ecosystem in coastal Georgia, from ancient live oak stands to salt marsh to maritime forest.

Melon Bluff has expanded its cultural tourism offerings, keying on the important recent discovery in the area of the earliest known artifact of the first European settlement in North America: a Spanish coin near the site of the fabled San Miguel de Gualdalpe colony. See a fascinating display on this little-known chapter in American history upstairs (free). Melon Bluff is three miles east of I-95 off Exit 76.

Further west off of Islands Highway is **Seabrook Village** (660 Trade Hill Rd., 912/884-7008, Tues.–Sat. 10 A.M.–4 P.M., $3 per person), a unique living history museum chronicling the everyday life of Liberty County's African American community, with a direct link to Sherman's famous "40 acres and a mule" Field Order No. 15. There are eight restored vernacular buildings on the 100-acre site, including the simple but sublime one-room Seabrook School.

Youmans Pond (daily, free) is a prime stop for migratory fowl. Its main claim to fame is being visited in 1773 by the great naturalist William Bartram on one of his treks across the Southeast. Youmans Pond has changed little since then, with its tree-studded pond and oodles of owls, ospreys, herons, egrets, wood storks, and many more. To get there, take I-95 south from Savannah to Exit 76. Take a left onto GA 38 (Islands Highway) and then a left onto Camp Viking Road. About a mile ahead take a right onto Pamira Road. About three-quarters of a mile ahead look for the pond on your right. It's unmarked but there's a wooden boardwalk.

Less easy to find is **LeConte-Woodmanston Botanical Garden** (912/884-6500, www.hist .armstrong.edu/publichist/LeConte/leconte-home.htm, Tues.–Sat. 9 A.M.–5 P.M., closed Dec. 18–Feb. 14, call first to verify times and road conditions, $2). Part of William Bartram's historic nature trail, this was the home of Dr. Louis LeConte, renowned 19th-century botanist, and his sons John LeConte, first president of the University of California at Berkeley, and Joseph LeConte, who with John Muir founded the Sierra Club. The highlight here is the rare tidally influenced freshwater wetland, featuring the blackwater Bulltown Swamp. This visit is best done in a four-wheel-drive vehicle. From Savannah, take I-95 south to Exit 76. Turn right on U.S. 84, then left on U.S. 17. Turn right on Barrington Ferry Road until pavement ends at Sandy Run Road. Continue until you see the historic markers. Turn left onto the dirt road, then drive another mile.

Dorchester Academy and Museum (8787 E. Oglethorpe Hwy., 912/884-2347, www.dorchesteracademy.com, open Tues.–Fri. 11 A.M.–2 P.M., Sat. 2–4 P.M., free) was built as a boarding and day school for freed African Americans after the Civil War. Liberty County was one of the earliest integrated school districts in Georgia, and Martin Luther King Jr. came to Dorchester in 1962 to plan the march on Birmingham. In 1997, an extensive renovation brought the multi-building facility to its current state. The museum is small but features an interesting display of memorabilia. Take Exit 76 off I-95 and go west on U.S. Highway 84, about two miles past the intersection with U.S. Highway 17.

Built to defend the once-proud port of Sunbury, **Fort Morris State Historic Site** (2559 Ft. Morris Rd., 912/884-5999, www.gastateparks.org/info/ftmorris, Tues.–Sat. 9 A.M.–5 P.M., Sun. 2–5:30 P.M., $3) was reconstructed during the War of 1812 and was an encampment during the Civil War. It was here that Colonel John McIntosh gave his famous reply to the British demand for his surrender: "Come and take it." The museum has displays of military and everyday life of the era. Reenactments and cannon firings are highlights. There's a visitors center and a nature trail. To get there, take Exit 76 off I-95 south. Go east on Islands Highway and take a left on Fort Morris Road; the site is two miles down.

A little ways south of Midway on the Liberty Trail, in tiny Riceboro, is **Geechee Kunda** (622 Ways Temple Rd., 912/884-4440, www.geecheekunda.net), a combination museum/outreach center dedicated to explaining and exploring the culture of Sea Island African Americans on the Georgia coast. (Don't be confused: "Geechee" is the Georgia word for

THE DEAD TOWN OF SUNBURY

If you spend much time in Liberty County you'll probably hear someone mention that a certain place or person is "over near Sunbury." Such is the lasting legacy of this long-gone piece of Georgia history on the Midway River that locals still refer to it in the present tense, though the old town itself is no more.

Founded soon after Midway in 1758, by 1761 Sunbury rivaled Savannah as Georgia's main commercial port, with a thriving trade in lumber, rice, indigo, corn, and, unfortunately, slaves as well. At one time, one writer recalls, seven square-rigged vessels called on the port in a single day. At various times, all three of Georgia's signers of the Declaration of Independence – Button Gwinnett, Lyman Hall, and George Walton – had connections to Sunbury.

The beginning of the end came with those heady days of revolution, however, when Sun-

bury was the scene of much fighting between colonists and the British army in 1776-1779. A British siege in 1778 culminated in this immortal reply from the colonial commander, Colonel John McIntosh, to a redcoat demand for surrender: "Come and take it."

By the beginning of 1779, however, a separate British assault did indeed "take it," adding to the increasingly violent pillage of the surrounding area. Though after American independence Sunbury remained the Liberty County seat until 1797, it was never the same, beset by decay, hurricanes, and yellow fever outbreaks. (Fort Morris, however, would defend the area against the British one more time, in the War of 1812, as Fort Defiance.)

By 1848, nothing of the town remained but the old cemetery, which you can find a short drive from the Fort Morris State Historic Site; ask a park employee for directions.

© JIM MOREKIS

reenactors at Fort Morris State Historic Site

the Gullah people. Both groups share similar folkways and history and the terms are virtually interchangeable.) There are artifacts from slavery and Reconstruction, including authentic Geechee/Gullah relics.

Liberty County is also home to part of the sprawling Fort Stewart army installation, home of the U.S. Army "Rock of the Marne" 3rd Infantry Division. The only thing open to the public is the **Fort Stewart Museum** (Bldg. T904, 2022 Frank Cochran Dr., 912/767-7885, Tues.–Sat. 10 a.m.–4 p.m., free), which chronicles the division's activity in World War II, Vietnam, Korea, Desert Storm, and Iraq. All visitors must stop at the main gate and provide proof of registration, insurance, and drivers license to receive a visitor's pass. To get there, take Exit 87 off I-95 south. Take a left on Hwy. 17, then veer right onto GA 196 west. Turn right at U.S. 84. Turn right onto General Stewart Way and follow directions to the main gate.

Accommodations and Food

While industry is coming quickly to Liberty County, it's still a small, self-contained community with not much in the way of tourist amenities (many would say that is part of its charm). A great choice for a stay is ◀ **Dunham Farms** (5836 Islands Hwy., 912/880-4500, www.dunhamfarms.com). The B&B ($165–205) is in the 1940s converted Palmyra Barn, and the self-catered circa-1840 Palmyra Cottage ($300) nearby is right on the river, with plenty of kayaking and hiking opportunities. Your hosts, Laura and Meredith Devendorf, couldn't be more charming or informed about the area, and the breakfasts are absurdly rich and filling in that hearty and deeply comforting Southern tradition.

Restaurants of note include the **Sunbury Crab Company** (541 Brigantine Dunmore Rd., 912/884-8640, lunch Sat.–Sun., dinner Wed.–Sun., $10–30), providing, you guessed it, great crab cakes in a casual atmosphere on the Midway River. Get there by taking GA 38 east of Midway and then a left onto Fort Morris Road.

Many locals eat at least once a week at **Holton's Seafood** (13711 E. Oglethorpe

Hwy., 912/884-9151, daily lunch and dinner, $7–17), an unpretentious and fairly typical family-run fried seafood place just off I-95 at the Midway exit.

RICHMOND HILL AND BRYAN COUNTY

Known as the "town that Henry Ford built," Richmond Hill is a growing bedroom community of Savannah in adjacent Bryan County. Sherman's March to the Sea ended here with much destruction, so little history before that time is left. Most of what remains is due to Ford's philanthropic influence, still felt in many place names around the area, including the main drag, GA 144, known as Ford Avenue.

After the auto magnate and his wife Clara made the area, then called Ways Station, a summer home, they were struck by the area's incredible poverty and determined to help improve living conditions, building hospitals, schools, churches, and homes. The Fords eventually acquired over 85,000 acres in Bryan County, including the former Richmond plantation. What is now known as Ford Plantation—currently a private luxury resort—was built in the 1930s and centered on the main house, once the central building of the famous Hermitage Plantation on the Savannah River, purchased and moved by Ford south to Bryan County.

Sights

The little **Richmond Hill Historical Society and Museum** (corner of Ford Ave. and Timber Trail Rd., 912/756-3697, daily 10 A.M.–4 P.M., donations encouraged) is housed in a former kindergarten built by Henry Ford.

Perhaps the main attraction here, especially for Civil War buffs, is **Fort McAllister State Historic Site** (3894 Ft. McAllister Rd., 912/727-2339, www.gastateparks.org/info/ ftmcallister, daily 7 A.M.–10 P.M., $5 adults, $3.50 children). Unlike the masonry forts of Savannah, Fort McAllister is an all-earthwork fortification on the Ogeechee River, the site of a short but savage assault by Sherman's troops in December 1864, in which 5,000 Union

soldiers quickly overwhelmed the skeleton garrison of 230 Confederate defenders. After the war, the site fell into disrepair until Henry Ford funded and spearheaded restoration of it in the 1930s, as he did with so many historic sites in Bryan County. The fort, which features many reenactments throughout the year, has a well-run new **Civil War Museum** (Mon.–Sat. 9 A.M.–5 P.M., Sun. 2–5 P.M.). An adjacent recreational site features a beautiful, oak-lined picnic ground, a nature trail, and the nearby 65-site Savage Island Campground. To get there off I-95, take Exit 90 and go 10 miles east on GA Spur 144.

Practicalities

There's no end to the chain food offerings here, but one of the better restaurants in town is **The Upper Crust** (1702 U.S. 17, 912/756-6990, Mon.–Sat. lunch and dinner, Sun. dinner only, $7–12), a casual American place with great pizza in addition to soups, salads, and hot sandwiches. Another popular place, also on Highway 17, is **Steamers Restaurant & Raw Bar** (4040 U.S. Hwy. 17, 912/756-3979, daily 5–10 P.M. $10–20), home of some good Lowcountry Boil.

To get to Richmond Hill, drive south of Savannah on I-95 and take Exit 90. Most lodgings in the area are clustered off I-95 at Exit 87 (Exit 90 also gets you to Richmond Hill). Keep in mind the two most important thoroughfares are the north–south U.S. 17 and the east–west GA 144, also known as Ford Avenue.

NEW EBENEZER

Few people visit New Ebenezer today, west of Savannah in Effingham County. Truth is, there's not much there anymore except for one old church. But oh, what a church. The **Jerusalem Evangelical Lutheran Church** (2966 Ebenezer Rd., Rincon, 912/754-3915, www.effga.com/jerusalem) hosts the oldest continuous congregation in the United States. Built out of local clay brick in 1769, its walls are 21 inches thick. Some original panes of glass remain, and its European bells are still rung before each service, which begins each Sunday at

SAVANNAH

NEW EBENEZER AND THE SALZBURGERS

Perhaps the most unsung chapter in Europe's great spiritual diaspora of the 1700s, the Salzburgers of New Ebenezer – a thrifty, peaceful, and hard-working people – were Georgia's first religious refugees and perhaps the most progressive as well.

The year after Oglethorpe's arrival, a contingent of devout Lutherans from Salzburg in present-day Austria arrived after being expelled from their home country for their beliefs. Oglethorpe, mindful of Georgia's mission to provide sanctuary for persecuted Protestants and also wishing for a military buffer to the west, eagerly welcomed them.

Given land about 25 miles west of Savannah, the Salzburgers named their first settlement Ebenezer ("stone of help" in Hebrew). Disease prompted them to move the site to better land nearer to the river and call it – in pragmatic Germanic style – New Ebenezer, and so it remains to this day.

Because they continued to speak German instead of English, the upriver colony maintained its isolation. Still, the Salzburgers were among Oglethorpe's most ardent and loyal supporters. Their pastor and de facto political leader Johann Martin Boltzius, seeking to build an enlightened agrarian utopia of small farmers, was an outspoken foe of slavery and the exploitative plantation system of agriculture.

His system largely worked: The fragile silk industry thrived in New Ebenezer where it had failed miserably in Savannah, and the nation's first rice mill was built here.

However, don't get the idea that the Salzburgers were all work and no play. They enjoyed their beer, so much so that Oglethorpe was forced to send regular shipments, rationalizing that "cheap beer is the only means to keep rum out."

For 10 years, Georgia hosted another progressive Lutheran sect, the Moravians, who John Wesley called the only genuine Christians he'd ever met. Despite their professed pacifism, however, they had to leave New Ebenezer because they didn't get along with the Salzburgers and their communal living arrangements led to internal discord.

The Trustees' turnover of Georgia back to the crown in 1750 signaled the final victory of pro-slavery forces – so much so that even Pastor Boltzius acquired a couple of slaves as domestic servants. New Ebenezer's influence began a decline that rapidly accelerated when British forces pillaged much of the town in the Revolution, even burning pews and Bibles.

Fifty years later nothing at all remained except the old Jerusalem Church, now the Jerusalem Evangelical Lutheran Church. Built in 1769, it still stands today and hosts regular worship services. Right around the corner is the New Ebenezer Retreat nestled along the banks of the Savannah, providing an ecumenical meeting and natural healing space for those of all faiths.

Though New Ebenezer's often called a "ghost town," this is a misnomer. Extensive archaeological work continues in the area, and the Georgia Salzburger Society works hard to maintain several historic buildings and keep the legacy alive through special events.

© BRUCE TUTEN

the Jerusalem Evangelical Lutheran Church

11 A.M. Several surrounding structures are also heirs to New Ebenezer's Salzburg legacy.

Around the corner from the church is a much newer spiritually themed site, the **New Ebenezer Retreat and Conference Center** (2887 Ebenezer Rd., 912/754-9242, www.new ebenezer.org). Built in 1977, the Retreat provides acres of calm surroundings, lodging, and meals in an ecumenical Christian setting.

Scenic, blackwater **Ebenezer Creek** is best experienced by putting in at the private Ebenezer Landing ($5).

To get to New Ebenezer, take Exit 109 off I-95. Go north on GA 21 to Rincon, Georgia, then east on GA 275 (Ebenezer Road).

The above-mentioned New Ebenezer Retreat and Conference Center offers a range of very reasonably priced lodgings, most including meals, in a beautiful setting. The extremely fast-growing town of Rincon, through which you will most likely drive on your way to New Ebenezer, offers an assortment of the usual chain food and lodging establishments.

WASSAW ISLAND NATIONAL WILDLIFE REFUGE

Totally unique in that it's the only Georgia barrier island never cleared for agriculture or development, the 10,000-acre Wassaw Island National Wildlife Refuge (www.fws.gov/ wassaw) is accessible only by boat. There are striking, driftwood-strewn beaches, while the interior of the island has some beautiful old-growth stands of longleaf pine and live oak.

Wassaw is a veritable paradise for nature-lovers and bird-watchers, with migratory activity in the spring and fall, waterfowl in abundance in the summer, and manatee and loggerhead turtle activity (about 10 percent of Georgia's transient loggerhead population makes use of Wassaw for nesting). There are also about 20 miles of trails and a decaying Spanish-American War–era battery, Fort Morgan, on the north end. National Wildlife Refuge Week is celebrated in October.

Because of its comparatively young status—it was formed only about 1,600 years ago—Wassaw also has some unique geographical features. You can still make out the parallel ridge features, vestiges of successive ancient shorelines. A central ridge forms the backbone of the island, reaching an amazing (for this area) elevation of 45 feet above sea level at the south end.

Native Americans first settled the island, whose name comes from an ancient word for "sassafras," which was found in abundance there. During the Civil War, both Confederate and Union troops occupied the island successively. In 1866 the wealthy New England businessman George Parsons bought the island, which stayed in that family's hands until it was sold to the Nature Conservancy in 1969 for $1 million. The Conservancy in turn sold Wassaw to the U.S. government for $1 to be managed as a wildlife refuge.

It's easiest to get to Wassaw Island from Savannah. Charters and scheduled trips are available from **Captain Walt's Charters** (Thunderbolt Marina, 3124 River Dr., 912/507-3811, www.waltsadventure.com/ charters), the **Bull River Marina** (8005 E. Hwy. 80, 912/897-7300), **Delegal Marina** (1 Marina Dr., 912/598-0023), **Capt. Joe Dobbs** (Delegal Marina, 1 Marina Dr., 912/598-0090, www.captjdobbs.com), and **Isle of Hope Marina** (50 Bluff Dr., 912/354-8187, www.isleofhopemarina.com). Most docking is either at the beaches on the north and south ends or in Wassaw Creek, where the Fish and Wildlife Service dock is also located (temporary mooring only).

There's no camping allowed on Wassaw Island; it's for day use only.

OSSABAW ISLAND

Owned and operated by Georgia as a heritage and wildlife preserve, the island was a gift to the state in 1978 from Eleanor Torrey-West and family, who still retain some property on the island. All public use of the island is managed by the **Ossabaw Island Foundation** (www.ossabawisland.org).

The 12,000-acre island is much older than Wassaw Island to its north, and so has traces of human habitation back to 2000 B.C. The island's name comes from an old Muskogean word referring to yaupon holly, found in abundance on the island and used by Native Americans in purification rituals to induce vomiting. Wading birds and predators such as bald eagles make their homes on the island, as do feral horses and a transient population of loggerhead turtles, who lay eggs in the dunes during the summer. There are several tabby ruins on the island, along with many miles of walking trails.

Unlike the much-younger Wassaw, Ossabaw Island was not only timbered extensively but hosted several rice and cotton plantations, particularly on the north end. The first property transfer in Georgia involved Ossabaw, St. Catherine's, and Sapelo Islands, which were ceded to the Yamacraws in exchange for the English getting the coastal region. The Yamacraws then granted those islands to Mary Musgrove, who began the modern era on the island by planting and introducing livestock.

Descendants of the island's slaves moved to the Savannah area after the Civil War, founding the community of Pin Point. Similarly to Jekyll Island to the south, Ossabaw was a hunting preserve for wealthy families in the Roaring Twenties. Even today hunting is an important activity on the island, with lotteries choosing who gets a chance to pursue its overly large populations of deer and wild hog, the latter of which are descended from pigs brought by the Spanish.

Now reserved exclusively for educational and scientific purposes, the island is accessible only by boat. Georgia law provides public access to all beaches up to the high-tide mark—which simply means that the public can ride out to Ossabaw and go on the beach for day-use, but any travel to the interior is restricted and you must have permission first. Contact the Ossabaw Island Foundation at info@ossabawisland.org for information. For day trips, call any of the numbers for tour operators listed under *Wassaw Island*.

THE GOLDEN ISLES

More than any other area in the region, the Georgia coast retains a timeless mystique evocative of a time before the coming of Europeans, even of humankind itself. Often called the Golden Isles because of the play of the afternoon sun on the vistas of marsh grass, its other nickname, "the Debatable Land," is a nod to its centuries-long role as a constantly shifting battleground of European powers.

Though on the map it looks relatively short, Georgia's coastline comprises the longest contiguous salt marsh environment in the world—a third of America's remaining salt marsh. Abundant with wildlife, vibrant with exotic, earthy aromas, constantly refreshed by a steady, salty sea breeze, it's a place with no real match anywhere else.

Filled with rich sediments from rivers upstream and replenished with nutrients from the twice-daily ocean tide, Georgia's marshes from the mainland to the barrier islands are an amazing engine of natural production. Producing more food energy than any estuary on the East Coast, each acre of marsh produces about 20 tons of biomass—four times more productive than an acre of corn.

Ancient Native Americans held the area in special regard, intoxicated not only by the easy sustenance it offered but its spiritual solace. Their shell middens, many still in existence, are not only a sign of a well-fed people, but one thankful for nature's bounty.

Avaricious for gold as they were, the Spanish also admired the almost monastic enchantment of Georgia's coast, choosing it as the site of their first colony in North America. Their

© JIM MOREKIS

HIGHLIGHTS

◖ Brunswick Historic District: A charming, pedestrian-friendly area of restored buildings, art galleries, and shrimp boats in the heart of Brunswick (page 109).

◖ Jekyll Island Historic District: Relax and soak in the salty breeze at this one-time playground of the world's richest people (page 117).

◖ The Village: The center of social life on St. Simons Island has shops, restaurants, a pier, and a beachside playground (page 126).

◖ Fort Frederica National Monument: An excellently preserved tabby fortress from the first days of English settlement in Georgia (page 127).

◖ Harris Neck National Wildlife Refuge: This former wartime airfield is now one of the East Coast's best birding locations (page 134).

◖ Cumberland Island National Seashore: Wild horses – such as the ones that live here – might not be able to drag you off of this evocative, undeveloped island paradise (page 143).

◖ Okefenokee National Wildlife Refuge: More than just a swamp, the Okefenokee is a natural wonderland that takes you back into the mists of prehistory (page 148).

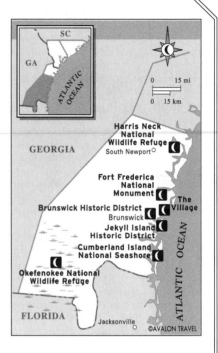

LOOK FOR ◖ TO FIND RECOMMENDED SIGHTS, ACTIVITIES, DINING, AND LODGING.

---

subsequent chain of Roman Catholic missions are now long gone, but certainly testified to their own quest here.

While the American tycoons who used these barrier islands as personal playgrounds had an avarice of their own, we must give credit where it's due: Their self-interest kept these places largely untouched by the kind of development that has plagued many of South Carolina's barrier islands to the north.

Though isolated even today, the Golden Isles played an irreplaceable role in the defense of the young United States. It was here that massive live oaks were forested and used in the construction of the bulked-up, super-fast frigates of the fledgling U.S. Navy. The USS *Constitution* got its nickname, "Old Ironsides," from the strength of these pieces of Georgia oak, so resilient as to literally repel British cannonballs during the War of 1812.

Though the South Carolina Sea Islands are generally seen as the center of Gullah culture, the African American communities of the Golden Isles, Georgia's Sea Islands, also boast a long and fascinating history of survival, resourcefulness, and proud cultural integrity carried on to this day.

HISTORY

For over 5,000 years, the Golden Isles of what would become Georgia were an abundant food and game source for Native Americans. In those days, long before erosion and channel dredging had taken their toll, each barrier island was an easy canoe ride away from the next one—a sort of early Intracoastal Waterway—and there was bounty for everyone.

But all that changed in 1526 when the Golden Isles became the site of the first European settlement in America, the fabled San Miguel de Guadalpe, founded nearly a century before the first English settlements in Virginia. Historians remain unsure where expedition leader Lucas de Ayllon actually set up camp with his 600 colonists and slaves, but recent research breakthroughs have put it somewhere around St. Catherine's Sound.

Though San Miguel disintegrated within a couple of months, it set the stage for a lengthy Spanish presence on the Georgia coast that culminated in the mission period of 1580–1684. Working with the coastal chiefdoms of Guale and Mocama, almost all of Georgia's barrier islands and many interior spots hosted Catholic missions, each with an accompanying contingent of Spanish regulars.

The missions began retreating with the English incursion into the American Southeast in the 1600s, and the coast was largely free of European presence until an early English outpost, Fort King George near modern-day Darien, Georgia, was established decades later in 1721. Fetid, isolated, and hard to provision, the small fort was abandoned seven years later.

The next English project was Fort Frederica on St. Simons Island, commissioned by General James Edward Oglethorpe following his establishment of Savannah to the north. Oglethorpe's settlement of Brunswick and Jekyll Island came soon afterward. With the final vanquishing of the Spanish at the Battle of Bloody Marsh near Fort Frederica, the Georgia coast became an exclusively British-dominated area. It quickly emulated the profitable rice-based plantation culture of the South Carolina Lowcountry, and indeed many notable Carolina planters expanded their holdings with marshland on the Georgia coast.

Though comparatively little fighting took place this far south, the American Revolution would find an affluent class of local planters energetically engaged in the cause of independence. The area's seaports hosted a steady stream of agricultural goods and naval stores for domestic and international markets.

The southern reaches of Sherman's March to the Sea came down as far as Darien, a once-vital trading port which was burned to the ground by Union troops. With slavery gone and the plantation system in disarray, the coast's African American population was largely left to its own devices. Though the famous "40 acres and a mule" land and wealth redistribution plan for freed slaves was not to see fruition, the black population of Georgia's Sea Islands, like that of South Carolina's, developed an inward-looking culture that persists to this day.

The generic term for this culture is Gullah, but in Georgia you'll also hear it referred to as Geechee, local dialect for the nearby Ogeechee River.

As with much of the South after the war, business carried on much as before, with the area becoming a center of lumber, the turpentine trade, and an increasing emphasis on fishing and shrimping. But by the start of the 20th century, the Golden Isles had become firmly established as a playground for the rich, who hunted and dined on the sumptuous grounds of exclusive retreats such as the Jekyll Island Club.

As it did elsewhere, World War II brought new economic growth in the form of military bases, even as German U-boats ranged off the coast. Today the federal presence is most notable in the massive Trident submarine base at Kings Bay toward the Florida border.

PLANNING YOUR TIME

Generally speaking, the peak season in this area is March through Labor Day. With the exception of some resort accommodations on St. Simons

THE GOLDEN ISLES

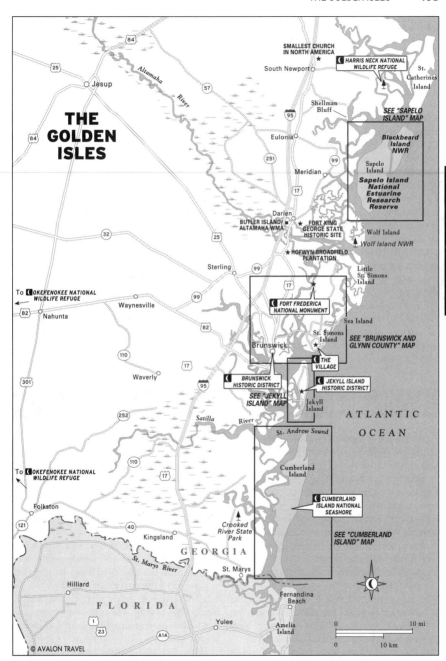

Island, Little St. Simons Island, and Sea Island, lodging is generally far more affordable than up the coast in either Savannah or Charleston.

Though many travelers take I-95 south from Savannah to the Golden Isles, U.S. 17 roughly parallels the interstate—in some cases so closely that cars on both roads can see each other—and is a far more scenic and enriching drive for those with a little extra time to spend. Indeed, U.S. 17 is an intrinsic part of the life and lore of the region and you are likely to spend a fair amount of time on it regardless.

Geographically, Brunswick is similar to Charleston in that it lies on a peninsula situated roughly north/south. And like Charleston, it's separated from the Atlantic by barrier islands, in Brunswick's case St. Simons Island and Jekyll Island. Once you get within city limits, however, Brunswick has more in common with Savannah due to its Oglethorpe-designed grid layout.

Brunswick itself can easily be fully experienced in a single afternoon. But really—as its nickname "Gateway to the Golden Isles" indicates—Brunswick's main role is as an economic and governmental center for Glynn County, to which Jekyll Island and St. Simons Island, the real attractions in this area, belong.

Both Jekyll Island and St. Simons Island are well worth visiting, and have their own separate pleasures—Jekyll more contemplative, St. Simons more upscale. Give an entire day to Jekyll so you can take full advantage of its relaxing, open feel. A half-day can suffice for St. Simons because most of its attractions are clustered in the Village area near the pier, and there's little beach recreation to speak of.

Getting to the undeveloped barrier islands, Sapelo and Cumberland, takes planning in advance because there is no bridge to either. Both require a ferry booking and a hence more substantial commitment of time. There are no real stores and few facilities on these islands, so pack along whatever you think you'll need, whether it be food, water, medicine, suntan lotion, insect repellant, or otherwise.

Sapelo Island is limited to day use unless you have prior reservations, with the town of Darien in McIntosh County as your gateway. The same is true for Cumberland Island National Seashore, with the town of St. Marys in Camden County as your gateway.

Brunswick and Glynn County

Consider Brunswick sort of a junior Savannah, sharing with that city twice its size to the north a heavily English flavor, great manners, a city plan with squares courtesy of General James Oglethorpe, a thriving but environmentally intrusive seaport, and a busy shrimping fleet.

While Brunswick never became the dominant commercial center, à la Savannah, that it was envisioned to be, it has followed the Savannah model in modern times, both in terms of downtown revitalization and an increasing emphasis on port activity. Sadly, unlike Savannah, Brunswick has not seen fit to preserve the integrity of its six existing squares, all but one of which (Hanover Square) have been bisected by streets and/or built on.

Though the first real English-speaking settler of the area, Mark Carr, began cultivating land near Brunswick in 1738, the city wasn't laid out until 1771, in a grid design similar to Savannah's. Originally comprising nearly 400 acres, Brunswick was named for Braunschweig, the seat of the House of Hanover in Germany and also for the Duke of Brunswick, a brother of King George III.

The Brunswick area hosted a number of profitable plantations and a burgeoning lumber industry, but a series of financial panics in the late 1830s hit particularly hard. When the Civil War started, most white citizens fled to nearby Waynesville, Georgia, and wharves and key buildings were burned to keep them out of Union hands.

Brunswick's longstanding status as "Gateway

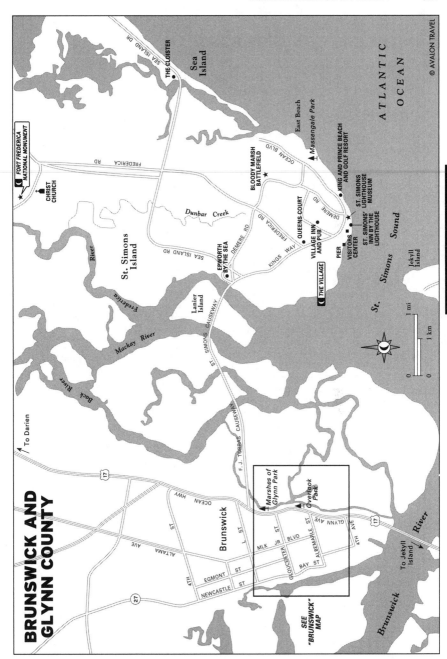

THE GOLDEN ISLES

© AVALON TRAVEL

BRUNSWICK AND GLYNN COUNTY

SEA ISLAND DR

THE CLOISTER

Sea Island

FORT FREDERICA NATIONAL MONUMENT

CHRIST CHURCH

FREDERICA RD

Dunbar Creek

St. Simons Island

Frederica River

SEA ISLAND RD

EPWORTH BY THE SEA

Lanier Island

Mackay River

Back River

To Darien

ST. SIMONS CAUSEWAY

F. J. TORRAS CAUSEWAY

Marshes of Glynn Park

Overlook Park

17

OCEAN HWY

Brunswick

ALTAMA AVE

L ST

MLK JR BLVD

GLOUCESTER ST

ALBEMARLE ST

BAY ST

GLYNN AVE

4TH AVE

4TH ST

EGMONT ST

NEWCASTLE ST

27

SEE "BRUNSWICK" MAP

To Jekyll Island

River

Brunswick

17

BLOODY MARSH BATTLEFIELD

OCEAN BLVD

East Beach

Massengale Park

KING AND PRINCE BEACH AND GOLF RESORT

ST. SIMONS LIGHTHOUSE MUSEUM

QUEENS COURT

DEMERE RD

FREDERICA RD

KINGS WAY

VILLAGE INN AND PUB

THE VILLAGE

PIER

VISITORS CENTER

ST. SIMONS INN BY THE LIGHTHOUSE

St. Simons Sound

Jekyll Island

St. Simons Sound

ATLANTIC OCEAN

1 mi

1 km

0
0

IN THE FOOTSTEPS OF BARTRAM

The West has its stirring tale of Lewis and Clark, but the Southeast has its own fascinating – if somewhat less dramatic – tale of discovery, in the odyssey of William Bartram.

In March 1733, the 36-year-old Bartram – son of royal botanist John Bartram and definitely a chip off the old block – arrived in Savannah to begin what would become a four-year journey through eight Southern states and colonies. As Lewis and Clark would do in the following century, Bartram not only exhaustively documented his encounters with nature and with Native Americans, he made discoveries whose impact has stayed with us to this day.

Young "Willie," born near Philadelphia in 1739, had a talent for drawing and for plants, which of course thrilled his father, who wrote to a friend that "Botany and drawing is his darling delight." A failure at business, Bartram was happy to settle on a traveling lifestyle that mixed both his loves: art and flora. After accompanying his father on several early trips, Bartram set out on his own at the request of an old friend of his father's in England, Dr. John Fothergill, who paid Bartram 50 pounds per year plus expenses to send back specimens and drawings.

Though Bartram's quest would eventually move farther inland and encompass much of the modern American South, most of the first year was spent in coastal Georgia. After arriving in Savannah he moved southward, roughly paralleling modern US 17, to the now-dead town of Sunbury, through Midway and on to Darien, where he stayed at the plantation of Lachlan McIntosh on the great Altamaha River, which inspired Bartram to some of his most beautiful writing. Bartram also journeyed to Sapelo Island, Brunswick, St. Marys, and even into the great Okefenokee Swamp.

Using Savannah and Charleston as bases, Bartram mostly traveled alone, either by horse, by boat, or on foot. Word of his trip preceded him, and he was usually greeted warmly by local traders and Indian chiefs (except for one encounter with a hostile tribesman near the St. Marys River). In many places, he was the first white man seen since De Soto and the Spanish.

His epic journey ended in late 1776, when Bartram gazed on his beloved Altamaha for the last time. Heading north and crossing the Savannah River south of Ebenezer, he proceeded to Charleston and from there to his hometown of Philadelphia – where he would remain for the rest of his days.

At its publication, his 1791 chronicle, *Travels Through North and South Carolina, Georgia, East and West Florida*, was hailed as "the most astounding verbal artifact of the early republic." In that unassuming yet timeless work, Bartram cemented his reputation as America's first native-born naturalist and practically invented the modern travelogue.

Thanks to the establishment of the William Bartram Trail in 1976, you can walk in his footsteps – or close to them, anyway, since historians are not sure of his route. The trail uses a rather liberal interpretation, including memorials, trails, and gardens, but many specific "heritage sites" in coastal Georgia have their own markers, as follows:

- River and Barnard Streets in Savannah to mark his disembarkation and the beginning of his trek

- LeConte-Woodmanston Plantation in Liberty County (Barrington Ferry Road south of Sandy Run Road near Riceboro)

- A mile and half south of the South Newport River off Highway 17

- St. Simon's Island on Frederica Road near the Fort Frederica entrance

- Off GA 275 at Old Ebenezer Cemetery in Effingham County

Among the indigenous species Bartram was the first to notate are:

- Fraser Magnolia

- Gopher Tortoise

- Florida Sandhill Crane

- Flame Azalea

- Oakleaf Hydrangea

to the Golden Isles" happened in the 1880s with the increasing popularity of nearby Jekyll Island as a millionaires' getaway. Two terrible hurricanes, one in 1893 and another in 1898, put the city underwater, but it was quickly rebuilt.

Brunswick saw a boom in population during World War II as a home of wartime industry such as the J. A. Jones Construction Company, which in a two-year span built 99 massive Liberty ships and at its peak employed 16,000 workers (they managed to build seven ships in a single month in 1944).

Since the war, the shrimping industry has played a big role in Brunswick's economy, so much so that it calls itself the "Shrimp Capital of the World." But lately the local shrimping industry is in steep decline, both from depleted coastal stocks and increased competition from Asian shrimp farms.

SIGHTS
🄲 Brunswick Historic District

Technically Brunswick has an "Old Town"

district on the National Register of Historic Places as well as an adjacent district called "Historic Brunswick" centering on the storefronts of Newcastle Street. Since it's all pretty close together, for our purposes here we'll consider it all one nice package.

Unlike Savannah, which renamed many of its streets in a fit of patriotism after the American Revolution, Brunswick's streets bear their original Anglophilic names, like Gloucester, Albemarle, and Norwich. You'd be forgiven for thinking that Brunswick's Union Street is a post–Civil War statement of national unity, but the name actually commemorates the union of Scotland and England in 1707!

Though its layout mimics Savannah's, Brunswick's downtown assortment of low, brick, Main Street America–style buildings actually gives it a feel more like Athens or Macon, Georgia, than Savannah. Most of the visitor-friendly activity centers on **Newcastle Street,** where you'll find the bulk of the galleries, shops, and restored buildings. Adjacent

THE GOLDEN ISLES

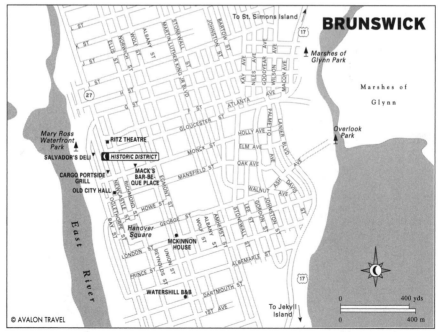

in the more historic areas are some nice residential homes.

The new pride of downtown is **Old City Hall** (1212 Newcastle St.), an amazing circa-1889 Richardsonian Romanesque edifice designed by noted regional architect Alfred Eichberg, who also planned many similarly imposing buildings in Savannah. City Hall reopened in 2004 after extensive renovations, bringing back to life its great vintage fireplaces and refitting its original gaslight fixtures.

Another active restored building is the charming **Ritz Theatre** (1530 Newcastle St., 912/262-6934, www.goldenislearts.org), built in 1898 to house the Grand Opera House and the offices of the Brunswick and Birmingham Railroad. This ornate three-story Victorian transitioned with the times, becoming a vaudeville venue, then a movie house. Under the management of the Golden Isles Arts and Humanities Association since 1989, the Ritz now hosts performances, studios, an art gallery, and classes.

the historic Ritz Theatre in downtown Brunswick

The privately owned **Mahoney-McGarvey House** (1705 Reynolds St.) is considered the finest example of "carpenter Gothic" architecture in Georgia.

Mary Ross Waterfront Park

This downtown gathering place at Bay and Gloucester Streets also has economic importance as a center of local economic activity—for it's here where Brunswick's shrimp fleet is moored and the town's large port facilities begin. Unfortunately, nearby is a huge factory, dispensing its unpleasant odor over the waterfront 24/7.

In 1989 the park was dedicated to Mary Ross, member of a longtime Brunswick shrimping family and author of the popular Georgia history book *The Debatable Land.* While the book is still a great read, sadly Ms. Ross was wrong when she wrote that the tabby ruins in the area were of Spanish origin. Devastated by the discovery that they actually dated from later and were of English construction, she vowed never to publish another word again.

At the entrance to the park is a huge and well-done model of a Liberty ship, like the thousands that were built in Brunswick during World War II.

Lover's Oak

At the intersection of Prince and Albany Streets, you'll find the Lover's Oak, a nearly 1,000-year-old tree. Local lore tells us that it's been a secret meeting place for young lovers for centuries (though one does wonder how much of a "secret" it actually could have been). It's about 13 feet in diameter and has 10 sprawling limbs.

Marshes of Glynn

Amid the light industrial sprawl of this area of the Golden Isles Parkway is the interesting little **Overlook Park,** just south of the visitors center on U.S. 17—a good, if loud, place for a picnic. From the park's picnic grounds or overlook you can see the fabled Marshes of Glynn, which inspired Georgia poet Sidney Lanier to write his famous poem of the same title under

© JIM MOREKIS

the Lanier Oak near the fabled Marshes of Glynn

the **Lanier Oak,** located a little farther up the road in the median.

Hofwyl-Broadfield Plantation

South Carolina doesn't own the patent on well-preserved old rice plantations, as the Hofwyl-Broadfield Plantation (5556 Hwy. 17, 912/264-7333, www.gastateparks.org, Thurs.–Sat. 9 A.M.–5 P.M., last main house tour 4:45 P.M., $5), a short drive north of Brunswick, proves. With its old paddies along the gorgeous and relatively undeveloped Altamaha River estuary, the plantation's main home is an antebellum wonder, with an expansive porch and a nice house museum inside, with silver, a rice plantation model, and a slide show. There's also a nice nature trail.

William Brailsford of Charleston finished the plantation in 1807, which soon passed into the hands of the Troup family, who expanded the holdings to over 7,000 acres. Rice finally became financially unfeasible in the early 20th century, and the plantation turned to dairy farming, a pursuit that lasted until World War II. Ophelia Troup Dent would finally will the site to the state of Georgia in 1973.

The best way to get there is by taking U.S. 17 north out of Brunswick until you see the signs; the plantation entrance is on the east side of the road.

ENTERTAINMENT AND EVENTS

The **Golden Isles Arts and Humanities Association** (1530 Newcastle St., 912/262-6934, www.goldenislesarts.org) is an umbrella organization for many arts activities in the Brunswick, Jekyll, and St. Simons area. They also manage the historic **Ritz Theatre** (1530 Newcastle St., 912/262-6934) in downtown Brunswick, which offers a yearly performance season that's worth checking out if you have a free weekend night.

Nightlife

Brunswick's a conservative place with little bar scene to speak of. But a few miles offshore is quite a different story, when the **Emerald**

Princess Dinner and Casino Cruises (Gisco Point, 912/265-3558, www.emeraldprincess casino.com, Mon.–Thurs. 7 P.M.–midnight, Fri.–Sat. 11 A.M.–4 P.M. and 7 P.M.–1 A.M., Sun. 1–6 P.M., $10) is operating. This is the classic gambling/party boat experience, with the action starting when the *Emerald Princess* slips into international waters and out of domestic gambling regulations. Ten bucks for the cruise gets you a light dinner. Drinks and chips, of course, are on you. No one under 21 is allowed, and minimum and maximum bets vary by table. Reservations required.

To get to the dock, take U.S. 17 over the massive Sidney Lanier Bridge. Take a left onto the Jekyll Island Causeway and then an immediate left onto Gisco Point Drive. Follow signs into the parking lot.

Performing Arts

Though based in St. Simons Island, the **Coastal Symphony of Georgia** (912/634-2006, www.coastalsymphonyofgeorgia.org), under the baton of Vernon Humbert, plays concerts in Brunswick during its season at different venues. Check the website for details.

Art Downtown (209 Gloucester St., 912/262-0628, www.artdowntowngallery 209.com) hosts locally written theater in its black box space, and showcases local visual artists in its attached Gallery 209.

The **Brunswick Community Concert Association** (912/638-5616, www.brunswick communityconcert.org, $25 adults, $5 students) brings an eclectic variety of high-quality national and regional vocal acts to various venues.

The **C.A.P.E. Theater** (916 Albany St., 912/996-7740, www.capetheater.org, $10 adult, $5 children), short for Craft, Appreciation, Performance, and Education, is a community group that performs a mix of classics and musicals at various venues. No reservations necessary unless you're attending a dinner theater show, which is about $30 for adults, $15 for students.

The town's main dance group is **Invisions Dance Company,** which performs out of

Studio South (1307 Grant St., 912/265-3255, www.studiosouthga.com).

Festivals and Events

Each Mother's Day at noon, parishioners of the local St. Francis Xavier Church hold the **Our Lady of Fatima Processional and Blessing of the Fleet** (www.brunswick.net), begun in 1938 by the local Portuguese fishing community. After the procession, at about 3 P.M. at Mary Ross Waterfront Park, comes the actual blessing of the shrimp-boat fleet.

Foodies will enjoy the **Brunswick Stewbilee** ($9 adults, $4 children), held on the second Saturday in October 11:30 A.M.–3 P.M. Pro and amateur chefs match skills in creating the local signature dish and vying for the title of "Brunswick Stewmaster." There are also car shows, contests, displays, and much live music.

SHOPPING

Right in the heart of the bustle on Newcastle is a good indie bookstore, **Hattie's Books** (1531 Newcastle St., 912/554-8677, www.hatties books.net, Mon.–Fri. 10 A.M.–5:30 P.M., Sat. 10 A.M.–4 P.M.). Not only do they have a good selection of local and regional authors, but you can get a good cup of coffee, too.

Like Beaufort, South Carolina, Brunswick has made the art gallery a central component of its downtown revitalization, with nearly all of them on Newcastle Street.

Near Hattie's you'll find the eclectic **Kazuma Gallery** (1523 Newcastle St., 912/279-0023, Mon.–Fri. 10 A.M.–5:30 P.M., Sat. 10 A.M.–2 P.M.) as well as the **Ritz Theatre** (1530 Newcastle St., 912/262-6934, Tues.–Fri. 9 A.M.–5 P.M., Sat. 10 A.M.–2 P.M.), which has its own art gallery inside. Farther down is **The Gallery on Newcastle Street** (1626 Newcastle St., 912/554-0056, Thurs.–Sat. 11 A.M.–5 P.M.), showcasing the original oils of owner Janet Powers.

SPORTS AND RECREATION
Hiking, Biking, and Bird-Watching

As one of the Colonial Coast Birding Trail sites, **Hofwyl-Broadfield Plantation** (5556

Hwy. 17, 912/264-7333, www.gastateparks.org, Tues.–Sat. 9 A.M.–5 P.M., Sun. 2–5:30 P.M.) offers a great nature trail along the marsh. Clapper rails, marsh wrens, and a wide variety of warblers come through the site regularly.

Birders and hikers will also enjoy the **Earth Day Nature Trail** (One Conservation Way, 912/264-7218), a self-guided, fully accessible walk where you can see such comparative rarities as the magnificent wood stork and other indigenous and migratory waterfowl. There are observation towers and binoculars available for checkout. To get there take U.S. 17 south through Brunswick. Just north of the big Sidney Lanier Bridge, turn left on Conservation Way and you'll see signage and come to a parking lot.

Just across the Brunswick River from town is **Blythe Island Regional Park** (6616 Blythe Island Hwy., 912/261-3805), a 1,100-acre public park with a campground, picnic area, and boat landing. The views are great, and it's big enough to do some decent biking and hiking. The best way there is to get back on I-95 and head south.

Another scenic park with a campground is **Altamaha Park of Glynn County** (1605 Altamaha Park Rd., 912/264-2342) northwest of Brunswick off U.S. 341, with 30 campsites and a boat ramp.

Golf

Compared to the more plentiful, high-dollar courses on the islands, golfing is reasonable in Brunswick. There are two main 18-hole public golf courses near the town: **Coastal Pines Golf Club** (1 Coastal Pines Circle, 912/261-0503, www.coastalpinesgolf.com, $47 green fees), open since 2001, and the older **Oak Grove Island Club** (126 Clipper Bay Rd., 800/780-8133, www.oakgroveislandgolf.com, $49 green fees). (Green fees are averages and fluctuate with season and time.)

Kayaking and Boating

Most recreational adventurers in the area prefer to launch from St. Simons Island. The key public landing in Brunswick, however, is **Brunswick Landing Marina** (2429 Newcastle St., 912/262-9264). You can also put in at the public boat ramps at **Blythe Island Regional Park,** which is on the Brunswick River, or the **Altamaha Park of Glynn County** (1605 Altamaha Park Rd., 912/264-2342), on the Altamaha River slightly north.

For expert guided tours at a reasonable price, check out **South East Adventures** (1200 Glynn Ave./Hwy. 17, 912/265-5292, www.southeastadventure.com), which has a dock right on the fabled "Marshes of Glynn."

ACCOMMODATIONS

In addition to the usual variety of chain hotels—most of which you should stay far away from—there are some nice places to stay in Brunswick if you want to make it a base of operations, at very reasonable prices.

In the heart of Old Town in a gorgeous Victorian is the ◖ **McKinnon House** (1001 Egmont St., 912/261-9100, www.mckinnonhousebandb.com, $125), which had a cameo role in the film *Conrack*. Today this bed-and-breakfast is Jo Miller's labor of love, a three-suite affair with some plush interiors and an exterior that's one of Brunswick's most photographed spots.

Surprisingly affordable for its elegance, the **WatersHill Bed & Breakfast** (728 Union St., 912/264-4262, www.watershill.com, $100) serves a full breakfast and offers a choice of five themed suites, such as the French country Elliot Wynell Room or the large Mariana Mahlaney room way up in the restored attic.

Without a doubt the most unique lodging in the area is the **Hostel in the Forest** (GA 82, 912/264-9738, $20, cash only), essentially a group of geodesic domes and whimsical treehouses a little ways off the highway. Formed over 30 years ago as an International Youth Hostel, the place initially gives off a hippie vibe, with an evening communal meal (included in the price) and a near-total ban on cell phones. But don't expect a wild time: No pets are allowed, the hostel discourages young children, and quiet time is strictly enforced at 11 P.M. It's an adventurous, peaceful, and very inexpensive place to stay, but

THE GOLDEN ISLES

BRUNSWICK STEW

Of course, Virginians being Virginians, they'll insist that the distinctive Southern dish known as "Brunswick Stew" was named for Brunswick County, Virginia, in 1828, where a political rally featured stew made from squirrel meat. But all real Southern foodies know the dish is named for Brunswick, Georgia.

Hey, there's a plaque to prove it in downtown Brunswick – though it says the first pot was cooked on July 2, 1898, on St. Simons Island, not in Brunswick at all. However, I think we can all agree that "Brunswick Stew" rolls off the tongue much easier than "St. Simons Stew."

In any case, it seems likely that what we now know as Brunswick Stew is based on an old colonial recipe, adapted from Native Americans, that relied on the meat of small game – originally squirrel or rabbit but nowadays mostly chicken or pork – along with vegetables like corn, onions, and okra, simmered over an open fire. Today this tangy, thick, tomato-based delight is a typical accompaniment to barbecue along the Lowcountry and Georgia coasts, as well as a freestanding entrée on its own.

Done traditionally and correctly, a proper pot of Brunswick Stew is an involved kitchen project taking most of a day. But it's worth it!

Here's a typical recipe from Glynn County, home of the famous Brunswick "Stewbilee" festival held the second Saturday of October:

© J_LAI

Sauce

Melt ¼ cup butter over low heat, then add:
1¾ cups ketchup
¼ cup yellow mustard
¼ cup white vinegar

Blend until smooth, then add:
½ tablespoon chopped garlic
1 teaspoon ground black pepper
½ teaspoon crushed red pepper
½ ounce Liquid Smoke
1 ounce Worcestershire sauce
1 ounce hot sauce
½ tablespoon fresh lemon juice

Blend until smooth, then add:
¼ cup dark brown sugar

Stir constantly and simmer for 10 minutes, being careful not to boil. Set aside.

Stew

Melt ¼ pound butter in a two-gallon pot, then add:
3 cups small diced potatoes
1 cup small diced onion
2 14.5-ounce cans chicken broth
1 pound baked chicken
8-10 ounces smoked pork

Bring to a boil, stirring until potatoes are near done, then add:
1 8.5-ounce can early peas
2 14.5-ounce cans stewed tomatoes
1 16-ounce can baby lima beans
¼ cup Liquid Smoke
1 14.5-ounce can creamed corn

Stir in sauce. Simmer slowly for two hours. Makes one gallon of Brunswick Stew.

be warned that there is no heating or cooling. To reach the hostel, take Exit 29 off I-95 and go west for two miles. Make a U-turn at the intersection at mile marker 11. Continue east on GA 82 for 0.5 mile. Look for a dirt road on the right with a gate and signage.

FOOD

For the most part, food comes in two flavors in Brunswick: barbecued and fried. A clear and notable exception is the relatively hip **(Cargo Portside Grill** (1423 Newcastle St., 912/267-7330, Tues.–Sat. 5:30–10 P.M., $20–30) in the historic Elliot Building downtown. Chef Alix Kinagy draws in a respectable crowd of mostly St. Simons residents from over the bridge to sample his rack of lamb with a seared rosemary/garlic crust and sesame catfish.

The premier barbecue in the Brunswick area is at the humble but nationally renowned **(Georgia Pig** (912/264-6664, Mon.–Thurs. 11 A.M.–7 P.M., Fri. and Sat. 11 A.M.–9 P.M., Sun. 11 A.M.–8 P.M., $6–10). Go over the South Brunswick River on I-95 and take Exit 29 onto U.S. 17 to find this roadside classic. It serves one of the more sublime pulled-pork sandwiches in a tangy tomato-based sauce you'll encounter.

For good BBQ closer into town on Highway 17, try **Mack's Bar-Be-Que Place** (2809 Glynn Ave./U.S. 17, 912/264-0605, www.macks bbqplace.com, Mon.–Sat. 10:30 A.M.–9 P.M., $5–8), which also has an $8 "Country Buffet" Monday–Friday 11 A.M.–3 P.M.

Right off the riverfront you'll find a fun breakfast and lunch joint with early hours, **Salvador's Deli** (205 Gloucester St., 912/264-1543, Mon.–Fri. 6:30 A.M.–3 P.M., $5–10).

INFORMATION AND SERVICES

The **Brunswick/Golden Isles Visitor Center** (2000 Glynn Ave., 912/264-5337, daily 9 A.M.–5 P.M.) is at the intersection of U.S. 17 and the Torras Causeway to St. Simons Island. It features the famous pot in which the first batch of Brunswick Stew was cooked over the bridge on St. Simons.

A downtown **information station** is in the Ritz Theatre (1530 Newcastle St., 912/262-6934, Tues.–Fri. 9 A.M.–5 P.M., Sat. 10 A.M.–2 P.M.).

The newspaper of record in town is the *Brunswick News* (www.thebrunswick news.com).

The main **U.S. Postal Service office** in downtown Brunswick is at 805 Gloucester Street (912/280-1250).

GETTING THERE AND AROUND

Brunswick is directly off I-95. Take Exit 38 to the Golden Isles Parkway and take a right on U.S. 17. The quickest way to the historic district is to make a right onto Gloucester Street. Though plans and funding for a city-wide public transit system are pending, currently Brunswick has no public transportation to speak of.

Jekyll Island

Few places in the United States have as paradoxical a story as Jekyll Island. Once the playground of the world's richest people—whose indulgence allowed it to escape the overdevelopment that plagues nearby St. Simons—Jekyll then became a dedicated vacation area for Georgians of modest means, by order of the state legislature.

Today, it's somewhere in the middle—a great place for a relaxing, nature-oriented vacation, with some of the perks of luxury owing to its Gilded Age pedigree.

HISTORY

In prehistoric times, Jekyll was mainly a seasonal getaway for Native Americans. Indigenous tribes visited the area during the winter to enjoy its temperate weather and abundant shellfish. The Spanish also knew it well, calling it *Isla de*

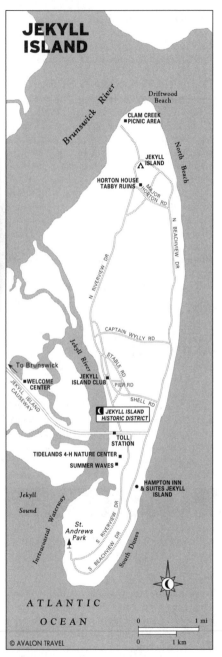

Las Ballenas ("Island of the Whales") for the annual gathering of calving right whale families directly off the coast every winter—a mystical event that happens to this day.

After securing safe access to the island from the Creeks in 1733, Georgia's founder General James Oglethorpe gave the island its modern name, after his friend Sir Joseph Jekyll. The first English settler was Major William Horton in 1735, recipient of a land grant from the general, and the tabby ruins of one of Horton's homes remain today. A Frenchman, Christophe Du Bignon, purchased the island in 1800 and remained a leading figure.

Another mysterious event came in 1858, when Jekyll Island was the final port of entry for the infamous voyage of *The Wanderer,* the last American slave ship. After intercepting the ship and its contraband manifest of 409 African slaves—the importation of slaves having been banned in 1807—its owners and crew were put on trial in Savannah.

As a home away from home for America's richest industrialists in the late 1800s and early 1900s—such as J. P. Morgan, William Rockefeller, and William Vanderbilt—Jekyll Island was the unlikely seat of some of the most crucial events in modern American history. It was at the Jekyll Island Club that the Federal Reserve banking system was originated, in a secret convocation of investors and tycoons in 1910. Five years later, AT&T President Theodore Vail, on the grounds of the Club, would listen in on the first transcontinental phone call.

Jekyll's unspoiled beauty prompted the state legislature in 1947 to purchase the island and—ironically, considering the island's former history—declare it a totally accessible "playground" for Georgians of low-to-middle income (though a causeway wasn't completed until the mid-1950s). This stated public mission is why prices on the island—currently administered on behalf of the state by the Jekyll Island Authority—have stayed so low and development has stayed so well managed.

Every so often a controversial redevelopment plan is proposed, with the potential to introduce high-dollar resort-style development to parts of Jekyll for the first time since the days of J. P. Morgan and company. Residents and conservationists alike continue to work together to protect this magical barrier island known as "Georgia's Jewel."

ORIENTATION

You'll have to stop at the entrance gate and pay a $5 "parking fee" to gain access to this state-owned island. A friendly attendant will give you a map and newsletter and from there you're free to enjoy the whole island at your leisure.

As you dead-end into Beachview Drive, you're faced with a decision to turn either left or right. Most scenic and social activity is to the north, with the left turn. For more peaceful beach-oriented activity with few services, turn right and head south. One historical reason for the lesser development at the south end is due to the fact that segregation laws were still in effect after the state's purchase of Jekyll in 1947. African American facilities were centered on the south end, while white activities went north.

SIGHTS
◖ Jekyll Island Historic District

A living link to one of the most glamorous eras of American history, the Jekyll Island Historic District is also one of the largest ongoing restoration projects in the southeastern United States. A visit to this 240-acre riverfront area is like stepping back in time to the Gilded Age, with croquet grounds, manicured gardens, and even ferry boats with names like the *Rockefeller* and the *J. P. Morgan.*

The Historic District essentially comprises the buildings and grounds of the old **Jekyll Island Club,** not only a full-service resort complex—consisting of the main building and several amazing "cottages" that are mansions in and of themselves—but a sort of living history exhibit chronicling that time when Jekyll was a gathering place for the world's richest and most influential people.

The Queen Anne–style main clubhouse, with its iconic turret, dates from 1886. But within a couple of years the club had already outgrown it, and the millionaires began building the ornate cottages on the grounds surrounding it.

THE GOLDEN ISLES

© JIM MOREKIS

the legendary Jekyll Island Club

THE GOLDEN ISLES

JEKYLL ISLAND'S MILLIONAIRE'S CLUB

After the Civil War, as the Industrial Revolution gathered momentum seemingly everywhere but Georgia's Golden Isles, a couple of men decided to do something to break the foggy miasma of Reconstruction that had settled into the area, and make some money in the process.

In the late 1870s, John Eugene DuBignon and his brother-in-law Newton Finney came up with a plan to combine DuBignon's long family ties to Jekyll with Finney's extensive Wall Street connections in order to turn Jekyll into an exclusive winter hunting club. Their targeted clientele was a no-brainer: the newly minted mega-tycoons of America's Industrial Age.

Finney found 53 such elite millionaires willing to pony up to become charter members of the venture, dubbed the Jekyll Island Club. Among them were William Vanderbilt, J. P. Morgan, and Joseph Pulitzer. As part of the original business model, in 1886 Finney purchased the island from DuBignon for $125,000.

With the formal opening two years later began Jekyll Island's half-century as a premier playground for America's richest citizens, centered on the Victorian winter homes, called "cottages," built by each member and preserved today in the Historic District. While it was formed as a hunt club, the Jekyll Island Club welcomed the millionaires' families. In the 1920s, the focus began shifting to golf, and you can still play a portion of the historic course at the Club today.

By 1900, the Club's membership represented a sixth of the world's wealth. And the word "exclusive" has never been more appropriate: Non-members were not allowed to enjoy the facilities, regardless of social stature. Winston Churchill and even President McKinley were refused admission.

As the mega-rich are wont to do even today, these influential men often mixed business with pleasure. In 1910, secret meetings of the so-called "First Name Club" led to the development of the Aldrich Plan that laid the groundwork for the modern Federal Reserve System. Under assumed names, Senator Nelson Aldrich, Assistant Treasury Secretary A. Piatt Andrew, Banker's Trust Vice President Benjamin Strong, National City Bank President Frank Vanderlip, investment banker Paul Warburg, and J. P. Morgan partner Henry P. Davison came into the Club with the cover story of participating in a duck hunt.

After they arrived by train at Brunswick, the stationmaster told them the cat was out of the bag and a gaggle of reporters had already gathered. But Davison took the stationmaster aside, saying, "Come out, old man, I will tell you a story." Returning a few minutes later, Davison told his colleagues, "That's all right. They won't give us away." What Davison's "story" was remains a mystery, but it must have been a pretty compelling one.

A few years later, AT&T president Theodore Vail, nursing a broken leg at his Mound Cottage on Jekyll, participated in the first transcontinental telephone call on January 25, 1915, between New York City, San Francisco, and the special line strung down the coast from New York and across Jekyll Sound to the Club grounds. Also on the line were the telephone's inventor Alexander Graham Bell, his assistant Thomas Watson, the mayors of New York and San Francisco, and President Woodrow Wilson himself.

The millionaires continued to frolic on Jekyll through the Great Depression, but worsening international economic conditions reduced membership, even though the cost of membership was lowered in 1933. The outbreak of World War II and the resulting drain of labor into the armed forces put a further cramp into the Club's workings, and it finally closed for good in 1942.

By the time prowling German U-boats began appearing off the Georgia coast, prompting island-wide blackouts, the Jekyll Island Club era already seemed like ancient history. The state would acquire the island after the war in 1947, turning the once-exclusive playground of millionaires into a playground for all the people.

The Chicora cottage is gone, demolished after the supposedly accidental gunfire death of Edwin Gould in 1917, with only a hole in the ground remaining, but most of the others have been fully restored as lodgings.

In 2000, a renovation took place for the most magnificent outbuilding, the 24-bedroom Crane Cottage, a Mediterranean villa that also hosts a fine restaurant. The most recent renovation was the 2010 reopening of the Indian Mound Cottage, once William Rockefeller's vacation getaway, to tours.

The **Jekyll Island Museum** (100 Stable Rd., 912/635-4036, www.jekyllisland.com, daily 9 A.M.–5 P.M., free), in the Historic District at the old Club stables, houses some good history exhibits. The Museum also provides a number of guided, themed tours (11 A.M., 1 P.M., 3 P.M., $16 adults, $8 for children 6–12) focusing on the Historic District, from the popular "Passport to the Century" (which includes entrance to two restored cottages) to "In the Service of Others" (focusing on the support staff of the golden age of the Jekyll Island Club). You can also purchase a guidebook for self-guided tours of the Historic District.

Georgia Sea Turtle Center

Within the grounds of the Historic District in a whimsically renovated, historic 1903 building is the Georgia Sea Turtle Center (214 Stable Rd., 912/635-4444, www.georgiaseaturtlecenter.org, Mon. 10 A.M.–2 P.M., Tues.–Sun. 9 A.M.–5 P.M., $6 adults, $4 children), which features interactive exhibits on these important marine creatures, for whom Jekyll Island is a major nesting ground. Don't miss the attached rehabilitation building, where you can see the Center's turtles in various states of treatment and rehabilitation before being released into the wild. Children and adults alike will enjoy this unique opportunity to see these creatures up close and learn about the latest efforts to protect them.

Helping to raise awareness about the need to protect the nesting areas of the big loggerheads that lay eggs on Jekyll each summer, the Sea Turtle Center also guides nighttime tours at 8:30 and 9:30 P.M. on the beach, in order to explain about the animals and their habitat and hopefully to see some loggerheads in action. Walks begin in early June and end in August. These fill up fast, so make reservations in advance.

Driftwood Beach

Barrier islands like Jekyll are in a constant state of southward flux, as currents erode the north end and push sand down the beach to the south end. Hence the creation of Driftwood Beach, as the soil erodes from under the large trees, causing them to fall and settle into the sand. In addition to a naturalist's wonderland, it's also a starkly beautiful and strangely romantic spot.

The newsletter you get as you enter the island has a map with Driftwood Beach on it, but here's a tip: Drive north on Beachview until you see a pullover on your right immediately after the Villas By The Sea (there's no signage). Park and take the short trail through the maritime forest and you'll find yourself right there among the fallen trees and sand.

© NORMANACK

Jekyll Island's Driftwood Beach

Horton House Tabby Ruins

Round the curve and go south on Riverview Drive, and you'll see the large frame of a two-story house on the left (east) side of the road. That is the ruins of the old Horton House, built by Jekyll's original English-speaking setter, William Horton. Horton's house has survived two wars, a couple of hurricanes, and a clumsy restoration in 1898 to its current state of preservation at the hands of the Jekyll Island Authority and various federal, state, and local partners.

His first house, also made of tabby, was burned by the Spanish during their retreat after losing the Battle of Bloody Marsh on nearby St. Simons Island. But the intrepid major rebuilt on the same spot in 1742, continuing to farm barley and indigo on the surrounding grounds as well as hosting Georgia's first brewery, ruins of which are nearby.

Frenchman Christophe Poulain Du Bignon would live in the Horton House for awhile after purchasing the island in the 1790s. Across the street from the house is the poignant little **Du Bignon Cemetery,** around which winds a nicely done pedestrian/bike path overlooking one of the most beautiful areas of marsh you'll see in all the Golden Isles.

ENTERTAINMENT AND EVENTS

There's no real nightlife to speak of on Jekyll, it being intended for quiet, affordable daytime relaxation. The focus instead is on several annual events held at the **Jekyll Island Convention Center** (1 N. Beachview Dr., 912/635-3400), which is likely to face major renovation if not outright replacement within the next few years.

In the beginning of the new year comes one of the area's most beloved and well-attended events, the **Jekyll Island Bluegrass Festival** (www.aandabluegrass.com). Many of the genre's biggest traditional names come to play at this casual, multiday gathering. The focus here is on the music, not the trappings, so come prepared to enjoy wall-to-wall bluegrass, played by the best in the business. Keep in mind that during this weekend the island is awash in RVs from all over the country, so if you're camping you better make reservations.

In September as the harvest comes in off the boats, the **Wild Georgia Shrimp and Grits Festival** (www.jekyllisland.com, free admission), seeks to promote the value of the Georgia shrimping industry by focusing on how good the little critters taste in various regional recipes.

SPORTS AND RECREATION

Hiking and Biking

Quite simply, Jekyll Island is a paradise for bicyclists and walkers, with a very well-developed and very safe system of paths (totaling about 20 miles) running the entire circumference of the island, going by all major sights, including the Jekyll Island Club in the Historic District. In addition, walkers and bicyclists can enjoy much of the seven miles of beachfront at low tide.

Rent your bikes at **Jekyll Island Miniature Golf** (100 James Rd., 912/635-2648, daily 9 A.M.–8 P.M., $5.25/hr., $11.50/day). Take a left when you dead-end after the entrance gate, then another left.

Bird-Watching

The **Clam Creek Picnic Area** on the island's north end is on the Colonial Coast Birding Trail, and without even trying you will see a wide variety of wading birds and shorebirds. Shell collectors will also have a blast, as will those with a horticultural bent, who will marvel at the variety of species presented in the various ecosystems on the island, from beach to marsh hammock to maritime forest.

Golf and Tennis

True to Jekyll Island's intended role as a playground for Georgians of low-to-medium income, its golf and tennis facilities—all centrally located at the middle of the island—are quite reasonably priced.

The **Jekyll Island Golf Resort** (322 Captain Wylly Rd., 912/635-2368, www.jekyll island.com, $40–60 green fees) comprises the largest public golf resort in Georgia. A total of 63 holes on four courses—Pine Lakes, Indian

Mound, Oleander, and Ocean Dunes (nine holes)—await. Check the website for "golf passport" packages that include local lodging.

The adjacent **Jekyll Island Tennis Center** (400 Captain Wylly Rd., 912/635-3154, www .gate.net/~jitc, $25/hr.) boasts 13 courts, seven of them lighted, as well as a pro shop (daily 9 A.M.–6 P.M.).

If a different kind of golf is your thing, try **Jekyll Island Miniature Golf** (100 James Rd., 912/635-2648, Sun.–Thurs. 9 A.M.–8 P.M., Fri. and Sat. 9 A.M.–10 P.M., $6).

Fishing

Continuing north on Beachview Drive at the very top of the island is the well-done **Clam Creek Picnic Area** (daily dawn–dusk). This free facility on the Colonial Coast Birding Trail has a spacious fishing pier over the Jekyll River and a trailhead through the woods and out onto the beach. About a 20-minute walk on the sand gets you to Driftwood Beach from the other side.

A good local fishing charter company is Captain Vernon Reynolds' **Coastal Expeditions** (3202 E. 3rd St., 912/265-0392, www.coastalcharterfishing.com), departing from the Jekyll Harbor Marina. Half-day and full-day trips are available; call for rates.

Kayaking and Boating

Most kayaking activity in the area centers on St. Simons across the sound. But **Tidelands 4-H Nature Center** (100 Riverview Dr., 912/635-5032, www.tidelands4h.org) offers a variety of Jekyll-oriented guided kayak tours and also rents kayaks and canoes March–October.

Water Parks

Summer Waves (210 S. Riverview Dr., 912/635-2074, www.jekyllisland.com, Memorial Day–Labor Day, $19.95 adults, $15.95 for children under 48 inches tall) is just what the doctor ordered for kids with a surplus of energy. The 11-acre facility has a separate section for toddlers to splash around in, with the requisite more daring rides for hard-charging preteens. Hours vary, so call ahead.

Horseback Riding and Tours

Victoria's Carriages and Trail (100 Stable Rd., 912/635-9500, Mon.–Sat. 11 A.M.–4 P.M.) offers numerous options, both on horseback as well as in a horse-drawn carriage. Carriage tours of the island depart every hour 11 A.M.–4 P.M. ($15 adults, $7 children). There's a night ride 6–8 P.M. ($38 per couple).

Horseback rides include a one-hour beach ride that leaves at 11 A.M., 1 P.M., and 3 P.M. ($55) and a sunset ride at 6:30 P.M. ($65) that lasts a little over an hour.

Victoria's is at the entrance to the Clam Creek Picnic Area on the north end of the island directly across the street from the Jekyll Island campground.

The **Tidelands 4-H Center** (912/635-5032) gives 1.5–2-hour Marsh Walks leaving Mondays at 9 A.M. from Clam Creek Picnic Area ($5 adults, $3 children), and Beach Walks ($5 adults, $3 children) leaving Wednesdays at 9 A.M. from the St. Andrews Picnic area and Fridays at 9 A.M. from South Dunes Picnic Area.

Captain Vernon Reynolds's **Coastal Expeditions** (3202 E. 3rd St., 912/265-0392, www.coastalcharterfishing.com, $24 adults, $10 children) provides dolphin tours March–May Tuesday–Saturday at 1:30 P.M., and three trips daily June–August.

ACCOMMODATIONS
Under $150

While most bargain lodging on Jekyll is sadly sub-par, the old **Days Inn** (60 S. Beachview Dr., 912/635-9800, www.daysinnjekyll.com, $100) has seen a remodeling lately and is the best choice if budget is a concern (and you don't want to camp, that is). It has a good location on the south side of the island with nice ocean views.

$150-300

Any discussion of lodging on Jekyll Island begins with the legendary ◖ **Jekyll Island Club** (371 Riverview Dr., 800/535-9547, www.jekyll club.com, $199–490), which is reasonably priced considering its history, postcard-perfect setting, and delightful rooms. Some of its 157 rooms in the club and annex areas are available for under $200 a night, and even the finest, the Presidential Suite, tops out at under $500 in the high season of March–October.

While 60 rooms are in the main Club building, several outlying cottages, chief among them the Crane, Cherokee, and Sans Souci Cottages, are also available. All rates include use of the big outdoor pool overlooking the river, and a neat amenity is a choice of meal plans for an extra daily fee.

Despite its auspicious beginnings, the Club has not been a total success story. The state tried to run it as a resort in the 1950s and '60s, but gave up in 1971. With Historic Landmark District status coming in 1978, restoration wasn't far behind, and the Club was first run as a Radisson. Now operated by Landmark, the Club is one of the "Historic Hotels of America" as ranked by the National Trust for Historic Preservation.

Keep in mind that not all the fixtures are original and the present interior design scheme was done with an eye to current commercial taste (those crusty old millionaires would never have gone for pastels).

The first hotel built on the island in 35 years, the brand-new **◖ Hampton Inn & Suites Jekyll Island** (200 S. Beachview Dr., 912/635-3733, www.hamptoninn.com, $180–210) was built according to an exacting set of conservation guidelines, conserving much of the original tree canopy and various low-impact design and building techniques. Quite simply, it's one of the best eco-friendly hotel designs I've experienced. An elevated wooden walkway to the beach preserves as much of the natural dunescape as possible, though keep in mind that the tradeoff is that you can't see the ocean from the hotel. Though the beach isn't far away, the walk-in, saltwater pool is particularly enjoyable and relaxing.

Camping

One of the niftiest campgrounds in the entire area is the **Jekyll Island Campground** (197 Riverview Dr., 912/635-3021). It's a friendly place with an excellent location at the north end of the island—a short drive or bike ride from just about anything and directly across the street from the Clam Creek Picnic Area, with easy beach access. There are more than 200 sites, from tent to full-service pull-through

© JIM MOREKIS

Jekyll Island Campground is a great place to spend the night.

RV sites. Tent sites are around $25 and RV sites are about $32. There's a two-night minimum on weekends and a three-night minimum on holiday and special event weekends. Reservations recommended.

FOOD

Cuisine offerings are few and far between on Jekyll. I'd suggest you patronize one of the three dining facilities at the **Jekyll Island Club** (371 Riverview Dr.), which are all open to the public. They're not only delicious, but pretty reasonable as well, considering the swank setting.

My favorite is the **C** **Courtyard at Crane** (912/635-2400, lunch Sun.–Fri. 11 A.M.–4 P.M., Sat. 11 A.M.–2 P.M., dinner Sun.–Thurs. 5:30–9 P.M., $27–38). In the circa-1917, beautifully restored Crane Cottage, one of the old tycoon villas, the Courtyard offers romantic evening dining (call for reservations) as well as tasty and stylish lunch dining, in the alfresco courtyard area or inside. The lunch menu—a great deal for the quality—is Mediterranean heavy, with wraps, sandwiches, and soups. The dinner menu moves more toward wine country casual chic, with a lot of pork, veal, and beef dishes to go with the requisite fresh seafood. As a plus, the coffee is great—not at all a given in Southern restaurants. Casual dress OK.

For a real and figurative taste of history, make a reservation at the **Grand Dining Room** (912/635-2400, breakfast Mon.–Sat. 7–11 A.M., Sun. 7–10 A.M., lunch Mon.–Sat. 11:30 A.M.–2 P.M., Sunday brunch 10:45 A.M.–2 P.M., dinner Mon.–Sun. 6–10 P.M., dinner $26–35), the Club's full-service restaurant. Focusing on Continental cuisine—ordered either à la carte or as a prix fixe "sunset dinner"—the Dining Room features a pianist each evening and for Sunday brunch. Jackets or collared shirts are required for men.

For a tasty breakfast, lunch, or dinner on the go and/or at odd hours, check out **Café Solterra** (912/635-2600, daily 7 A.M.–10 P.M.), great for deli-type food and equipped with Starbucks coffee.

There are two places for seaside dining and

cocktails at the historic Jekyll Island Club Wharf. **Latitude 31** (1 Pier Rd., 912/635-3800, www.crossoverjekyll.com, Tues.–Sun. 5:30–10 P.M., $15–25, no reservations) is an upscale seafood-oriented fine-dining place, while the attached **Rah Bar** (Tues.–Sat. 11 A.M.–close, Sun. 1 P.M.–close, depending on weather) serves up oysters and shellfish in a very casual setting; try the Lowcountry boil or the crab legs.

INFORMATION AND SERVICES

The **Jekyll Island Visitor Center** (901 Downing Musgrove Cswy., 912/635-3636, daily 9 A.M.–5 P.M.) is on the long causeway along the marsh before you get to the island. Set in a charming little cottage it shares with the Georgia State Patrol, the Center has a nice gift shop and loads of brochures on the entire Golden Isles region. Don't hesitate to ask questions of the person taking your $5 entrance fee when you get to the island itself.

The **U.S. Postal Service** keeps an outpost at 18 South Beachview Drive (912/635-2625).

GETTING THERE AND AROUND

Jekyll Island is immediately south of Brunswick. Take Exit 38 off I-95 to the Golden Isles Parkway. Take a right onto U.S. 17 and keep going until you cross the huge Sidney Lanier Bridge over the Brunswick River. Take an immediate left at the foot of the bridge onto the Downing Musgrove Cswy. (Jekyll Island Rd.). This long, scenic route over the beautiful marshes eventually takes you directly onto Jekyll, where you'll have to pay a $5 per vehicle fee to get onto the island.

Once on the island, most sites are on the north end (a left as you reach the dead-end at Beachview Dr.). The main circuit route around the island is Beachview Drive, which suitably enough changes into Riverview Drive as it rounds the bend to landward at the north end.

Many visitors choose to bicycle around the island once they're there, which is certainly the best way to experience both the sights and the beach itself at low tide.

St. Simons Island

Despite a certain and somewhat deserved reputation for aloof affluence, the truth is that St. Simons Island is also very visitor-friendly, and there's more to do here than meets the eye. Think of St. Simons—with a year-round population of about 13,000—as a smaller, less-polished Hilton Head and you've got the right idea. For those looking for island-style relaxation with no high-rise, cookie-cutter development—but still all the modern amenities and luxuries—St. Simons fits the bill perfectly.

HISTORY

St. Simons Island and its much smaller, symbiotic neighbor Sea Island (originally Long Island) were well known to Native Americans as a hunting and fishing ground. Eventually the Spanish would have two missions on St. Simons, one at the south end and one at the north end, as well as a town for non-converted native peoples called San Simon, which would eventually give the island its modern name.

A lasting European influence didn't come until 1736 with General James Oglethorpe's construction of Fort Frederica. The fort and surrounding town (also called Frederica) were a key base of operations for the British struggle to evict the Spanish from Georgia—which culminated in the decisive Battle of Bloody Marsh south of the fort—but fell into decline after the Spanish threat subsided.

In the years after American independence, St. Simons woke up from its slumber as acre after acre of virgin live oak was felled to make the massive timbers of new warships for the U.S. Navy, including the USS *Constitution*. In their place was planted a new crop—cotton. The island's antebellum plantations boomed to world-class heights of profit and prestige when the superior strain of the crop known as "Sea Island Cotton" came in the 1820s.

It's on St. Simons in 1803 that one of the most poignant chapters in the dark history of American slavery was written. In one of the first documented slave uprisings in North America, a group of slaves from the Igbo region of West Africa escaped custody and took over the ship that was transporting them to St. Simons from Savannah. But rather than do any further violence, immediately upon reaching shore on the west side of St. Simons, the slaves essentially committed mass suicide by walking into the swampy waters nearby, which forever after would be known as Ebo Landing (a corruption of the original Igbo).

The Civil War came to St. Simons in late 1861 with a Union blockade and invasion, leading Confederate troops to dynamite the lighthouse. Initially St. Simons was a sanctuary for freed slaves from the island's 14 plantations, and by late 1862 over 500 former slaves lived on St. Simons, including Susie King Taylor, who began a school for African American children. But in November of that year all former slaves were dispersed to Hilton Head and Fernandina, Florida.

St. Simons was chosen as one of the implementation sites of General William Sherman's Special Field Order No. 15, the famous "40 acres and a mule" order giving the Sea Islands of South Carolina and Georgia to freed slaves. However, after Sherman's order was quickly rescinded by President Andrew Johnson, life on St. Simons settled back into a disturbingly familiar pattern, with many local African Americans coming back to work the land as before—only as sharecroppers instead of slaves.

The next landmark development for St. Simons didn't come until the building of the first causeway in 1924, which led directly to the island's resort development by the mega-rich industrialist Howard Coffin, of Hudson Motors fame, who also owned nearby Sapelo Island to the north. By 1928, Coffin had completed the Sea Island Golf Club on the grounds of the old Retreat Plantation on the south end of St. Simons Island. He would move on to develop the famous Cloisters resort on Long Island (later Sea Island) itself.

GOLDEN ISLES ON THE PAGE

*And now from the Vast of the Lord will
    the waters of sleep
Roll in on the souls of men,
But who will reveal to our waking ken
The forms that swim and the shapes
    that creep
Under the waters of sleep?
And I would I could know what swimmeth
    below when the tide comes in
On the length and the breath of the
    marvelous marshes of Glynn.*
                                    – Sidney Lanier

Many authors have been inspired by their time in the Golden Isles, whether to pen flights of poetic fancy, page-turning novels, or politically oriented chronicles. Here are a few of the most notable names:

- Sidney Lanier: Born in Macon, Georgia, Lanier was a renowned linguist, mathematician, and legal scholar. Fighting as a Confederate during the Civil War, he was captured while commanding a blockade runner and taken to a POW camp in Maryland, where he came down with tuberculosis. After the war, he stayed at his brother-in-law's house in Brunswick to recuperate, and it was during that time that he took up poetry, writing the famous "Marshes of Glynn," quoted above.

- Eugenia Price: Though not originally from St. Simons, Price remains the best-known local cultural figure, setting her "St. Simons Trilogy" there. After relocating to the island in 1965, she stayed there until her death in 1996. She's buried in the Christ Church cemetery on Frederica Road.

- Tina McElroy Ansa: Probably the most notable literary figure currently living on St. Simons Island is award-winning African American author Tina McElroy Ansa. Though few of her books deal with the Golden Isles region, they all deal with life in the South and Ansa is an ardent devotee of St. Simons and its relaxed, friendly ways.

- Fanny Kemble: In 1834, this renowned English actress married Georgia plantation heir Pierce Butler, who would become one of America's largest slave-owners. Horrified by the treatment of Butler's slaves at Butler Island just south of Darien, Georgia, Kemble penned one of the earliest anti-slavery chronicles, *Journal of a Residence on a Georgian Plantation in 1838-1839*. Kemble's disagreement with her husband over slavery hastened their divorce in 1849.

© MOULTRIE CREEK

the Marshes of Glynn, which inspired Sidney Lanier to write his famous poem of the same name

ORIENTATION

Because it's only a short drive from downtown Brunswick on the Torras Causeway, St. Simons has much less of a remote feel than most other Georgia barrier islands, and is much more densely populated than any other Georgia island except for Tybee.

Most visitor-oriented activity on this 12-mile-long, heavily residential island about the size of Manhattan is clustered at the south end, where St. Simons Sound meets the Atlantic. The main reasons to travel north on the island are to golf or visit the historic site of Fort Frederica on the landward side.

The main roads to remember are Kings Way, which turns into Ocean Boulevard as it nears the active south end of the island, "the Village"; Demere Road (pronounced "DEMM-er-ee"), which loops west to east around the little island airport and then south, joining up with Ocean Boulevard down near the Lighthouse; Frederica Road, the dominant north–south artery; and Mallory Street, which runs north–south through the Village area and dead-ends at the Pier on St. Simons Sound. (You'll notice that Mallory Street is sometimes spelled "Mallery," which is actually the correct spelling of the avenue's namesake: Mallery King, child of Thomas King, owner of the historic Retreat Plantation.)

SIGHTS
◖ The Village

Think of "the Village" at the extreme south end of St. Simons as a mix of Tybee's downscale accessibility and Hilton Head's upscale exclusivity. This compact, bustling area only a few blocks long offers not only boutique shops and stylish cafés, but vintage stores and busking musicians. While visitors and residents here tend toward the affluent, they also tend not to be as flashy about it as in some other locales. You'll find the vast majority of quality eating spots, as well as most quality lodging, here.

It's fun to meander down Mallory Drive, casually shopping or noshing, and then make your way out onto the short but fun **St. Simons Pier** to enjoy the breeze and occasional spray coming off the sound.

© JIM MOREKIS

the view of the beach from the St. Simons Pier

© JIM MOREKIS

St. Simons Lighthouse Museum

St. Simons Lighthouse Museum

Unlike many East Coast lighthouses, which tend to be in hard-to-reach places, anyone can walk right up to the St. Simons Lighthouse Museum (101 12th St., 912/638-4666, www.saintsimonslighthouse.org, Mon.–Sat. 10 A.M.–5 P.M., Sun. 1:30–5 P.M., $6 adults, $3 children). Once inside, you can enjoy the museum's exhibit and take the 129 steps up to the top of the 104-foot beacon—which is, unusually, still active—for a gorgeous view of the island and the ocean beyond. (The museum offers a "Family of Four" package admission—$25 for two adults and two children, as well as a combo ticket to the nearby Maritime Center for $10 adults, $5 children.)

The first lighthouse on the spot came about after planter John Couper sold this land, known as Couper's Point, to the government in 1804 for a dollar. This original beacon was destroyed by retreating Confederate troops in 1862 to hinder Union navigation on the coast. Traces of its foundations are near the current facility. The current lighthouse dates from 1872, built by Irishman Charles Cluskey, responsible for a lot of Greek Revival architecture up and down the Georgia coast. Attached to the lighthouse is the oldest brick structure in Glynn County, the 1872 lighthouse keeper's cottage, now the museum and gift shop run by the Coastal Georgia Historical Society.

Maritime Center

A short walk from the lighthouse and likewise administered by the Coastal Georgia Historical Society, the Maritime Center (4201 First St., 912/638-4666, www.saintsimonslighthouse.org, Mon.–Sat. 10 A.M.–5 P.M., Sun. 1:30–5 P.M., $6 adults, $3 children) is at the historic East Beach Coast Guard Station. Authorized by President Franklin Roosevelt in 1933 and completed in 1937 by the Works Progress Administration, the East Beach Station took part in military action in World War II, an episode chronicled in exhibits at the Maritime Center. On April 8, 1942, the German U-boat U-123 torpedoed and sank two cargo ships off the coast of St. Simons Island. The Coast Guardsmen of East Beach station mounted a full rescue effort, saving many crewmen of the merchant ships, including one ship's canine mascot.

With the increase in tourism to St. Simons in the late 20th century, the Coast Guard's job was made more difficult as traffic and development hindered the route from the station, where they kept watch, to their boathouse on the Frederica River on the other side of the island. The Coast Guard's tenure on East Beach ended after a fire in 1993 burned down their boathouse. Two years later the station was decommissioned and the Coasties moved to a new station in Brunswick.

The Maritime Center offers a "Family of Four" package admission—$25 for two adults and two children, as well as a combo ticket to the St. Simons Lighthouse for $10 adults, $5 children.

◖ Fort Frederica National Monument

The starkly beautiful, historically vital Fort Frederica National Monument (Frederica

Rd., 912/638-3639, www.nps.gov/fofr, daily 9 A.M.–5 P.M., $3 adults, free for children under 15) lies on the landward side of the island, overlooking the key waterway of the Frederica River. Established by General James Oglethorpe in 1736 to protect Georgia's southern flank from the Spanish, the fort (as well as the village that sprang up around it, in which the Wesley brothers preached for a short time) was named for Frederick Louis, the Prince of Wales. The feminine "a" was added as a suffix to distinguish it from the older Fort Frederick in South Carolina.

Unlike the more imposing post-colonial installations, like Fort Pulaski on Tybee Island, Frederica is compact and easy to take in, and its tabby construction is more photogenic and pleasing to the eye. Examine the parapets of the sturdy little fortress and instantly see why this was such a strategic location, guarding the approach to the great Altamaha River. Take in the accompanying exhibits in the visitors center, including a 23-minute film every half-hour 9 A.M.–4 P.M. A park ranger also gives informative talks throughout the day.

Though the fort itself was not directly involved in a military clash, its garrison took part in the unsuccessful attack on St. Augustine, Florida in 1740 and was the force that swept south on St. Simons to decisively defeat the Spanish at Bloody Marsh two years later. With the ebbing of the Spanish threat, the need for a military presence on St. Simons subsided. By 1749 the fort was no longer active and the town of Frederica was largely destroyed in a disastrous fire in 1758. Fort Frederica became a National Monument in 1936 and was put on the National Register of Historic Places in 1966.

Bloody Marsh Battlefield

There's not a lot to see at the site of the Battle of Bloody Marsh (Frederica Rd., 912/638-3639, www.nps.gov/fofr, daily 8 A.M.–4 P.M., free), but—as with the similarly stirring site of Custer's Last Stand at the Little Bighorn—your imagination fills in the gaps, giving it perhaps more emotional impact than other, more substantial historic sites.

Essentially just a few interpretive signs overlooking a beautiful piece of salt marsh, the site is believed to be near the place where British soldiers from nearby Fort Frederica ambushed a force of Spanish regulars on their way to besiege the fort. Frederica's garrison, the 42nd Regiment of Foot, was augmented by a company of tough Scottish Highlanders from Darien, Georgia who legend says attacked to the tune of bagpipes.

Though the battle wasn't actually that "bloody"—some accounts say the Spanish lost only seven men—the stout British presence convinced the Spanish to leave St. Simons a few days later, never again to project their once-potent military power that far north in America. You'll often hear it claimed that the Battle of Bloody Marsh is the reason we speak English instead of Spanish. That's certainly hyperbolic, but there's no doubt that had the battle gone the other way the course of American history would have been changed.

While the Battle of Bloody Marsh site is part of the National Park Service's Fort Frederica site, it's not at the same location. Get to the battlefield from the fort by taking Frederica Road south, and then a left (east) on Demere Road. The site is on your left as Demere veers right, in the 1800 block.

Christ Church

Just down the road from Fort Frederica is historic Christ Church (6329 Frederica Rd., 912/638-8683, www.christchurchfrederica .org, daily 2–5 P.M.). Though the first sanctuary dates from 1820, the original congregation at the now-defunct town of Frederica held services under the oaks at the site as early as 1736. The founder of Methodism, John Wesley, and his brother Charles both ministered to island residents during 1736 and 1737.

The original church was rendered unusable by Union occupation during the Civil War. A new church, the one you see today, was funded and built in 1883 by a local mill owner, Anson Dodge, as a memorial to his first wife. But Christ Church's claim to fame in modern culture is as the setting of local novelist Eugenia

Price's *The Beloved Invader,* the first work in her Georgia trilogy. The late Price, who died in 1996, is buried in the church cemetery.

Tours

St. Simons Island Trolley Tours (912/638-8954, www.stsimonstours.com, daily 11 A.M., $22 adults, $10 children 4–12, under 4 free) offers just that, a ride around the island in comparative comfort, leaving from the Pier.

ENTERTAINMENT AND EVENTS
Nightlife

St. Simons is far from Charleston's or Savannah's league when it comes to partying, but there is a fairly active nightlife scene, with a strong dose of island casual. Unlike some areas this far south on the Georgia coast, there's usually a sizeable contingent of young people out looking for a good time.

The island's premier club, **Rafters Blues and Raw Bar** (315½ Mallory St., 912/634-9755, www.raftersblues.com, Mon.–Sat. 4:30 P.M.–2 A.M.), known simply as "Rafters," brings in live music most every Thursday, Friday, and Saturday night, focusing on the best acts on the regional rock circuit.

A popular meeting-and-eating place is **Loco's Deli & Pub** (2463 Demere Rd., 912/634-2002, www.locosgrill.com, daily 11 A.M.–11 P.M.), which has a full menu heavy on burgers and finger food, along with live music on weekends. A similar blend of food, libation, and live music is at **Ziggy Mahoney's** (5514 Frederica Rd., 912/634-0999, Thurs.–Sat. 8 P.M.–2 A.M.).

Inside the Village Inn is the popular nightspot, the **Village Pub** (500 Mallory St., 912/634-6056, www.villageinnandpub.com, Mon.–Sat. 5 P.M.–midnight, Sun. 5–10 P.M.). Slightly more upscale than most watering holes on the island, this is the best place for a quality martini or other premium cocktail.

Performing Arts

Because of its close proximity to Brunswick, a short drive over the bridge, St. Simons has a symbiotic relationship with that larger city in areas of art and culture.

Each summer, beginning Memorial Day weekend and continuing into September, there are several "Jazz in the Park" concerts by regional artists. The shows are usually on Sundays at 7–9 P.M. on the lawn of the St. Simons Lighthouse, and the beautiful setting and calming breeze is a delight. Admission is charged; bring a chair or blanket if you like.

Cinema

The island has its own multiplex, the **Island Cinemas 7** (44 Cinema Lane, 912/634-9100, www.georgiatheatrecompany.com).

SHOPPING

Most shopping on St. Simons is centered in the Village and is a typical beach town mix of hardware/tackle and casual clothing and souvenir stores. A funky highlight is **Beachview Books** (215 Mallory St., 912/638-7282, Mon.–Sat. 10:30 A.M.–5:30 P.M., Sun. 11:30 A.M.–3 P.M.), a rambling used bookstore with lots of regional and local goodies, including books by the late great local author Eugenia Price. The best antique shop in this part of town is **Village Mews** (504 Beachview Dr., 912/634-1235, Mon.–Sat. 10 A.M.–5 P.M.).

The closest thing to a mall is farther north on St. Simons at **Redfern Village** with some cute indie stores like **Beach Cottage Linens** (912/634-2000, Mon.–Fri. 10 A.M.–5:30 P.M., Sat. 10 A.M.–5 P.M.), **Thomas P. Dent Clothiers** (912/638-3118, Mon.–Sat. 9:30 A.M.–6 P.M.), and the craftsy **Rarebbits and Pieces** (912/638-2866, Mon.–Sat. 10 A.M.–5:30 P.M.). Redfern Village is on Frederica Road, one traffic light past the corner of Frederica and Demere.

SPORTS AND RECREATION
Beaches

Keep going from the pier past the lighthouse to find **Massengale Park** (daily dawn–dusk), with a playground, picnic tables, and restrooms right off the beach on the Atlantic side. The beach itself on St. Simons is underwhelming compared to some in these parts, but nonetheless it's easily accessible from the pier area and good for a romantic stroll if it's not high tide. There's a great playground, Neptune Park, right next to the pier overlooking the waterfront.

Kayaking and Boating

With its relatively sheltered landward side nestled in the marsh and an abundance of wildlife, St. Simons Island is an outstanding kayaking site, attracting connoisseurs from all over.

A good spot to put in on the Frederica River is the **Golden Isles Marina** (206 Marina Dr., 912/634-1128, www.gimarina.com), which is actually on little Lanier Island on the Torras Causeway right before you enter St. Simons proper. For a real adventure, put in at the ramp at the end of South Harrington Street off Frederica Road, which will take you out Village Creek on the seaward side of the island.

Undoubtedly the best kayaking outfitter and tour operator in this part of the Golden Isles is **SouthEast Adventure Outfitters** (313 Mallory St., 912/638-6732, www.southeast adventure.com, daily 10 A.M.–6 P.M.), which also has a location in nearby Brunswick. Michael Gowen and company offer an extensive range of guided tours all over the St. Simons marsh and sound area, as well as trips to undeveloped Little St. Simons Island to the north. Prices vary, so call or go to the website for information.

Hiking and Biking

Like Jekyll Island, St. Simons is a great place for bicyclists. Bike paths go all over the island, and a special kick is riding on the beach almost the whole length of the island (but only at high tide!).

There are plenty of bike rental spots, with rates generally $15–20 per day depending on season. The best place to rent bikes is **Monkey Wrench Bicycles** (1700 Frederica Rd., 912/634-5551).

You can rent another kind of pedal-power at **Wheel Fun Rentals** (532 Ocean Blvd., 912/634-0606), which deals in four-seat pedaled carts with steering wheels.

Golf and Tennis

A popular place for both sports is the **Sea Palms Golf and Tennis Resort** (5445 Frederica Rd., 800/841-6268, www.seapalms .com, $70–80 green fees) in the middle of the island, with three nine-hole public courses and three clay courts.

The **Sea Island Golf Club** (100 Retreat Rd., 800/732-4752, www.seaisland.com, $185–260 green fees) on the old Retreat Plantation as you first come onto the island has two award-winning 18-hole courses: the Seaside and the Plantation.

Another public course is the 18-hole **Hampton Club** (100 Tabbystone Rd., 912/634-0255, www.hamptonclub.com, green fees $95) on the north side of the island, part of the King and Prince Beach and Golf Resort.

ACCOMMODATIONS
Under $150

A charming and reasonable place a stone's throw from the Village is **(Queens Court** (437 Kings Way, 912/638-8459, $85–135), a traditional roadside motel from the late '40s, with modern upgrades including a nice outdoor pool in the central courtyard area. Despite its convenient location, you'll feel fairly secluded.

One of the most interesting lodgings in the Lowcountry and Georgia coast is **Epworth by the Sea** (100 Arthur J. Moore Dr., 912/638-8688, www.epworthbythesea.org, $90–100). This Methodist retreat in the center of the island boasts an entire complex of freestanding motels and lodges on its grounds, in various styles and configurations. Cafeteria-style meetings are the order of the day, and there are plenty of recreational activities on-site, including tennis, volleyball, baseball, football, soccer, and basketball. They also rent bikes, which is always a great way to get around St. Simons. Everyone loves the **Lovely Lane Chapel,** a picturesque sanctuary that's a favorite spot for weddings and holds worship services each Sunday at 8:45 A.M. (casual dress OK). Researchers can utilize the resources of the **Arthur J. Moore Methodist Museum and Library** (Tues.–Sat. 9 A.M.–4 P.M.).

$150-300

The most well-known lodging on St. Simons Island is the **(King and Prince Beach and Golf Resort** (201 Arnold Rd., 800/342-0212, $249–320). Originally opened as a dance club in 1935, the King and Prince brings a swank, old-school glamour similar to the Jekyll Island Club (though less imposing). And like the Jekyll Island Club, the King and Prince is also designated as one of the Historic Hotels of America.

Its nearly 200 rooms are spread out over a complex that includes several buildings, including the historic main building, beach villas, and freestanding guesthouses. Some standard rooms can go for under $200 even in the spring high season. Winter rates for all rooms are appreciably lower, and represent a great bargain.

For a dining spot overlooking the sea, try the **Blue Dolphin** (lunch daily 11 A.M.–4 P.M., dinner daily 5–10 P.M., $15–30). The Resort's Hampton Club provides golf for guests and the public.

You couldn't ask for a better location than the **St. Simons' Inn by the Lighthouse** (609 Beachview Dr., 912/638-1101, www.saintsimonsinn.com, $120–300), which is indeed in the shadow of the historic lighthouse and right next to the hopping Village area. A so-called "condo-hotel," each of the standard and deluxe suites at the Inn are individually owned by off-site owners-however, each guest gets full maid service and a complimentary breakfast.

An interesting B&B on the island that's also within walking distance of most of the action on the south end is the 28-room **Village Inn & Pub** (500 Mallory St., 912/634-6056, www.villageinnandpub.com, $160–245), nestled among shady palm trees and live oaks. The Pub, a popular local hangout in a renovated 1930 cottage, is a nice plus.

Over $300

Affiliated with the Sea Island Resort, the **Lodge at Sea Island** (100 Retreat Ave., 912/638-3611, $650–2500) is actually on the south end of St. Simons Island on the old Retreat Plantation.

Its grand assortment of 40 rooms and suites all have great views of either the Atlantic Ocean, the associated Plantation Course links, or both. Full butler service makes this an especially pampered and aristocratic stay.

FOOD

While the ambience at St. Simons has an upscale feel, don't feel like you have to dress up to get a bite to eat—the emphasis is on relaxation and having a good time.

Breakfast and Brunch

(Dressner's Village Cafe (223 Mallory St., 912/634-1217, www.dressners.com, Mon.–Fri. 7:30 A.M.–7 P.M., Sat. and Sun. 8 A.M.–7 P.M., $5–10) right in the middle of the Village's bustle is one of the island's most popular places, but still with enough seats so you usually don't have to wait. Lunches are very good, with an awesome blackened grouper sandwich and great burgers. But breakfast all day is the real attraction here, and includes omelets, steak and eggs, and a full range of griddle items.

Named for the birthday that the original three co-owners share, **Fourth of May Deli** (444 Ocean Blvd., 912/638-5444, breakfast daily 7 A.M.–1 P.M., lunch daily 11 A.M.–9 P.M., $8–20) is a popular breakfast and lunch place in the Village. Breakfast focuses on specialties like eggs Benedict and huevos rancheros, along with some fantastic breakfast burritos, a comparative rarity in the South.

Seafood

Despite its somewhat unappetizing name, **Mullet Bay** (512 Ocean Blvd., 912/634-9977, daily 11:30 A.M.–10 P.M., $7–18) in the Village is a favorite, good old-fashioned Southern seafood place, the kind where you get a big fried platter with two sides and hushpuppies.

A popular seafood place right in the action in the Village is **(Barbara Jean's** (214 Mallory St., 912/634-6500, www.barbarajeans.com, Sun.–Thurs. 11 A.M.–9 P.M., Fri.–Sat. 11 A.M.–10 P.M., $7–20), which also has a great variety of imaginative veggie dishes to go along with its formidable seafood menu, including some excellent she-crab soup and crab cakes. They also have plenty of good landlubber treats for those not inclined to the marine critters.

Fine Dining

◖ **J. Mac's Island Restaurant** (407 Mallory St., 912/634-0403, www.jmacsislandrestaurant .com, Tues.–Sat. 6–9 P.M., $20–30) is the Village's high-end restaurant, one that wouldn't be out of place in downtown Charleston or Savannah. Owner J. Mac Mason and head chef Connor Rankin conspire to bring a fresh take on Southern and seafood classics, with adventurous entrées like seared "Creamsicle" marlin with jumbo asparagus and sweet corn puree—seared filet with gorgonzola and herb gratin.

Inside the King and Prince Resort, you'll find the old-school glory of the **Blue Dolphin** (201 Arnold Rd., 800/342-0212, lunch daily 11 A.M.–4 P.M., dinner daily 5–10 P.M., $15–30), redolent of the Great Gatsby era. The Blue Dolphin claims to be the only oceanfront dining on the island, and the views are certainly magnificent.

INFORMATION AND SERVICES

The **St. Simons Visitors Center** (530-B Beachview Dr., 912/638-9014, www.bgivb .com, daily 9 A.M.–5 P.M.) is in the St. Simons Casino Building near Neptune Park and the Village.

The main newspaper in St. Simons is the **Brunswick News** (www.thebrunswicknews .com).

The **U.S. Postal Service** (800/275-8777) has an office at 620 Beachview Drive.

GETTING THERE AND AROUND

Get to St. Simons through the gateway city of Brunswick. Take the Golden Isles Exit 38 off I-95, which will take you to the Golden Isles Parkway. Take a right onto U.S. 17 and look for the intersection with the Torras Causeway, a toll-free road which takes you the short distance onto St. Simons.

Immediately as you cross the Frederica River onto the island, look for a quick right onto

Kings Way to take you directly to the Village area. Or you can take a quick left onto Demere Road to reach Frederica Road and the more northerly portion of the island, where you'll find Fort Frederica and Christ Church.

LITTLE ST. SIMONS ISLAND

This 10,000-acre, privately owned island, accessible only by water, is almost totally undeveloped—thanks to its salt-stressed trees, which discouraged timbering—and boasts seven miles of beautiful beaches.

All activity centers on the circa-1917 ◖ **Lodge on Little St. Simons Island** (1000 Hampton Point Dr., 888/733-5774, www.little stsimonsisland.com, $625 and up), named by *Condé Nast Traveler* as the top U.S. mainland resort in 2007. Within it lies the famed Hunting Lodge, where meals and cocktails are served. With 15 ultra-plush rooms and suites in an assortment of historic buildings, all set amid gorgeous natural beauty—there are five full-time naturalists on staff—the Lodge is a reminder of what St. Simons proper used to look like. Guest count is limited to 30 people.

Getting There and Around

Unless you enlist the aid of a local kayaking charter company, you have to be a guest of the Lodge to have access to Little St. Simons. The ferry, a 15-minute ride, leaves from a landing at the northern end of St. Simons at the end of Lawrence Road. Guests have full use of bicycles once on the island and can also request shuttle transportation just about anywhere.

SEA ISLAND

The only way to enjoy Sea Island—basically a tiny appendage of St. Simons facing the Atlantic Ocean—is to be a guest at ◖ **The Sea Island Resort** (888/732-4752, www.seaisland .com, $700 and up). And guests visiting now are truly lucky; the legendary facility, routinely ranked as one of the best resorts on the planet, completed extensive renovations in 2008.

Unfortunately, the economic downturn put the institution into bankruptcy as of this writing; however, they do plan to stay in business.

The rooms at the Resort's premier lodging institution, **The Cloister,** nearly defy description—enveloped in Old World luxury, they also boast 21st-century technology. And the service at The Cloister is equally world-class, featuring 24-hour butler service in the European tradition.

There are hundreds of cottages for rental on Sea Island as well, all of which grant temporary membership in the Sea Island Club and full use of all its many amenities and services.

Getting There and Around

Get to Sea Island by taking Torras Causeway onto the island and then making a left onto Sea Island Causeway, which takes you all the way to the gate marking the only landward entrance to Sea Island.

Darien and McIntosh County

THE GOLDEN ISLES

It doesn't get near the attention or amount of visitors as Savannah to the north or the St. Simons/Jekyll area to the south, but the tiny town of Darien in McIntosh County, Georgia, has an interesting historic pedigree of its own—and is centrally located near some of the best treasures the Georgia coast has to offer, from the Harris Neck National Wildlife Refuge to the sea island of Sapelo.

HISTORY

Unlike Anglophilic Savannah to the north, the Darien area has had a distinctly Scottish flavor almost from the beginning (with the exception of the Spanish mission era, of which almost no trace remains). In 1736, Scottish Highlanders established a settlement at this area at the mouth of the Altamaha River at the bequest of General James Oglethorpe, who no doubt wanted the tough Scots protecting his southern border against the resurgent Spanish.

Though their colony was at the site of an earlier English effort, the abandoned Fort King George, they came up with a new name: Darien, honoring the failed 1697 settlement in Panama. Leading them was John McIntosh Mohr, who would go on to father several sons (who would become famous in their own right) and eventually lend his surname to the county in which Darien was contained.

The Scots brought a singularly populist sentiment to the New World. When Georgia planters lobbied to legalize slavery, which was outlawed by Oglethorpe, the Scots of Darien signed a petition against them in 1739—believed to be the first organized protest of slavery in America. The Darien settlers were also known for keeping more cordial relations with the Native Americans than the area's English settlements. Of course they were a frugal bunch, too, and The Bank of Darien was the largest bank south of Philadelphia in the early 1800s.

Unquestionably Darien's heyday was in that antebellum period, when for a brief time the town was the world's largest exporter of cotton, floated downriver on barges and shipped out through the port of Darien. A prosperous rice culture grew up around the Altamaha estuary as well, relying on the tidal flow of the area's acres and acres of marsh.

Almost none of this period remains, however, because on June 11, 1863, a force of mostly African American Union troops under the command of Colonel Robert G. Shaw (of the movie *Glory* fame) burned Darien to the ground, with all its homes and warehouses going up in smoke.

After the Civil War, lumber became the new cash crop, and Darien once again became a thriving seaport and lumber mill headquarters. Also, the late 1800s saw a new reliance on shrimping and oystering, industries that survive to this day (barely) despite the toll of overfishing and drought.

A different kind of industry prospered in the years after World War II. In those pre-Interstate days, U.S. 17 was the main route south to booming Florida. McIntosh County got a bad reputation for "clip joints," which would fleece gullible travelers with a variety of illegal schemes. This period is recounted in the best seller *Praying for Sheetrock* by Melissa Fay Greene.

SIGHTS
Smallest Church in North America

While several other churches claim that title, in any case fans of the devout and of roadside kitsch alike will enjoy the tiny and charming little **Memory Park Christ Chapel** (U.S. 17, daily 24 hrs.). Built in 1949 by local grocer Agnes Harper, the church—which contains a pulpit and chairs for a dozen people—was intended as a round-the-clock travelers' sanctuary on what was then the main coastal road, U.S. 17. Upon her death, Mrs. Harper simply willed the church to Jesus Christ. The stained-glass windows are imported from England, and there's a guestbook so you can leave any note of appreciation. Get there by taking Exit 67 off I-95 and going south a short way on U.S. 17; the church is on the east side of the road.

◖ Harris Neck National Wildlife Refuge

Literally a stone's throw away from the "Smallest Church" is the turnoff east onto the seven-mile Harris Neck Road leading to the Harris Neck National Wildlife Refuge (912/832-4608, www.fws.gov/harrisneck, daily sunrise–sunset, free). In addition to being one of the single best sites in the South from which to view wading birds and waterfowl in their natural habitat, Harris Neck also has something of a poignant backstory.

For generations after the Civil War, an African American community descended from the area's original slaves quietly struggled to eke out a living by fishing and farming. But their land was taken by the federal government in World War II to build a U.S. Army Air Force base, primarily to train pilots on the P-40 Tomahawk fighter, the same plane used by the famed Flying Tigers.

© JIM MOREKIS

the "Smallest Church in North America"

© JIM MOREKIS

Harris Neck National Wildlife Refuge

After the war, the base was decommissioned and given to McIntosh County as a municipal airport. But the notoriously corrupt local government so mismanaged the facility that the feds once again took it over, eventually transferring it to the forerunner of the U.S. Fish and Wildlife Service.

Now a nearly 3,000-acre nationally protected refuge, Harris Neck gets about 50,000 visitors a year to experience its mix of marsh, woods, and grassland ecosystems, and for its nearly matchless bird-watching. Its former life as a military base has the plus of leaving behind a decent system of roads, many of them based on old runways. Most visitors use the four-mile "wildlife drive" to travel through the refuge, stopping occasionally for hiking or bird-watching.

In the summer, look for egrets, herons, and wood storks nesting in rookeries. In the winter, waterfowl like mallards and teal flock to the brackish and freshwater pools. You can see painted buntings from late April until late September.

Kayaks and canoes can put in at the public boat ramp on the Barbour River. Near the landing is an old African American cemetery, publicly accessible, with some charming handmade tombstones that evoke the post-Civil War era of Harris Neck before the displacement of local citizens to build the airfield.

To get there, take Exit 67 off of I-95 and go south on U.S. 17 about a mile, then east on Harris Neck Road (GA 131) for seven miles to the entrance gate on your left.

Shellman Bluff

Just northeast of Darien is the old oystering community of Shellman Bluff. It's notable not only for the stunning views from the high bluff but for fresh seafood. Go to **Shellman's Fish Camp** (912/832-4331) to put in for a kayak or canoe ride. Save room for some food; there are some great seafood places here.

To get to Shellman Bluff, take the South Newport Exit 67 off I-95 and get on U.S. 17 south. There are two easy ways to get to Shellman Bluff from Highway 17: East on

Minton Road and then left onto Shellman Bluff Road, or east on Pine Harbor Road followed by an immediate left onto Shellman Bluff Road. In either case take Shellman Bluff Road until it dead ends, then a right onto Sutherland Bluff Drive.

Darien Waterfront Park

Right where U.S. 17 crosses the Darien River, find the **Darien Welcome Center** (corner U.S. 17 and Fort King George Dr., 912/437-6684, daily 9 A.M.–5 P.M.). From there it's a short walk down some steps to the newly refurbished little Darien Waterfront Park. This small but charming area on a beautiful bend of the Darien River—a tributary of the mighty Altamaha just to the south—features some old tabby warehouse ruins, some of the only remnants of Darien's glory days as a major seaport and old enough to have century-old live oaks growing around them. To the east are the picturesque docks where the town shrimp boat fleet docks.

Vernon Square

Right around the corner from the Welcome Center on Washington Street is Vernon Square, a charming little nook of live oaks and Spanish moss that was the social center of Darien in the town's antebellum heyday. The Methodist Church on the square was built in 1843, damaged during the Civil War, then rebuilt in 1884 using materials from the first church. The nearby St. Andrews Episcopal Church, built in 1878, was once the site of the famous Bank of Darien.

Fort King George State Historic Site

The oldest English settlement in what would become Georgia, Fort King George State Historic Site (1600 Wayne St., 912/437-4770, www.gastateparks.org/fortkinggeorge, Tues.–Sun. 9 A.M.–5 P.M., $5 adults, $2.50 children) for a short time protected the Carolinas from attack, with its establishment in 1721 to its abandonment in 1727. Walking onto the site, with its restored, 40-foot-tall cypress blockhouse fort, shows you instantly why this place

was so important: It guards a key bend in the wide Altamaha River, vital to any attempt to establish transportation and trade in the area.

In addition to chronicling the ill-fated English occupation of the area—plagued by insects, sickness, danger, and boredom—the site also has exhibits about other aspects of local history, including the Guale Indians, the Spanish missionary presence, and the era of the great sawmills. Nature lovers will enjoy the site as well, as it offers gorgeous vistas of the marsh.

Fort King George holds regular reenactments, living history demonstrations, and cannon firings; go to the website for details. To get there, take U.S. 17 to the Darien River Bridge, and go east on Fort King George Drive. There's a bike route to the fort if you want to park in town.

Butler Island

South of Darien is the Altamaha River, Georgia's largest river (and only undammed one) and one of America's great estuarine habitats, with the second-largest watershed on the East Coast. It's a paradise for outdoors enthusiasts, one that amazed and delighted famed naturalist William Bartram on his journey here in the late 1700s. Over 30,000 ducks visit each year from mid-October through mid-April on this key stop on the Colonial Coast Birding Trail.

A great way to enjoy the river ecosystem is at the **Altamaha Waterfowl Management Area** (912/262-3173, http://georgiawildlife.dnr. state.ga.us). This was the site of Butler Island Plantation, one of America's largest and most successful tidewater plantations in the antebellum era. (The 75-foot brick chimney just off U.S. 17 is part of an old rice mill belonging to the plantation.)

In 1834, planter Pierce Butler II married English actress Fanny Kemble, who would go on to write one of the earliest anti-slavery chronicles, *Journal of a Residence on a Georgian Plantation in 1838–39,* about what she saw during her short stay at Butler Island. Just past the chimney is a large plantation house, which now houses offices of the Nature Conservancy. There's a picnic ground nearby.

© JIM MOREKIS

remains of the old Butler Island Plantation south of Darien

The dominance of the plantation culture in this area is proved by the dikes and gates throughout the marsh, still plainly visible from the road. Many are still used by the Georgia Department of Natural Resources to maintain bird habitat. Birds you can see throughout the area include endangered wood storks, painted bunting, white ibis, all types of ducks, and even bald eagles.

Some of the best hiking and birding in the area is just south of the chimney on U.S. 17. Park on the east side of the road at an old dairy barn and from there you'll find the trail head for a four-mile round-trip hike on the Billy Cullen Memorial Trail, which offers great bird-watching opportunities and interpretive signage. On the other side of U.S. 17 is the entrance to the Ansley Hodges Memorial, where a quarter-mile hike takes you to an observation tower. Be aware that hunting goes on near this area on some Saturdays during the year.

Kayaks and canoes can easily put in at the state-run landing at **Champney River Park** right there where U.S. 17 crosses the Champney River. There are a variety of fish camps up and down this entire riverine system, providing fairly easy launching and recovery.

ACCOMMODATIONS

If you want to stay in McIntosh County, I strongly recommend booking one of the five charming rooms at ◖ **Open Gates Bed and Breakfast** (301 Franklin St., 912/437-6985, www.opengatesbnb.com, $125–140). This lovingly restored and reasonably priced inn is on historic and relaxing Vernon Square in downtown Darien. Owners Kelly and Jeff Spratt are not only attentive innkeepers who rustle up a mean breakfast, they're also biologists who can hook you up with the best nature-oriented experiences and tours on this part of the coast.

FOOD

As you might expect, fresh seafood in a very casual atmosphere is the order of the day here. Though a good ways off the main roads, the community of Shellman Bluff is by far the best pick and well worth the drive.

Find ◖ **Hunter's Café** (912/832-5771, lunch Mon.–Fri. 11 A.M.–2 P.M., dinner 5–10 P.M., Sat. and Sun. 7 A.M.–10 P.M., $10–20) and get anything that floats your boat—it's all fresh and local. Wild Georgia shrimp are a particular specialty, as is the hearty cream-based crab stew. Take a right off Shellman Bluff Road onto Sutherland Bluff Drive, then a left onto New Shellman Road. Take a right onto the unpaved River Road and you can't miss it.

Another Shellman Bluff favorite is ◖ **Speed's Kitchen** (912/832-4763, Thurs.– Sat. 5 P.M.–close, Sun. noon–close, $10–20), where people move anything but fast and the fried fish and crab-stuffed flounder are out of this world. Take a right off of Shellman Bluff Road onto Sutherland Bluff Drive. Take a right onto Speed's Kitchen Road.

On the Darien waterfront, you'll find **Skipper's Fish Camp** (85 Screven St., 912/437-3579, www.skippersfishcamp.com, daily 11 A.M.–9 P.M., $15–25), which, as is typical for this area, also hosts a marina. Try the fried wild Georgia Shrimp, fresh from local waters.

THE GOLDEN ISLES

South of Darien just off U.S. 17 on the Altamaha River, try **Mudcat Charlie's** (250 Rice Field Wy., 912/261-0055, daily 8 A.M.–2 P.M., $10–20), where fresh seafood is served in a friendly and very casual atmosphere, yes, right in the middle of a busy fish camp.

INFORMATION AND SERVICES

The **Darien Welcome Center** (1111 Magnolia Bluff Way, www.visitdarien.com, Mon.–Sat. 10 A.M.–8 P.M., Sun. 11 A.M.–6 P.M.) is located within the Preferred Outlets mall just off I-95 at Exit 49.

Within Darien proper is the **McIntosh Old Jail Art Center and Welcome Center** (404 Northway, 912/437-7711, www.visitdarien.com, Tues.–Sat. 10 A.M.–4 P.M.), which also doubles as a small art gallery for the local arts association.

The closest hospital is the Brunswick campus of **Southeast Georgia Health System** (2415 Parkwood Dr., Brunswick, 912/466-7000, http://sghs.org).

GETTING THERE AND AROUND

Highway 17 goes directly through Darien. The closest exit off I-95 is Exit 49.

Once you get off Highway 17, Darien is a pretty bike-friendly place; you can park the car downtown and ride your bike east on Fort King George Drive and visit Fort King George.

SAPELO ISLAND

Another of those amazing, undeveloped Georgia barrier islands that can only be reached by boat, Sapelo also shares with some of those islands a link to the Gilded Age.

History

The Spanish established a Franciscan mission on the north end of the island in the 1500s. Sapelo didn't become fully integrated into the Lowcountry plantation culture until its purchase by Thomas Spalding in the early 1800s. After the Civil War, many of the nearly 500 former slaves on the island remained, with a partnership of freedmen buying land as early as 1871.

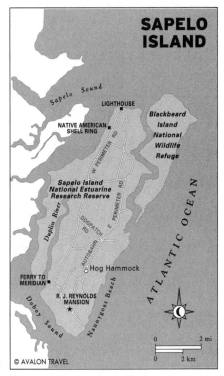

Hudson Motors mogul Howard Coffin bought all of Sapelo, except for the African American communities, in 1912, building a palatial home and introducing a modern infrastructure. Among Coffin's visitors were two presidents, Calvin Coolidge and Herbert Hoover, and aviator Charles Lindbergh.

Coffin hit hard times in the Great Depression and in 1934 sold Sapelo to tobacco heir R. J. Reynolds, who consolidated the island's African Americans into the single Hog Hammock community. By the mid-1970s the Reynolds family had sold the island to the state, again with the exception of the 430 acres comprising Hog Hammock, with a little over 100 residents.

Today most of the island is administered for marine research purposes under the designation of **Sapelo Island National Estuarine Research Reserve** (www.sapelonerr.org).

Sights

Once on the island, you can take guided tours under the auspices of the Georgia Department of Natural Resources. Wednesdays 8:30 A.M.–12:30 P.M. is a tour of the **R. J. Reynolds Mansion** (www.reynoldsonsapelo.com) on the south end, and the rest of the island, including Hog Hammock and the Long Tabby ruins. Saturdays 9 A.M.–1 P.M. is a tour of the historic **Sapelo Lighthouse** on the north end, and the rest of the island. June through Labor Day there's an extra lighthouse/island tour Fridays 8:30 A.M.–12:30 P.M. On the last Tuesday of the month March–October they do an extra-long day trip, 8:30 A.M.–3 P.M.

Tours are $10 adults, $6 children, free for those under age 6. Call 912/437-3224 for reservations. You can also arrange private tours.

Another key sight on Sapelo is a 4,500-year-old **Native American shell ring** on the north end, one of the oldest and best preserved anywhere.

Beach-lovers will especially enjoy the unspoiled strands on Sapelo, including the famous **Nannygoat Beach.**

Accommodations

While it's theoretically possible to stay overnight at the **R. J. Reynolds Mansion** (www.reynoldsonsapelo.com), it is limited to groups of at least 16 people.

Realistically, to stay overnight on Sapelo you need a reservation with one of the locally owned guesthouses. One recommendation is Cornelia Bailey's six-room **The Wallow** (912/485-2206, call for rates) in historic Hog Hammock.

The Baileys also run a small campground, **Comyam's Campground** (912/485-2206, $10 per person per night).

Another option is **The Weekender** (912/485-2277, call for rates).

Getting There

Visitors to Sapelo must embark on the ferry at the **Sapelo Island Visitors Center** (912/437-3224, www.sapelonerr.org, Tues.–Fri. 7:30 A.M.–5:30 P.M., Sat. 8 A.M.–5:30 P.M., Sun.

1:30–5 P.M., $10 adults, $6 ages 6–18) in little Meridian, Georgia, on GA 99 out of Darien. The visitors center actually has a nice nature hike of its own, and an auditorium where you can see an informative video. From there it's a half-hour trip over the Doboy Sound.

Keep in mind you must call in advance for reservations *before* showing up at the visitors center. In April–October it's recommended to call at least a week in advance.

ST. CATHERINE'S ISLAND

The interior of this beautiful island off the coast of Midway, Georgia, is off-limits to the public, but you can visit the beach up to the high-water mark by boat, enjoy its beautiful, unspoiled beaches, and spy on local wildlife. While that's about all you can do, it's important to know a little of the interesting background of this island.

Owned and administered by the St. Catherine's Island Foundation, it's unusual in that it has a 25-foot-high bluff on the northern end, an extraordinarily high geographic feature for a barrier island in this part of the world. Once central to the Spanish missionary effort on the Georgia coast, St. Catherine's was found to be home to over 400 graves of Christianized Native Americans (a large shell ring also exists on the island).

Declaration of Independence signer Button Gwinnett made a home here for a while until his death from a gunshot wound suffered in a duel in Savannah in 1777. After Sherman's famous "40 acres and a mule" order, a freed slave named Tunis Campbell was governor of the island, living in Gwinnett's home. But when the order was rescinded, all former slaves had to leave for the mainland.

In 1986, American Museum of Natural History archaeologist David Hurst Thomas began extensive research on Spanish artifacts left behind from the Santa Catalina de Guale mission, including foundations of living quarters, a kitchen, and a church—possibly the first Christian church in the modern-day United States. Today, however, the island, a National Historic Landmark, is better known as host to a New York Zoological Society project to recover injured or sick animals of endangered species and nurse them back to health for a possible return to the wild.

The closest marinas for the trip to the island's peaceful beaches are Shellman Fish Camp (912/832-4331) in McIntosh County and Halfmoon Marina (912/884-5819) in Liberty County.

BLACKBEARD ISLAND

While no one is positive if the namesake of Blackbeard Island actually landed here, the legends tell us he used it as a layover—even leaving some treasure here. Now federally administered as **Blackbeard Island National Wildlife Refuge** (912/652-4415, www.fws.gov/black beardisland), the island is accessible to the public by boat and gets about 10,000 visitors a year.

Plenty of hiking trails exist and the bird-watching is fantastic. It's also a major nesting ground for the endangered loggerhead turtle. Biking is permitted, but overnight camping is not.

For charters to Blackbeard, I recommend **SouthEast Adventures** (313 Mallory St., 912/638-6732) on St. Simons Island.

Cumberland Island and St. Marys

Actually comprising two islands—Great Cumberland and Little Cumberland—Cumberland Island National Seashore is the largest and one of the oldest of Georgia's barrier islands, and also one of its most remote and least developed. Currently administered by the National Park Service, it's accessible only by ferry or private boat.

Most visitors to Cumberland get there from the "gateway" town of St. Marys, Georgia, a nifty little fishing village that has so far managed to defy the increasing residential sprawl coming to the area.

ST. MARYS

Much like Brunswick to the north, the fishing town of St. Marys plays mostly a gateway role, in this case to the Cumberland Island National Seashore. That being said, it's a very friendly little waterfront community with undeniable charms of its own and a historic pedigree going back to the very beginnings of the nation.

History

As early as 1767, once the Spanish threat subsided, plans were made to establish a town in the area near the Florida border then known as Buttermilk Bluff. But it wasn't until 20 years later that a meeting was held on Cumberland Island to close the deal with Jacob Weed to purchase the tract—acquired by confiscation from two loyalist landowners—for the grand sum of $38.

The first influx of immigration to the area came as French Canadian refugees from Acadia (who would become known as Cajuns in Louisiana) came to St. Marys after being deported by the British. Another group of French-speakers came, fleeing Toussaint L'Ouverture's slave rebellion in Haiti.

During the colonial period, St. Marys was the southernmost U.S. city, and enjoyed not only importance as a seaport but was militarily important as well. Ironically, this strategic importance came into play more during America's conflict with Great Britain than with anything having to do with the Spanish.

In 1812 a British force took over Cumberland Island and St. Marys, with a contingent embarking up the river to track down the customs collection. However, in a bloody skirmish they were ambushed by American troops firing from the riverbanks. Though vowing to avenge their loss by burning down every building between the St. Marys and the Altamaha Rivers, the ensuing peace treaty ending the War of 1812 brought a ceasefire.

Unlike towns such as Darien, which was put to the torch by Union troops, St. Marys was saved from destruction in the Civil War. The lumber industry boomed after that conflict,

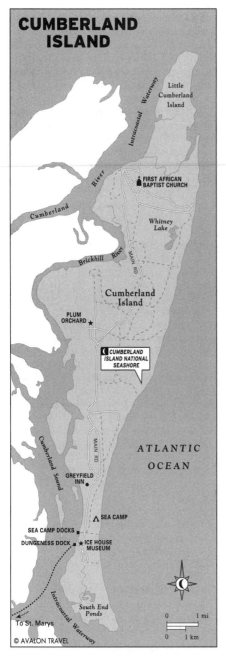

CUMBERLAND ISLAND

Little Cumberland Island

Intracoastal Waterway

FIRST AFRICAN BAPTIST CHURCH

Cumberland River

Whitney Lake

Brickhill River

MAIN RD

Cumberland Island

PLUM ORCHARD ★

CUMBERLAND ISLAND NATIONAL SEASHORE

Cumberland Sound

MAIN RD

ATLANTIC OCEAN

GREYFIELD INN ●

▲ SEA CAMP

SEA CAMP DOCKS ■

DUNGENESS DOCK ★ ICE HOUSE MUSEUM

Intracoastal Waterway

South End Ponds

To St. Marys

© AVALON TRAVEL

0   1 mi
0   1 km

as well as the local fishing and shrimping industry.

A hotel was built in 1916 (and hosted Marjorie Kinnan Rawlings, author of *The Yearlings*), but tourists didn't discover the area until the 1970s. It was also then that the U.S. Navy built the huge nuclear submarine base at Kings Bay, currently the area's largest employer, with almost 10,000 employees.

Development has increased in the area, with suburban sprawl beginning to cover the area like mushrooms after a heavy rain. Indeed, there's so much growth in the St. Marys/Camden County area that it's increasingly considered an outpost of the huge Jacksonville, Florida, metropolitan area to the south.

Orientation

Like Brunswick, the waterfront faces opposite the ocean and is instead oriented west toward a river, in this case the St. Marys River. Most activity in downtown St. Marys happens up and down Osborne Street, which perhaps not coincidentally is also how you get to the **Cumberland Island Visitor Center** (113 St. Marys St., 912/882-4335, daily 8 A.M.–4:30 P.M.) and from there board the *Cumberland Queen* for the trip to the island itself.

Sights

Tying the past to the present, it's only fitting that the home of the Kings Bay Submarine Base (which is not open to the public) has a museum dedicated to the "Silent Service." The **St. Marys Submarine Museum** (102 St. Marys St., 912/882-2782, www.stmarys submuseum.com, Tues.–Sat. 10 A.M.–4 P.M., Sun. 1–5 P.M., $4 adults, $2 children) on the riverfront has a variety of exhibits honoring the contribution of American submariners. There's a neat interactive exhibit where you can look out of the genuine sub periscope that sticks out of the roof of the museum.

The most notable historic home in St. Marys is the **Orange Hall House Museum** (311 Osborne St., 912/576-3644, www.orangehall .org, Tues.–Sat. 9 A.M.–4 P.M., Sun. 1–4 P.M., $3 adults, $1 children). This beautiful Greek

Revival home, circa 1830, survived the Civil War and was the center of town social life during the Roaring Twenties, when it was owned by a succession of socialites from up north. The home is gorgeous inside and out, particularly during the holidays when it gets the full decorative treatment.

Events and Recreation

As a nod to its Cajun history, St. Marys hosts a heck of a **Mardi Gras Festival** each February, closing down six blocks of the riverfront for a parade. There's also live entertainment, vendors, and a costume ball.

For outdoor recreation near St. Marys, go to the **Crooked River State Park** (6222 Charlie Smith Sr. Hwy., 912/882-5256, www.gastateparks .org, daily office hours 8 A.M.–10 P.M., Thurs. 8 A.M.–5 P.M.), which is not only a great place to put in for kayaking trips, including jaunts to Cumberland itself, but also has a wide range of lodging options as well.

A key stop on the Colonial Coast Birding Trail, Crooked River features its own nature center and is near a historic site just upriver, the tabby ruins of the McIntosh Sugar Works— actually a lumber mill from the early 1800s. The easiest way to get there is Exit 3 off I-95 and go about eight miles east.

For renting kayaks or booking kayak and eco-tours, try **Up the Creek Xpeditions** (111 Osborne St., 912/882-0911, www.upthecreek tours.com), which can take you all around the area including out to Cumberland Island.

Accommodations

Don't even think about staying at a chain hotel when you're in St. Marys. Stay at one of these cute historic inns for a song.

The most notable lodging for historic as well as economic value is the 18-room **Riverview Hotel** (105 Osborne St., 912/882-3242, www .riverviewhotelstmarys.com, under $100). This waterfront locale, like many old hotels in this area, has a great retro feel. It was built in the 1920s and has hosted such notables as author Marjorie Rawlings, John Rockefeller, poet Sidney Lanier, and Andrew Carnegie.

◖ Emma's Bed and Breakfast (300 West Conyers St., 912/882-4199, www.emmas bedandbreakfast.com, under $200) is situated on four beautiful acres in downtown St. Marys in a grand, Southern-style mansion with all the trappings and hospitality you'd expect.

You can also hang out on the veranda at the historic **◖ Goodbread House** (209 Osborne St., 912/882-7490, www.goodbreadhouse.com, under $200), which offers rates below $100 in the off-season. The 1870 house features a stunning veranda and sumptuous interiors, including a classic dining room in which awesome breakfasts are served.

More outdoorsy visitors can stay at cottage, tent, or RV sites at **Crooked River State Park** (6222 Charlie Smith Sr. Hwy., 912/882-5256, www.gastateparks.org). There are 62 tent and RV sites (about $22) and 11 cottages ($85– 110), as well as primitive camping ($25).

Food

St. Marys cannot compete in culinary sophistication with Charleston or Savannah, but it does have some of the freshest seafood around. One of the best places to eat seafood on the waterfront in St. Marys is at **Lang's Marina Restaurant** (307 W. St. Marys St., 912/882-4432, lunch Tues.–Fri. 11 A.M.–2 P.M., dinner Wed.–Sat. 5–9 P.M., $15–20). The other premier seafood place is **Trolley's** (109 W. St. Marys St., 912/882-1525, Sun.–Thurs. 11 A.M.–9 P.M., Fri. and Sat. 11 A.M.–10 P.M., $15–20).

Information and Services

The **St. Marys Convention and Visitors Bureau** (406 Osborne St., 912/882-4000, www.stmaryswelcome.com) is a good source of information not only for the town but for Cumberland Island, though keep in mind that this is not actually where you catch the ferry to the island.

Getting There and Around

Take Exit 3 off I-95 to Kingsland-St. Marys Road (GA 40). This becomes Osborne Road, the main drag of St. Marys, as it gets closer into town. The road by the waterfront is St. Marys Street.

◖ CUMBERLAND ISLAND NATIONAL SEASHORE

Not only one of the richest estuarine environments in the world, Cumberland Island National Seashore (912/882-4335, www.nps.gov/cuis) is quite simply one of the most beautiful and romantic places on the planet, as everyone learned when the "it" couple of their day, John F. Kennedy Jr. and Carolyn Bessette were wed on the island in 1996. With more than 16 miles of gorgeous beach and an area of over 17,000 acres, there's no shortage of beauty either, and the island's already-remote feel is enhanced further by the efforts that have been taken to protect it from development.

Cumberland is far from pristine—it's been used for timbering and cotton, is dotted with evocative, abandoned ruins, and hosts a band of beautiful but voracious wild horses. But it is still a remarkable island paradise in a world where those kinds of locations are getting harder and harder to find.

History

Like modern-day Americans, the Timucuan Indians also revered this site, visiting it often

THE GOLDEN ISLES

WILD HORSES OF CUMBERLAND

© DOUGANDME

Cumberland Island's famous wild horses are not actually direct descendants of the first horses brought to the island by Spanish and English settlers, though certainly feral horses have ranged the island for most of recorded history. The current population of 250 or so is actually descended from horses brought to the island by the Carnegie family in the 1920s.

Gorgeous and evocative though these mag- nificent animals are, they have a big appetite for vegetation and are frankly not the best thing for this sensitive barrier island ecosystem. But their beauty and visceral impact on the visitor is undeniable, which means the horses are likely to stay as long as nature will have them. And yes, these really are *wild* horses, meaning you shouldn't feed them even if they approach you for food, and you certainly won't be riding them.

for shellfish and for sassafras, a medicinal herb common on the island. Cumberland's size and great natural harbor made it a perfect base for Spanish friars, who established the first missionary on the island, San Pedro Mocama in 1587. In fact, the first Christian martyr in Georgia was created on Cumberland, when Father Pedro Martinez was killed by Indians.

As part of his effort to push the Spanish back into Florida for good, General James Oglethorpe established Fort William at the south end of Cumberland—the remains of which are now underwater—and a hunting lodge named Dungeness—an island place name which persists today. While land grants were made in the 1760s, they saw little followthrough, and by the time of naturalist William Bartram's visit in 1774, Cumberland Island was almost uninhabited.

But inevitably, the Lowcountry planters' culture made its way down to Cumberland, which was soon the site of 15 thriving plantations and small farms. After the Revolution, the heirs of one of its heroes, General Nathanael Greene, established Dungeness Plantation in 1802, its central building a now-gone tabby structure right on top of an ancient shell mound.

Actual military action wouldn't come to Cumberland until the War of 1812, when the British came in force and occupied the island for two months, using Dungeness as their headquarters. In the process they freed 1,500 slaves, who would then emigrate to various British colonies.

In 1818, Revolutionary War hero General "Lighthorse" Harry Lee—father of Robert E. Lee—arrived on Cumberland's shore, in failing health and determined to see the home of his old friend General Greene one last time. He died a month later and was buried there, his son returning later to erect a gravestone. Lighthorse Harry remained on Cumberland until 1913, when his remains were taken to Lexington, Virginia, to be beside those of his son. However, the gravestone on Cumberland remains to this day.

War—and another freeing of slaves—came again in the 1860s, when Union troops occupied the island. Though at war's end Cumberland was set aside as a home for freed African Americans—part of the famous and ill-fated "40 acres and a mule" proposal—politics intervened. Most of Cumberland's slaves were rounded up and taken to Amelia Island, Florida, though some settled at the north end (the "Settlement" area today).

As elsewhere on the Georgia coast, the Industrial Revolution came to Cumberland in the form of a vacation getaway for a mega-tycoon, in this case Thomas Carnegie, industrialist and brother of the better-known Andrew Carnegie of Carnegie Library fame. Carnegie built a new, even grander Dungeness, which in a 1959 fire suffered the same fate as its predecessor.

Cumberland Island narrowly avoided becoming the next Hilton Head—literally—in 1969 when Hilton Head developer Charles Fraser bought the northern tip of the island and began bulldozing a runway. The dwindling but still influential Carnegies joined with the Georgia Conservancy to broker an agreement which resulted in dubbing Cumberland a National Seashore in 1972, saving it from further development. A $7.5 million gift from the Mellon Foundation enabled the purchase of Fraser's tract and the eventual incorporation of the island within the National Park system.

Sights

The ferry typically stops at two docks a short distance from each other, the Sea Camp dock and the Dungeness dock. At 4 P.M., Rangers offer a "Dockside" interpretive program at the Sea Camp. A short ways farther north at the Dungeness Dock, Rangers offer a "Dungeness Footsteps Tour" at 10 A.M. and 12:45 P.M., concentrating on the historic sites at the southern end of the island. Also at the Dungeness dock is the little **Ice House Museum** (912/882-4336, daily 9 A.M.–5 P.M., free) containing a range of exhibits on the island's history from Native American times to the present day.

Down near the docks are also where you'll find the stirring, almost spooky **Dungeness Ruins** and the nearby grave marker of Lighthorse Harry

Lee. Controversy continues to this day as to the cause of the fire in 1866 that destroyed the old Dungeness home. Some say it was those freed slaves on the north end who lit the blaze, but others say it was the plantation's final owner, Robert Stafford, who did it out of spite after his former slaves refused to work for him after the war.

Moving north on the Main Road/Grand Avenue you come to **Greyfield Inn** (904/261-6408, www.greyfieldinn.com). Because it is a privately owned hotel, don't trespass through the grounds. A good ways farther north, just off the main road, you'll find the restored, rambling 20-room mansion **Plum Orchard,** another Carnegie legacy. Guided tours of Plum Orchard are available on the second and fourth Sunday of the month for $6 plus ferry fare; reserve a space at 912/882-4335.

At the very north end of the island, accessible only by foot or by bike, is the former freedmen's community simply known as **the Settlement,** featuring a small cemetery and the now world-famous **First African Baptist Church** (daily dawn–dusk)—a 1937 version of the 1893 original—a humble and rustic one-room church made of whitewashed logs in which the Kennedy/Bessette marriage took place.

Sports and Recreation

There are more than 50 miles of trails all over Cumberland, about 17 miles of nearly isolated beach to comb, and acres of maritime forest to explore—the latter an artifact of Cumberland's unusually old age for a barrier island. Upon arrival, you might want to rent a bike at the **Sea Camp docks** (no reservations, arrange rentals on the ferry, $16 per day for adult bikes, $10 youth bikes, $20 overnight).

Shell-and-sharks-teeth collectors might want to explore south of Dungeness Beach as well as between the docks. Unlike some parks, you are allowed to take shells and fossils off the island.

Wildlife enthusiasts will be in heaven. More than 300 species of birds have been recorded on the island, which is also a favorite nesting ground for female loggerhead turtles in the late summer. Of course the most iconic image of Cumberland Island is its famous **wild horses,** a free-roaming band of feral equines who traverse the island year-round, grazing as they please.

THE GOLDEN ISLES

© PWBAKER

the Dungeness Ruins

Accommodations

The only "civilized" lodging on Cumberland is the 13-room 【 **Greyfield Inn** (main road and Grand Ave., 904/261-6408, www.grey fieldinn.com, $475), ranked by the American Inn Association as one of America's "Ten Most Romantic Inns." Opened in 1962 as a hotel, the Greyfield was originally built in 1900 as the home of the Carnegies. The rate includes meals, transportation, tours, and bike usage.

Many visitors opt to camp on Cumberland (reservations 877/860-6787, $4 per day, limit of up to seven nights) in one of three basic ways: at the **Sea Camp,** which has restrooms and shower facilities and permits fires; the remote **Stafford Beach,** a good hike from the docks and with no facilities; and pure wilderness camping farther north at **Hickory Hill, Yankee Paradise,** and **Brickman Bluff,** all of which are a multiple-mile hike away, do not permit fires, and have no facilities of any kind.

Reservations are needed for camping. *All* trash must be packed out on departure, as there are no refuse facilities on the island. Responsible alcohol consumption is limited to those 21 and over.

Getting There and Around

The most vital information about Cumberland is how to get ashore in the first place. Most visitors do this by purchasing a ticket on the *Cumberland Queen* at the **Cumberland Island Visitor Center** (113 St. Marys St., 912/882-4335, daily 8 A.M.–4:30 P.M., $17 adults, $12 children 12 and under, and $15 seniors) on the waterfront at St. Marys. The ferry ride is 45 minutes each way. Hours to call for reservations are Monday–Friday 10 A.M.–4 P.M.

The ferry does *not* transport pets, bicycles, kayaks, or cars. However, you can rent bikes at the Sea Camp docks once you're there. Every visitor to Cumberland over 16 years old must pay a $4 entry fee, including campers.

March 1–November 30, the ferry leaves St. Marys at 9 A.M. and 11:45 A.M., returning from Cumberland at 10:15 A.M. and 4:45 P.M. March 1–September 30, Wednesday–Saturday, there's an additional 2:45 P.M. departure from Cumberland back to St. Marys. December 1–February 28, the ferry does not operate on Tuesdays or Wednesdays, and there is no 2:45 P.M. departure from Cumberland.

One of the quirks of Cumberland, resulting from the unusual way in which it passed into federal hands, is the existence of some private property on which you mustn't trespass except where trails specifically allow it. Also, unlike the general public, these private landowners are allowed to use vehicles. For these reasons, it's best to make sure you have a map of the island, which you can get before you board the ferry at St. Marys.

There are no real stores and very few facilities on Cumberland. *Bring whatever you think you'll need,* whether it be food, water, medicine, suntan lotion, insect repellant, or otherwise.

The Okefenokee Swamp

Scientists often refer to Okefenokee as an "analogue," an accurate representation of a totally different epoch in earth's history. In this case it's the Carboniferous Period of about 350 million years ago, when the living plants were lush and green and the dead plants simmered in a slow-decaying peat that would one day end up as the oil that powers our entire civilization.

But for the casual visitor, Okefenokee might also be simply a wonderful place to get almost completely away from human influence and witness firsthand some of America's most interesting and gorgeous wildlife in its natural habitat. Despite the devastating wildfires of the spring of 2007—the largest the Southeast has seen in half a century, so large they were visible from space—the swamp has bounced back and is once again hosting visitors to experience its timeless beauty.

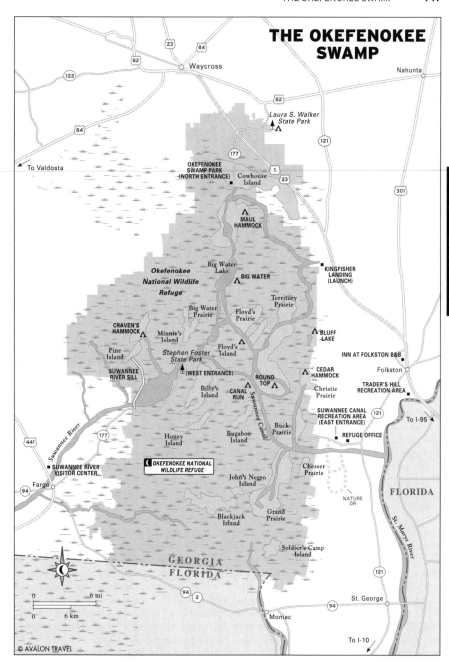

THE OKEFENOKEE SWAMP

THE GOLDEN ISLES

Waycross

Nahunta

To Valdosta

Laura S. Walker State Park

OKEFENOKEE SWAMP PARK (NORTH ENTRANCE)

Cowhouse Island

MAUL HAMMOCK

Big Water Lake

BIG WATER

Okefenokee National Wildlife Refuge

KINGFISHER LANDING (LAUNCH)

Territory Prairie

Big Water Prairie

Floyd's Prairie

CRAVEN'S HAMMOCK

Minnie's Island

BLUFF LAKE

Floyd's Island

Pine Island

Stephen Foster State Park

INN AT FOLKSTON B&B

SUWANNEE RIVER SILL

(WEST ENTRANCE)

CEDAR HAMMOCK

Folkston

ROUND TOP

TRADER'S HILL RECREATION AREA

Billy's Island

CANAL RUN

Christie Prairie

Suwannee Canal

SUWANNEE CANAL RECREATION AREA (EAST ENTRANCE)

Buck Prairie

Honey Island

Bugaboo Island

REFUGE OFFICE

To I-95

Suwannee River

OKEFENOKEE NATIONAL WILDLIFE REFUGE

SUWANNEE RIVER VISITOR CENTER

Chesser Prairie

John's Negro Island

NATURE DR

FLORIDA

Fargo

St. Marys River

Blackjack Island

Grand Prairie

Soldier's Camp Island

GEORGIA
FLORIDA

0   6 mi
0   6 km

Moniac

St. George

To I-10

© AVALON TRAVEL

a resident of the Okefenokee Swamp

◖ OKEFENOKEE NATIONAL WILDLIFE REFUGE

It's nearly the size of Rhode Island and just a short drive off I-95, but the massive and endlessly fascinating Okefenokee National Wildlife Refuge (Route 2, Box 3330, 912/496-7836, www.fws.gov/okefenokee, Mar.–Oct. daily dawn–7:30 P.M., Nov.–Feb. daily dawn–5:30 P.M., $5 per vehicle) is one of the lesser-visited national parks. Is it that very name "swamp" that keeps people away, with its connotations of fetid misery and lurking danger? Or simply its location, out-of-sight and out-of-mind in South Georgia?

In any case, while it long ago entered the collective subconscious as a metaphor for the most untamed, darkly dangerous aspects of the American South—as well as the place where Pogo the Possum lived—the Okefenokee remains one of the most intriguing natural areas on the planet.

The nearby old rail town of Folkston is the gateway to the swamp for most visitors off of I-95, which is to say the bulk of them. In true Georgia fashion, the town is insular but friendly, slow but sincere.

History

The Okefenokee Swamp was created by an accident of geology. About 250,000 years ago, the Atlantic Ocean washed ashore about 70 miles farther inland from where it does today. Over time, a massive barrier island formed off this primeval Georgia coastline, running from Jesup, Georgia, south to what is now Starke, Florida.

When the ocean level dropped during the Pleistocene Era, this sandy island became a topographical feature known today as the Trail Ridge, its height effectively creating a basin to its west. Approximately 90 percent of the Okefenokee's water comes from rainfall into that basin, which drains slowly via the Suwannee and St. Mary's rivers.

Ordinarily, what the summer heat evaporates from the Okefenokee is more than replenished by rain, unless there's a severe drought like the one that caused the 2007 wildfires. But even the fires can't hold the swamp back. In fact, the Okefenokee is a fire ecosystem, meaning some plant species, like the cypress, depend on heat generated by wildfires to open their seed cones and perpetuate their lifecycle.

Because of constant rejuvenation by water

and fire, biologists estimate that the oldest portion of this supposedly "ancient" swamp is actually no older than 7,000 years—the faintest blink of an eye in geological terms. Unlike Florida's Everglades, which actually comprise a single large and very slow-moving river—the Okefenokee is a true swamp.

Native Americans used the swamp as a hunting ground and gave us its current name, which means "Land of the Trembling Earth," a reference to the floating peat islands, called "houses," that dominate the landscape. The Spanish arrived about 1600, calling the swamp *Laguna de Oconi* (Lake Oconi), and establishing at least two missions in the area of two nearby Timucuan villages.

During the Seminole Wars of the 1830s, that tribe took refuge within the swamp for a time before continuing south into Florida. While trade had occurred on the outskirts for nearly a century before, it wasn't until the 1850s that the first white settlers set up camp inside the swamp itself.

It's a common mistake to call the Okefenokee "pristine," because like much of the heavily timbered and farmed southeastern coast, it is anything but. The swamp's ancient cypress stands and primordial longleaf pine forests were heavily harvested in the early 20th century. About 200 miles of old rail bed through the swamp still remain as a silent testament to the scope of that logging operation.

But the pace of logging gradually slowed to a stop, as the cost of the operation became prohibitive. In 1918, the Okefenokee Society was formed in nearby Waycross, Georgia, the first organized attempt to protect the habitat. In 1937, President Franklin Roosevelt brought the area within the federal wildlife refuge system.

In recent years, large deposits of titanium prompted several mining interests, including DuPont, to exercise rights in the area, to a great outcry from conservationists who worried that the intrusive 24-hour mining operations would destroy the swamp's habitat. However, a series of transactions involving the state and conservation trusts have, so far, resulted in halting those mining efforts.

Sights

Contrary to the popular image of a nasty, dank swamp, the Okefenokee is anything but a monoculture. It features a wide variety of ecosystems, from peat bogs to sandhills to blackgum and bay forests. Perhaps most surprising is the wide open vista of the swamp's many prairies or extended grasslands, 22 all told, which besides being stirring to the eye are also great places to see birds. So you see, not all of the Okefenokee is wet!

There is water aplenty here, though, with over 60 named lakes and 120 miles of boating trails. And as you kayak or canoe on one of the water trails or on the old **Suwanee Canal** from the logging era, you'll notice the water's all very dark. This blackwater is not due to dirt or silt, but to natural tannic acid released into the water from the decaying vegetation that gave the swamp its name. While I don't recommend that you drink the water, it's actually very clean despite its color.

As you'd expect on a national wildlife refuge, the Okefenokee hosts a huge variety of animal life—more than 400 species of vertebrates, including over 200 varieties of birds and more than 60 types of reptiles. Birders get a special treat in late November/early December, when sandhill cranes come south to winter in the swamp. In January, their colonies are at their peak and the swamp echoes with their loud cries. Other common bird species you'll see are herons, egrets, and endangered wood storks and red-cockaded woodpeckers. The white ibis has seen a big spike in population in the refuge recently, as has the bald eagle.

A great way to see the sandhill cranes and other birds of the Okefenokee is to hike the three-quarter-mile boardwalk out to the 50-foot **Chesser Island Observation Tower** on the eastern end of the swamp. You get there by driving or biking the eight-mile round-trip **Wildlife Drive,** which also takes you by the old **Chesser Homestead,** the remnants of one of the oldest settlements in the swamp. You can also hike out to Chesser; indeed there are many miles of hiking trails through the upland areas of the swamp near the East Entrance.

Probably the first creature one thinks of when one thinks of a swamp is the alligator. Certainly Okefenokee has plenty of them, and no one who has heard the roar of a male alligator break the quiet of the night will ever forget the experience. Most of the time, though, alligators are quite shy, and spotting them is an acquired skill. They often look like floating logs. Conversely, in warm weather you might see them out in the open, sunning themselves.

While no one can remember an incident of a gator attacking a human in the refuge, whatever you do, don't feed alligators in the wild. As a Fish and Wildlife ranger in Okefenokee once told me: "If a gator attacks a human, at some point in the past someone has fed that gator. Gators get used to being fed. Unfortunately, they can't tell the difference between the person and the food."

Believe it or not, the alligator is not even the top predator in the Okefenokee. That title belongs to the black bear. Biologists estimate that as many as 90 percent of alligator eggs laid in the refuge are eaten by the local black bear population. And as with the gators, please don't feed the bears.

Recreation and Accommodations

For most visitors, the best way to enjoy the Okefenokee is to book a guided tour through **Okefenokee Adventures** (866/843-7926, www.okefenokeeadventures.com), the designated concessionaire of the refuge. They offer a 90-minute guided boat tour ($16 adults, $10 children) that leaves each hour, and a 2.5-hour reservation-only sunset tour ($25 adults, $17 children) that takes you to see the gorgeous sunset over Chesser Prairie. Extended and/or custom tours, including multiday wilderness excursions, are also available. They also rent bikes, canoes, and camping gear, and even run a decent little café where you can either sit down and have a meal or take it to go out on the trail.

It's possible to stay the night in the swamp, canoeing to one of the primitive camping "islands" in the middle of the refuge. You need to make reservations up to two months in

advance, however, and you do this by calling **U.S. Fish and Wildlife** (912/496-3331, Mon.–Fri. 7–10 A.M.). A non-refundable fee of $10 per person (which also covers your entrance fee) must be received 16 days before you arrive (mailing address is Okefenokee National Wildlife Refuge, Route 2, Box 3330, Folkston, GA 31537). Campfires are allowed only at Canal Run and Floyds Island. A camp stove is required for cooking at all other shelters.

Privately owned canoes and boats with motors under 10 horsepower may put in with no launch fee, however you must sign in and out. No ATVs are allowed on the refuge, and bikes are allowed only on designated bike trails. Keep in mind that some hunting goes on in the refuge at designated times. Pets must be leashed at all times.

At the **Stephen Foster State Park** (17515 Hwy. 177, 912/637-5274, fall and winter daily 7 A.M.–7 P.M., spring and summer daily 6:30 A.M.–8:30 P.M.), a.k.a., the **West Entrance,** near Fargo, Georgia, there are 66 tent sites ($24) and nine cottages ($100). Several miles away the state has recently opened the **Suwanee River Visitor Center** (912/637-5274, www.gastateparks.org, Wed.–Sun. 9 A.M.–5 P.M.), a "green" building featuring an orientation video and exhibits.

Getting There and Around

For the purposes of anyone using this guide as a travel resource, the best way to access the Okefenokee—and the one I recommend—is the **East Entrance** (912/496-7836, www.fws.gov/okefenokee, Mar.–Oct. daily dawn–7:30 P.M., Nov.–Feb. daily dawn–5:30 P.M., $5 per vehicle), otherwise known as the **Suwanee Canal Recreation Area.** This is the main U.S. Fish and Wildlife Service entrance and the most convenient way to hike, rent boating and camping gear, and observe nature. The **Richard S. Bolt Visitor Center** (912/496-7836) has some cool nature exhibits and a surround-sound orientation video.

Get to the East Entrance by taking the Kingsland Exit 3 off I-95 to Georgia Highway 40 west. Go through Kingsland and into

Folkston until it dead-ends. Take a right, then an immediate left onto Main Street. At the third light, make a left onto Okefenokee Drive (Hwy. 121 south).

Families with kids may want to drive a bit farther and hit the **North Entrance** at the privately run **Okefenokee Swamp Park** (US 1 south, 912/283-0583, www.okeswamp.com, daily 9 A.M.–5:30 P.M., $12 adults, $11 children 3–11) near Waycross, Georgia (fans of the old "Pogo Possum" will recall Waycross from the comic strip; and yes, there's a real "Fort Mudge" nearby). There you will find a more-touristy vibe, with a reconstructed pioneer village, serpentarium, and animals in captivity. From there you can take various guided tours for an additional fee. There's camping at the nearby but unaffiliated **Laura S. Walker State Park** (5653 Laura Walker Rd., 800/864-7275, www.gastateparks.org). Be aware the state park is not in the swamp and isn't very swampy.

Get to the North Entrance by taking Exit 6 off I-95 and go west on US 90 about 45 miles to GA 177 (Laura Walker Rd.). Go south through the state park; the Swamp Park is several miles from there.

If you really want that cypress-festooned, classic swamp look, take the long way around the Okefenokee to the **Stephen Foster State Park** (17515 Hwy. 177, 912/637-5274, fall and winter daily 7 A.M.–7 P.M., spring and summer daily 6:30 A.M.–8:30 P.M.), a.k.a., the **West Entrance**, near Fargo, Georgia. Guided tours are available.

Get to Stephen Foster State Park by taking Exit 3 off I-95 and take the signs to Folkston. Get on GA 121 south to St. George, and then go west on GA 94.

FOLKSTON

The chief attraction in Folkston, the little town right outside the refuge's East Entrance, is the excellent [C **Inn at Folkston Bed and Breakfast** (509 W. Main St., 888/509-6246, www.innatfolkston.com, $120–170). There is nothing like coming back to its cozy Victorian charms after a long day out in the swamp. The four-room inn boasts an absolutely outstanding breakfast, an extensive reading library, and whirlpool tub.

A five-minute drive from the Inn is another Folkston claim to fame, the viewing depot for the **Folkston Funnel** (912/496-2536, www.folkston.com), a veritable train-watcher's paradise. This is the spot where the big CSX double-track rail line—following the top of the ancient Trail Ridge—hosts 60 or more trains a day. Railroad buffs from all over the South congregate here, anticipating the next train by listening to their scanners. The first Saturday each April brings buffs together for the all-day "Folkston RailWatch."

www.moon.com

DESTINATIONS | ACTIVITIES | BLOGS | MAPS | BOOKS

MOON.COM is ready to help plan your next trip! Filled with fresh trip ideas and strategies, author interviews, informative travel blogs, a detailed map library, and descriptions of all the Moon guidebooks, Moon.com is all you need to get out and explore the world—or even places in your own backyard. While at Moon.com, sign up for our monthly e-newsletter for updates on new releases, travel tips, and expert advice from our on-the-go Moon authors. As always, when you travel with Moon, expect an experience that is uncommon and truly unique.

MAP SYMBOLS

▨▨▨	Expressway	**◖**	Highlight	✈	Airport	⚲	Golf Course
▨▨▨	Primary Road	○	City/Town	✗	Airfield	**P**	Parking Area
▨▨▨	Secondary Road	◉	State Capital	▲	Mountain	⬟	Archaeological Site
▨▨▨	Unpaved Road	⊛	National Capital	✦	Unique Natural Feature	♦	Church
------	Trail	★	Point of Interest			⛽	Gas Station
········	Ferry	●	Accommodation	🐚	Waterfall		Glacier
✖✖✖	Railroad	▼	Restaurant/Bar	⚑	Park		Mangrove
▨▨▨	Pedestrian Walkway	■	Other Location	⬛	Trailhead		Reef
▥▥▥	Stairs	⋀	Campground	⛷	Skiing Area		Swamp

CONVERSION TABLES

°C = (°F - 32) / 1.8
°F = (°C x 1.8) + 32
1 inch = 2.54 centimeters (cm)
1 foot = 0.304 meters (m)
1 yard = 0.914 meters
1 mile = 1.6093 kilometers (km)
1 km = 0.6214 miles
1 fathom = 1.8288 m
1 chain = 20.1168 m
1 furlong = 201.168 m
1 acre = 0.4047 hectares
1 sq km = 100 hectares
1 sq mile = 2.59 square km
1 ounce = 28.35 grams
1 pound = 0.4536 kilograms
1 short ton = 0.90718 metric ton
1 short ton = 2,000 pounds
1 long ton = 1.016 metric tons
1 long ton = 2,240 pounds
1 metric ton = 1,000 kilograms
1 quart = 0.94635 liters
1 US gallon = 3.7854 liters
1 Imperial gallon = 4.5459 liters
1 nautical mile = 1.852 km

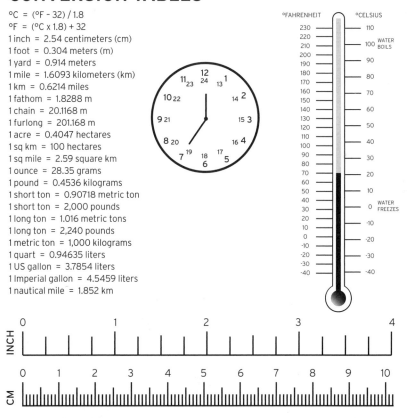

**MOON SPOTLIGHT SAVANNAH &
THE GEORGIA COAST**
Avalon Travel
a member of the Perseus Books Group
1700 Fourth Street
Berkeley, CA 94710, USA
www.moon.com

Editor and Series Manager: Kathryn Ettinger
Copy Editor: Jamie Andrade
Graphics Coordinator: Elizabeth Jang
Production Coordinator: Elizabeth Jang
Cover Designer: Kathryn Osgood
Map Editor: Brice Ticen
Cartographers: Kat Bennett, Chris Markiewicz,
    Allison Rawley

ISBN: 978-1-59880-681-6

Front cover photo: a great egret perches on a tree
limb in Savannah © Rose Waddell / Dreamstime.com
Title page photo: Cathedral of St. John the Baptist
in Savannah © Jim Morekis

Printed in the United States

ABOUT THE AUTHOR

Jim Morekis

Maybe it's because he was born in the same hospital as Flannery O'Connor – the old St. Joseph's in downtown Savannah – but there's no doubt that Jim Morekis has writing in his blood. As the longtime editor-in-chief of the weekly newspaper *Connect Savannah*, the University of Georgia graduate has written about and experienced pretty much every cultural happening in the area. He credits his love of travel to his mother, Elizabeth, who was John Berendt's travel agent during his stint in Savannah while writing *Midnight in the Garden of Good and Evil*.

Jim currently serves on Savannah's Cultural Affairs Commission, happily spending taxpayer money on the city's many festivals. As for the ongoing debate over which city is better, Charleston or Savannah, Jim calls it a tie: Charleston has better long-term planning, but Savannah has to-go cups (allowing anyone to explore the Historic District with a beer or cocktail in hand).

When not busy writing, Jim enjoys spending time with his two beautiful daughters, Alex and Sophia, and his dear wife, Sonja, who gets his deepest gratitude for opening his eyes to the true wonder and mystery of the Georgia coast.

Jim chronicles the history of the old Morekis family dairy online at www.morekisdairy.com.